THE CATHOLIC

REVOLUTION

THE CATHOLIC REVOLUTION

BY DOUGLAS J. ROCHE

DAVID McKAY COMPANY, INC.

New York

THE CATHOLIC REVOLUTION

Library of Congress Catalog Card Number: 68-31283

MANUFACTURED IN THE UNITED STATES OF AMERICA

VAN REES PRESS • NEW YORK

For E.N.R.

Acknowledgments

Anyone who tries to comprehend and report the Catholic Church of our times needs wide-ranging assistance. I received help in abundance.

My first debt of gratitude belongs to Gary MacEoin, author of (among many books) *What Happened at Rome?*, and a combination journalist-historian-theologian who, John Cogley says, is "stupendously sophisticated about Catholicism." In many conversations with me in Rome, the United States, and Canada, Mr. MacEoin shared a lifetime of insights. His commentaries on my own research and technical assistance enabled the book to take shape.

Many other persons were of direct help to me in a variety of ways: Mathew Ahmann, Frank Dolphin, Father Gilbert Graham, O.P., Father Edward Heston, C.S.C., William Holub, John Hodgson, Father Robert Kanka, Father John Kirvan, C.S.P., Romeo Maione, Barrett McGurn, James Norris, James O'Neill, Thomas Quigley, Donald Quinn, William Restivo, Father James Sheehan, Father John Sheerin, C.S.P., Edward Wakin, Martin Work.

Several bishops went out of their way to enlarge my viewpoint: the late Archbishop Paul J. Hallinan, Archbishop Anthony Jordan, OMI, Archbishop Philip Pocock, Bishop Remi De Roo, Bishop Ernest Primeau, Bishop James P. Shannon.

I am particularly grateful for the continuing confidence

of my editor, Charles N. Heckelmann, the mood-setting foreword by Donald J. Thorman, and the manuscript preparation by my secretary, Mrs. Marie Beck. I want to acknowledge the influence of two men in the shaping of my thoughts over many years: John E. Thompson and Father Ralph Gorman, C.P.

It meant a great deal to me to have the understanding of my family during long separations brought on by traveling for research and the necessary lonely hours in my study.

D.J.R.

April, 1968

Foreword

by

Donald J. Thorman, Publisher,
National Catholic Reporter

In these days of super-colossal expressions and gimmicky phrases, "revolution" may appear to be a relatively quiet word, even when preceded by Catholic. Yet, nothing less than "revolution" can adequately describe the changing mood of Roman Catholicism, especially as we know it in practice in contemporary United States and Canada.

Moderately enough, Mr. Roche describes it as "the radical change in thought and action within the Catholic Church," beginning with Vatican II and now in the hands of those impatient with the failure of the institution to implement the reforms it freely legislated at the Council.

Despite its implications, though, one cannot help but wonder if revolution is a word adequate to the task of describing what is happening to Catholicism today. For lack of a better one, it is perhaps the best and most suggestive description available to us. But, unless we examine some of its multiple implications, its real depths of meaning may escape us.

As surprising as it may seem, one of the most difficult and potentially dangerous problems we face is the simple fact that apparently a significant percentage of our ecclesiastical (read bishops, religious superiors, pastors) leadership is not easily willing to acknowledge the existence of a revolution or even a crisis within the Church. They put their faith in history—in the historical fact that the Church has always survived periods of crisis in the past. History is on their side, they reason, and thus they have only to wait out the unrest and upheavals of the post-conciliar period and—inevitably, magically—the institutional Church will emerge triumphant, as always.

The catch is that those who clutch this view to their bosom with all the intensity of a security blanket have misjudged history. Things are not as they were in the past. As historian Msgr. John Tracy Ellis noted not long ago, "the Catholic Church finds herself today in the midst of the gravest crisis she has experienced since the Protestant Revolt, and the American branch of the Church Universal is no exception." (*Commonweal*, 3/10/67)

Not only has the Church changed dramatically, in a revolutionary manner, but the world has changed, as well. The Church is not Big Daddy or Big Mommy to the secular society. Instead, it is often regarded as a scarcely credible relic of the past which has to prove itself to the present generation. The world is no longer coming to the Church, but now the Church must go to the world. Ecclesiastical leadership is no longer conferred automatically in the real world with ordination or consecration; instead, it must be earned and worked for as in the case of other leadership centers in our society—for example, the political, racial, or educational.

Prelates who sit on their episcopal thrones awaiting the obeisance of the contemporary world or the acknowledgment of their apostolic succession will increasingly become lonely figures, even within the Church, if they do not somehow reflect Christ and his life-style and message to the 1960s and 70s. To those on the front lines of the real world of the mid-20th century it all too often seems, as one layman magazine editor phrased it to me, that "Rome is fiddling while the world burns."

It is, of course, easy enough to sit back and take pot shots at bishops. They are easy targets and quickly shot down—and shooting them down is a favorite parlor game in some lay circles today, just as more than one emerging layman has bit the dust in innumerable rectory or chancery conversations.

All of this madness might make sense were it not for the reality of the world today, the fact of Vatican II and the fact of the layman's stake and role in the Church. The reality is that we are all in this Church together—Pope, bishops, priests, religious, lay people. It is easy enough to note that our Church is not the Church of the Pope, the bishops, and the clergy and religious alone. But we are simply going to stay on dead center if we lay people do not also realize and openly acknowledge that this is not the laymen's Church alone, either. We are all the Pilgrim People together, or we are nothing. We need each other. We are members of the same community. We are all members of Christ joined together by him or facing the danger of being torn apart by him. There is no middle ground with the man called Christ.

I think this is what Mr. Roche's report on the Church in revolution is telling us. It is relating how every segment of the Church is beginning to awaken to its own responsibilities, its own dimensions, its own stake in the total mission of the Church. Mr. Roche is really a modern author of contemporary Acts of the Holy Spirit within his Church in the 1960s. The Holy Spirit shook up the bishops at the Council, and now it is the turn—as the ripples of the Council spread out—of every element within the Church to face up to its own self-examination, within the context of the total mission of Christ in the 20th century.

And this is precisely what gives me as an individual some

element of hope for the future: The very existence of our unsettled and revolutionary times concomitantly opens up opportunities for dynamic development and fruitful change within the institutional Church which would never have been present in a self-satisfied and complacent community. Leaders who would never consider experimentation in a smoothly running organization are much more easily frightened into willingness to consider realities and alternatives in the midst of a swirling, changeable, mercurial period with an uncertain present and an indefinite future. Fear is not the best of all human motives, but it is better than none. And if Mr. Roche's expert report does not upset the guardians of the institution, they are not listening. The Church and the world around us are in change and in flux, and unless we begin to try to get with it, there is no reason to believe the institution that has meant too much to so many will survive in recognizable form.

But examining the evidence which comes across my desk daily as a newspaper publisher and reading such reports as Mr. Roche's makes me more than ever feel and hope that the Holy Spirit is as much abroad today in New York and Chicago and Los Angeles and Edmonton as he was in ancient Jerusalem. He is stirring up and unsettling, but most of all, he is present.

And I repeat that it is really the story of his presence which Mr. Roche is recording in this volume. Within the Catholic press, the name of Douglas J. Roche has long stood for professionalism and journalistic skill. Mr. Roche's abilities as both a magazine and a newspaper editor have been highly respected for years by his colleagues and peers, and now it is a privilege for me to introduce him to a new and broader audience as the author of an insightful and timely book.

Contents

Introduction:
Conflicting Signposts

On December 8, 1965, the Second Vatican Council ended with a festive celebration in St. Peter's Square, and some twenty-three hundred bishops of the Catholic Church went home, the final words of Pope Paul VI their guide: "In the name of Our Lord Jesus Christ, go in peace!"

But peace was not to be found. Instead, discord became the chief characteristic of the post-conciliar age. The Catholic Church, which had traditionally presented a united front to the world, suddenly became a house divided. Hostility, bewilderment, suspicion, fear, disillusionment, wonder, boredom, rejection—all these became the qualities of Catholics who fell or drifted into different camps.

The progressives, who wanted fast renewal, found themselves split into two schools, the first willing to let the reform be paced by the institution's leaders, the second veering around what they considered an institutional roadblock to launch their own kind of non-institutional Christianity. The traditionalists varied from those who resisted every change as a capitulation to the secular world to those who gave only a grudging submission to the updating process. The great majority of Catholics, who were not intellectually prepared for the dynamic of Vatican II and did not understand it, felt themselves hardly touched by it.

Within two years, the glory of Vatican II had changed

into the crisis of reform. The Church, which had won new admiration from non-Catholics for its attempts at updating, suddenly came under a barrage of attacks from within. Some who were the most ardent supporters of *aggiornamento*—the Italian word that came to mean the modernizing of the Church—charged that the institutional Church is so enmeshed in medieval anachronisms that it cannot be reformed quickly enough to make any impact on a world that is racing ahead technologically. The institution is so bound in legalisms, according to this view, that it chokes off the love of Christ from the millions who want the love Christ talked about. The bishops appear to be more worried about the priests and nuns who are rebelling against authoritarianism than they are about the millions of laity who are gradually drifting farther away from any meaningful relationship with the Church.

Three books, written by men who are or have been priests, captured the frustration coming to a boil in the Catholic Church.

The first, *The Grave of God* by Father Robert Adolfs, a young Dutch theologian, proclaims that if God is dead for modern man, the Church is guilty because it has buried Christ in the trappings of imperial power. The Christian faith plays hardly any part today, Adolfs avers, in the really dynamic spheres of central importance in modern society—science, politics, economics, business life, trade, technology, and the social services. "What is more, the Church is unprepared, clumsy, and impotent in the face of such phenomena as urbanization, automation, the population explosion, and the denationalization tendencies in politics and economics."

Adolfs insists that the Church is no longer relevant to these or other developments that are taking place within society. "That is why perhaps the Church means so little to the great masses in the world today. There are, of course, certain spheres in which she still exerts an influence—in education, for example—but even there her witness is diminishing. The Church, then, would appear to be still relevant only in the clerical sphere, in family life, and in the private life of those individuals who still believe."

The second book, *A Modern Priest Looks at His Outdated Church,* by James Kavanaugh, is an impassioned plea for a Church shorn of the legalisms that bring unhappiness to so many. Rooted in anguish and written in heat, the book indicts the Church for failing to put into practice the charity of Christ. The author jabs a dozen exposed nerve-ends in Catholic life, centering mostly on the rigidity of the Church's laws on sex and marriage. As the book jumped to the top of the bestseller lists, Kavanaugh immediately became a national figure. He toured the U.S., becoming angrier with each public appearance. Finally, before an audience of Notre Dame University students, he slashed away at the institutional Church for keeping men "guilty, frightened, docile, loyal, and silent." Then he proclaimed, "Your institution can go to hell," and he resigned his priesthood.

The third book, *A Question of Conscience,* is the most powerful of the three. It is by Charles Davis, who, as Britain's leading theologian, shook the entire Catholic world by leaving both his priesthood and the Church. In his moderate, scholarly manner, Davis attacks the credibility of the Roman Catholic Church. He asserts it is no longer the sign of Christ as a credible embodiment of faith, hope, and love, and secondly, that Biblical and historical data do not support the hierarchical structure of the Church and its teaching authority.

Davis intends to remain a Christian while rejecting the institutional Church. He calls for an "open" Christian community without any "over-arching organization." He suggests that the attitude of Christians toward the Church today should be one of "creative disaffiliation." Davis' book is more than an apologia, more than a personal account of his struggle for intellectual and spiritual freedom. It is an argument against the integrity of the structure of the Church, and as such it is the embodiment of a great question mark rippling through the Catholic world.

What is evident in the sparks struck by Adolfs, Kavanaugh, and Davis is that these men do not speak just for themselves. Developing their serious protests, they have embodied the major phenomenon of modern Christianity: the Catholic Church is in a state of revolution.

The revolution is not confined to writers of books. It is operative today in dozens of areas within the Catholic Church and is fermenting as much in the grass roots as in the intellectuals' studies. I do not use the word revolution in the sense of a violent overthrow of the bishops who comprise the legitimate government of the Catholic Church. Rather, I use the word, in the belief that any lesser term would be inadequate, to indicate the radical change in thought and action within the Catholic Church.

The revolution had its identifiable beginning with the Second Vatican Council and in that sense was institutional in character. But the continuing surge of the revolution is in the hands of those Catholics who want to blaze a trail to the Vatican II goal and are not content with the ambivalence of an institution that resists the implementation of legislated reforms. Like all revolutions, this one is full of conflicting ideas and forces.

A Church that had a closed mentality is opening up; a Church that was protective of its own institutional power is now committed to the service of mankind; a Church that was circumscribed by law is now accenting freedom of action in deeper love of God and neighbor; a Church that was regimented as an institution is now accommodating the interplay of people within a community; a Church that was identified as a clerical preserve is giving way to lay influence. This does not mean that a great deal of the Church is still not closed, power-conscious, legalistic, institutional, and clerical. Rather, the developing new style, service, love, community, and lay involvement are tension points that are erupting with increasing frequency into flash fires.

Thus, we see priests leaving their ministry in greater numbers. Nuns are leaving their convents, too, and even forming new lay communities to live as religiously committed laywomen in the modern world. Many people, bored by weekly compulsory attendance at cold liturgical services in huge churches, are forming their own Christian communities with many of the features of an underground. Committed priests, sisters, and laymen, despairing of any real leadership from the hierarchy on peace and race—the two great social issues of our time—go off on their own to demonstrate and protest. The Berrigan brothers, Father Daniel and Father Philip, lead the way into the desperate tactics of civil disobedience to strengthen the peace movement. And Father James Groppi shows the Negroes that there is at least one Catholic who will suffer and march with them, endlessly if need be, to penetrate the consciences of the whites.

Since the revolution is basically the action and reaction of committed people caught in the conflict between the aspirations of a timeless Church and the reality of a time-conscious world, it can be best described as a new mood within the Catholic Church. This new mood has to be sensed, touched, and probed at many different places in the fullness of the Church in order to be understood.

To acquire first-hand evidence, I spent three months in the fall of 1967 traveling throughout the United States and Canada and to Rome for the First World Synod of Bishops and the Third World Congress for the Lay Apostolate. I interviewed bishops, pastors, curia officials, sisters and former sisters, priests and former priests, laity who believe and disbelieve, bureaucrats, college presidents, ecumenical leaders, Negroes, Peace Corps volunteers, college students, editors, liberals, and conservatives.

I attended theology conferences, priests' seminars, education symposiums, and discussions in many living rooms where men and women talked frankly about their changing attitudes to the changing Church. I watched Pope Paul carried triumphantly through St. Peter's to the acclaim of thousands. I climbed filthy tenements in urban American slums with courageous women trying to help Negro riot victims. I spent hours with former priests listening to them explain why they left the priesthood. In poverty areas I watched women who ceased being sisters in order to get closer to the poor.

I spent long sessions with interracial leaders to get insights into what the Church is doing to help Negroes. I prayed with people at unauthorized experimental Masses in living rooms in many towns. I watched a midnight session of lay leaders making history at the world congress in Rome by proving that democracy can work within the authoritarian Church. I conducted group interviews with college students to find out why they are turning off the institutional Church. I examined parish councils from the viewpoint of both the pastors and the laity.

This book, then, records my findings as a journalist. It is neither a history of the forces evolving in the Church in the past decade that set the stage for a renewal that turned into revolution, nor is it a scientific survey pinpointing the causes and effects of all the changes. In my bibliography, I list those books that are particularly helpful in understanding the Second Vatican Council and many of the new theological and sociological trends. I have been concerned with observing, as a journalist, the life of the Church today at the various levels, insofar as anyone can get hold of the events rushing by with such rapidity.

Two impressions from my investigation stand out in my mind. The first is that bishops are being challenged by an increasingly articulate band of priests, sisters, and laity to provide the continuing kind of leadership in the post-conciliar Church that they demonstrated while the Council was in progress. Everywhere I traveled I found people either disappointed or unimpressed with bishops as leaders. The handful of courageously progressive bishops greatly overshadow their brothers who are regarded by widening circles of people as being afraid to go on with the spirit and style of conciliar thinking.

Most bishops see their authority being challenged, and in fact it is. However, it is being challenged not so much by eruption as by a silent schism of persons who are dropping out of involvement with the institutional Church while still maintaining a selection of Christian beliefs. People are weighing their bishops as leaders, and when they do not measure up to the standards of leadership, the tendency today is to regard them as irrelevant. The anguish and restlessness of those who want the Church to be a meaningful expression of Christ's love just as applicable to modern man in the secular city as in apostolic times are not reflected by the bishop's statements. Despite the accent of Vatican II on the Church as a family or people of God, there is very little communication between the bishops and the people.

This reaction, which is so much a part of the revolution, was bluntly expressed by *Commonweal*, a liberal Catholic weekly: "Your Holiness, Your Excellencies: Are you reading what the polls have to say? Do you hear the rustle of the petitions from your priests piling up on your desks? Do you hear Sister Nora slamming the door as she leaves the convent? Do you hear the echoes in the corridors of half-empty seminaries? Have your ears discerned that there are not quite so many small feet noisily rushing to the schools and more small change rattling in the baskets?"

The community of Christians needs authority—visible, meaningful, spirit-filled authority, *Commonweal* insisted. "What it does not need is a naked power masquerading as authority." Open rebellion against unjust Church laws and practices was urged so that the bishops' real authority could be saved from misuse.

Against this crisis of authority must be balanced the new creativity working its way into the life of the Church. What I see as a creative revolution is the second major impression of my travels. The old-style ghetto Church of Trent is dead but not buried. The new-style open Church of Vatican II has been conceived but not yet born. It is easier to discern the negative results of an old-style Church clashing with new ideas. That is what makes headlines. But underneath the clamor is the stirring of a new Church which gives every sign of being a far more relevant expression of Christian love. This does not make headlines. But the creativity at work today in the new form of government at the top level in the Church, the social concerns of committed Christians, the new ecumenical fellowship, the maturity of priests and nuns who have grasped their responsibility to get out of pre-cast molds, the growing awareness of laity that they have a vital place in the decision-making processes in the Church, and finally the demythologizing of theology so that the beliefs of the Catholic Church become less culturally and more scripturally oriented—all are marks of this new creativity.

The new age is one of transition from the stereotypes of the past to a free-flowing style, from convention to conviction, from certainties to inquiries. Most of all, there is a new sense of discovery in the Catholic Church, which for ages thought she knew everything. From the false security of the supposition that the Church possessed all truth and could stand like a rock in the midst of a changing world, Catholics have discovered that they are on a pilgrimage through history in constant search of truth. The tensions, the emotional reactions, and the threat to vested interests from this discovery are all still too strong to permit a clear vision of the route ahead. But the signposts are becoming visible for those who will look up at them.

THE CATHOLIC

REVOLUTION

CHAPTER 1

A New Government — Tomorrow

The bar was complete, a long table covered with enticing hors d'oeuvres and the crowd elbow to elbow in the Renaissance halls of the Columbus Hotel on the Via della Conciliazione. The journalists, the Rome insiders, even several Synod Fathers had come as guests of five British and Irish Catholic publishing firms to celebrate the opening of a book display.

Cardinal William Conway, Archbishop of Armagh and Primate of all Ireland, one of the three Synod Presidents, graced the occasion with a few words of paternal pride in his hosts' intellectual endeavors. An even greater coup was the presence of a lustrous star, new-risen in the curial firmament—Archbishop Giovanni Benelli, Subsecretary of State for Ordinary Affairs—who unrolled a scroll and read a modest address.

An American woman radio producer, in black cocktail dress, came up to me when the formalities were over and said, "I just got in from the States. Listen, what's really happening at the Synod? Has a new age begun or are they still giving us the same old crap?"

The October mornings in Rome make the human spirit soar. The pale blue sky and light breeze provide a sense of well-being as you walk along the streets past the monuments and fountains that have stood during the ages, past the Romans who at this hour have a spring in their step. The lassitude of the siesta hour, when the sun beams straight down, will come later. Then the streets will quickly become deserted. Even the Fiats, now hurtling by in a gay nightmare of Roman traffic patterns, take refuge.

But at this hour, about 8:30 a.m. on Tuesday, October 10, 1967, many of these cars, skilled chauffeurs having once more conquered the traffic, rolled across the invisible boundary of the 107.8 acres of Vatican City, an absolute monarchy smaller than Monaco and politically more important than Italy. The first glimpse of this power, the Swiss Guard in blue-and-gold-striped tunics that were in vogue several centuries ago, tends to be a joke. The real power is invisible, but you know it is there as you become swallowed up in the ocher buildings, fresco-lined passages, and marble staircases, and catch glimpses of rustling scarlet, purple, and black cassocks.

Here in the Vatican, where everything is at once forbidden and possible, the preservation of power makes a cold impression on every interloper. Not that there are many of these. The multitudes throng St. Peter's Square, in the embrace of the Bernini columns, to cheer the radiant figure in white who blesses them from his window, but no more than the tiniest fraction of the world's five hundred million Catholics have ever seen or have any idea what goes on behind the Vatican façade. It is here and in a room appropriately called "The Hall of Broken Heads" that a power struggle took place, a struggle full of nuances and niceties and shielded from public glare, but a struggle regarded by experts as the acid test of the reforms legislated by the Second Vatican Council.

The cars swung into the Belvedere Court and the prelates got out to attend the ninth session of the First World Synod of Bishops called by Pope Paul VI to advise him on five specific questions. The month-long Synod was an experiment in collegial government of the Church. Collegiality, the sharing by bishops in the government of the universal Church, was the most important element in the creative revolution launched by the Council. If collegiality works, it will break the suffocating strangle-hold on the development of Catholic life maintained by the curialists in the recesses of the Vatican. It is the curialists, wielding the enormous, invisible power of the Holy See, who for long years have stood between the Pope and the bishops.

The Synod was the first meeting in the history of the Vatican where the bishops were elected by their national hierarchies and sent to Rome with specific wishes for the development of reform. The Curia had the upper hand in the planning of the Synod, and some of the more recalcitrant officials hoped that the free-wheeling spirit of Vatican II would blow away with the winds. But the bishops came to demonstrate the new principle that it is they, under and with the Pope, who govern the Church, not the careerists in the Vatican who through mere survival frequently find themselves in power positions.

One by one the prelates disappeared through a brick wall that looks like the entrance to a catacomb. Some of the most famous names in the Christian world were there. The tall, friendly Cardinal Leo Suenens of Belgium, a favorite of the progressives and one of the most impressive figures of Vatican II, stopped to chat with the Frenchman, Cardinal Jean Villot, another of the three Synod presidents. Cardinal Valerian Gracias, silver-haired and majestic, swept by.

The Americans appeared from their residence at the North American College on the Janiculum just a few minutes away—Archbishop John Dearden of Detroit, president of the United States Conference of Bishops; Cardinal John Krol of Philadelphia, newly elevated to the College of Cardinals; Cardinal Lawrence Shehan of Baltimore; and Bishop John J. Wright of Pittsburgh. These four were elected by the American bishops. With them was Bishop Fulton J. Sheen of Rochester, the 71-year-old former U.S. head of the Society for the Propagation of the Faith, who startled America with his innovations upon taking over Rochester and who was personally appointed by the Pope to the Synod.

The four elected Canadians came into the courtyard, led by Cardinal Paul-Emile Leger of Montreal, another of the great progressives of Vatican II, the secret still locked in his breast that he would shortly resign his office, even though only 63, and set out for Africa to devote the rest of his life to aiding lepers. With him was Archbishop Louis Levesque of Rimouski, Quebec, and the two representatives of English-speaking Canada—Archbishops Philip Pocock of Toronto and George Flahiff of Winnipeg, both sturdy moderates. A fifth Canadian, Metropolitan Maxim Hermaniuk of Winnipeg, represented Ukrainian Byzantine Catholics.

The tiny Cardinal Franziskus Koenig of Austria came by, then the strapping, youthful Bishop Mark McGrath of Panama, the sturdy Cardinal Julius Doepfner of West Germany, Cardinal John Heenan of Westminster, Cardinal Giovanni Urbani of Venice, and the aging, half-blind Cardinal Alfredo Ottaviani, the "old policeman," as he called himself.

Altogether there were 199 Synod Fathers. About two-thirds of them had been elected by 37 national and regional conferences of bishops around the world under a formula that gave one representative to each conference with 25 or fewer members, two to those with 26 to 50 members, three to those with 51 to 100, and four to bigger conferences. Patriarchs, major archbishops, and most metropolitans of the Eastern rites were included by virtue of the importance of their offices. Religious superiors elected ten delegates to represent religious orders. Also by virtue of their office,

4

16 cardinals of the Roman Curia were admitted. The others were nominees of the Pope under a provision authorizing him to appoint up to 15 percent of the total.

The Hall of the Broken Heads is one of the ancient rooms in the unknown Vatican. It was suddenly brought to life through its new prominence as the site of the first Synod. The old statues were cleared out and new lighting installed. Even so, with two huge pillars in the room and scarcely room for more than the Synod Fathers plus a few secretaries, the visibility was poor.

Grayish-brown brick dominated the dull appearance which seemed to contrast with the gilded court effect in many other rooms of the Vatican. A bronze sculpture hung on the wall over a rectangular table where the three presidents—Cardinals Felici, Conway, and Villot—took their places. The Synod Fathers sat in cream-upholstered seats, and some pulled out a board on the back of the seat in front of them to write on. Between each two seats was a microphone. Three television cameras in the corners were controlled from a central booth. Simultaneous translators were standing by upstairs equipped to cross-translate Latin, English, French, Spanish, Italian, and German, thereby making possible for the Synod Fathers the immediate dialogue which exclusive use of Latin, combined with set speeches to be handed in several days ahead of delivery, had prevented at the Council. The Synod speeches, however, were still made in Latin.

A bell rang in the foyer and the opening prayer, the *Adsumus*, was recited, the same prayer that opened each day of the Vatican Council's four sessions. On this day, the first half of the meeting was presided over by Cardinal Conway. There was an added sense of expectancy because the bishops knew the Pope would come in at the coffee break and stay for the remainder of the morning session.

The general secretary, Bishop Ladislaus Rubin of

5

Poland, announced that, in order to become more personally acquainted with the Synod Fathers, the Pope would receive various national groups beginning that day. The announcement caused some surprise. Everyone knew how ill the Pope was and that his doctors were struggling to keep him well enough to function until the Synod closed and they could go ahead with a prostatectomy.

October 10 was the turning point of the Synod, a day that provided another milestone in the brief and turbulent history of the Catholic revolution. It was the day the Fathers irrevocably confirmed their decision to exercise the most important of their powers under the rules of procedure, namely, to elect their own commission to draw up a report on the most contentious issue under discussion—a Curia-prepared document ominously entitled, "Dangerous Modern Opinions and Atheism."

They had been tempted to take similar action during the debate on Canon Law a few days previously, but had drawn back because of uncertainty among themselves as to where the majority lay, and had settled for a compromise. But now the issues were too clearly drawn. The Congregation for the Doctrine of the Faith, the renamed Holy Office, was seeking to reassert its age-old supremacy. It was a direct challenge to the letter and spirit of the Second Vatican Council. The progressive leaders recognized that they had to take the risk of direct confrontation. They need not have worried. The outcome was even more decisive than the great battles of the Council.

To put the issues in proper perspective, I must go back a little.

Following the inspired initiatives of Pope John XXIII, the Second Vatican Council had laid the groundwork for the Catholic revolution between 1962 and 1965 by formulating a concept of Church membership, organization, and function very different from that which had prevailed since the proclamation of papal infallibility in 1870, and before. Incorporation into Christ by baptism was exalted as the identifying mark of the Christian, giving him an active part in building up the kingdom of God, a rejection of the former two-class society that in practice gave rights to the clergy and duties to the laity.

Although collegial rule was expressly affirmed by Vatican II only for the top echelons, making the bishops co-responsible with the Pope as the final authority, the logic of that affirmation clearly implied a collegial relationship between each bishop and his priests, and between each pastor and the laity he served. This approach to the exercise of authority was further emphasized by a stress on decentralization. From the purely pragmatic viewpoint, the operation of the Church had been strangled by the absorption of decision-making into a small and extremely inefficient bureaucracy surrounding the Pope—the Roman Curia.

One archbishop summed up the situation during the Council by saying that it took him ten years to get a decision on a marriage case, by which time nobody cared whether the verdict was favorable or unfavorable. The Council provided a base on which to rebuild the Church as an institution of love and service. It proclaimed the authority given the bishop by his consecration and the autonomy of the local churches for the settlement of their own problems, an autonomy subsequently given legal expression in the creation of national or regional conferences of bishops where they did not exist, and an enlargement of the powers of existing conferences, such as those of the United States and Canada.

Starting from the same concept of incorporation into Christ by baptism, the Council also began a reevaluation of the status of other Christians, of the extent to which their Churches enshrine Christian values (including many long neglected by Roman Catholics) and are for their members

7

the legitimate channels of Christ's grace and mercy. It pursued this line of thought far enough to recognize an implicit presence of Christ in the great non-Christian religions and even in the hearts of agnostics and atheists who honestly seek the promotion of the positive human values which have been revealed to them.

In addition, it proclaimed the objective worth and importance of these human values, in terms that shocked those Catholics who had been taking literally the narrow exhortations of their traditional spiritual guides. It told Catholics they should no longer seek salvation in the isolation of their churches, cells, or ghettoes, but should join enthusiastically with all who would accept their help in building up a truly human society, an essential prerequisite to the reign of Christ over all men.

The records of the Council describe the tremendous struggle involved in formulating these conclusions. The struggle was twofold. There was the open conflict between those who formulated the programs and led the movement for renewal and reform, and those who wanted to retain the previous closed, self-sufficient, dictatorial system. I do not question the good faith of the latter group. My study and observation in Rome during the exciting Council years satisfied me that they believed what they defended. But it is a significant commentary on human motivations that their nucleus, the Pope's own civil service—the Roman Curia—was the entity immediately threatened by change.

More cataclysmic than this open conflict, however, was the hidden one in the hearts of the many bishops who had come to the Council with an obscure sense of malaise, but with no appreciation of just what was wrong or what must be done to get back on course. The reformulation of beliefs and goals I have just synthesized ran counter to all they had previously accepted without question. They had been picked by the Roman Curia for the jobs they held. The Curia had selected them, not necessarily for independence or originality of thought, but for their records as conservative and obedient administrators, and it had chosen most of them from among the graduates of the Roman universities. It is remarkable that an overwhelming majority of them had the illumination and the courage to rise above their conditioning and endorse the substance of the programs of updating and reform. For many observers, this was a clear indication of the presence of the Holy Spirit in the Council. But rise above it they did, to the extent that every major proposal of the progressives was voted by an overwhelming majority.

The Council, nevertheless, was a political body. An extreme effort to minimize conflict hedged around crisp formulas with restrictions and ambiguities that in many cases permitted everyone to draw his own conclusions. The progressives were satisfied with documents that left doors open to advance. They believed, and subsequent events have largely confirmed their belief, that the internal dynamism of the Church would accomplish the rest. But their opponents found solace in the ambiguities to resist implementation of what was the clear intention of the Council. When Pope Paul promulgated its sixteen documents, they consoled themselves with an observation widely attributed to Cardinal Giuseppe Siri of Genoa: "They are not definitions; they will never bind us."

The two years following the Council showed that the bishops had only postponed conflict by acceptance of numerous ambiguities, and that the postponement had moved the conflict to a field where they would have far less ability to control its conduct and define its scope. The bishops as a group went home well satisfied, but with little understanding of the practical implications of what they had done. The Catholic avant-garde, exhilarated after long years when the notion of change was suspect, was impatient to put the Council into practice. The traditionalists at home were not emotionally prepared for change.

The vast bulk of Catholics in between had not yet begun to suspect the true dimension of the Council. Conflict and chaos at the grass roots were inevitable. The bishops' total reevaluation of their own principles and prejudices left them emotionally exhausted, while simultaneously giving them an image of themselves as venturous innovators marked for history's Hall of Fame. They could now rest on their laurels, scattering tokens of implementation of a few of the great changes they had approved—a layman to read the Epistle at Mass here, an advisory council for a pastor there, three inches chopped off a nun's habit somewhere else.

That was largely the attitude of the bishops of the United States. Notwithstanding their numbers (the 1968 total of active bishops is 220) and the significant influence they exercised on the universal Church, they had gone to the Council with little real awareness of the ferment of discontent among Catholics. Episcopal isolation from the rank-and-file had removed them from deep problems of faith and religious practice now about to burst open. Apart from the one issue of freedom of religion, an issue in which their involvement was less ideological than based on the pragmatic needs of their pluralist society, they made little original contribution. At the same time, they readily joined with the majority in the consensus in favor of progress, though without any real change of heart. Even the idea of collegial autonomy for their national conference was distasteful to many. They preferred the old system under which that conference could not bind its members, leaving distant Rome to make the laws while each bishop could administer them in his own way in his own bailiwick.

Progressive Council leaders had anticipated this reaction

—a reaction certainly not confined to the United States—and they had urged as strongly as they could the creation of an institution to ensure the continuation of the Council's work after its close.

"This government could take the form of a large college, a kind of episcopal council beside the Pope, to include patriarchs, cardinals who are residential bishops or archbishops, and delegates from episcopal conferences or missionary areas." Such was the formulation offered by Archbishop Hermaniuk on the Council floor in October, 1963.

Maximos IV Saigh, Melchite Patriarch of Antioch, added that it should be in permanent session, some members "taking their place in turn beside the Pope . . . the supreme executive and decision-making council of the universal Church, to which all Roman offices would be subject."

Pope Paul announced in November, 1964, that he would accede to the request of the bishops for a collegial body to help him in governing the Church. But the constitution of the Synod of Bishops published in September, 1965, fell far short of a full implementation of the projections of Archbishop Hermaniuk, Patriarch Maximos, and many other Council leaders. While most of its members were to be elected by episcopal conferences, they would be called into session if and when the Pope decided. They would have no control over the content of their agenda, which would be fixed by the Pope. Unless the Pope determined to the contrary in particular cases, they would have no decision-making function. They would offer their advice, and he could accept or reject. The Pope would name the president, the secretaries, and other officials.

This was the body which Pope Paul convoked for the first time to meet in Rome in the last days of September, 1967. Some in the interval had grumbled at its limited authority, complaining that it was a grudging and inadequate implementation of the Council's request. Others had stressed that forms always tend to lag behind reality, that the living dynamics of the situation would count for more than the juridic boundaries, that it was a beginning which could be expected, in the normal course of evolution, to grow from a puny infant to a driving youth and powerful adult. Meanwhile, the situation with which the institutional Church had to deal had changed significantly through the interplay of the forces released by the Council with those previously existing and permitted to survive in the interests of compromise.

First of all, the advance wing of the "People of God"—to use the phrase chosen by the Council to describe everyone who is baptized—embraced the role allotted to it with an alacrity which taxed all efforts of the bishops to keep up with their previously docile flocks. The result was what Catholic commentator John Cogley has called "a revolutionary mood." It was basically anti-legalist and ecumenical, seeking common expression of the faith with other Christians, not only in social and community affairs, but in worship. It proclaimed a change from anathematization of the world to a respect for the claims of the secular unprecedented in Catholic history, a change that quickly started a new evaluation of the role of religious orders and of Catholic education.

The specifics of this revolution will be detailed in later chapters. We need only note here that within two years of the close of Vatican II, the chains of legalism had given way to a surge of freedom. Increasing numbers of Catholics had decided for themselves that they could, without sin, use methods of contraception traditionally disapproved by the Church. A papal encyclical had failed to stop them from discussing in private and in public the desirability of allowing priests to marry. In increasing numbers they were joining groups of people who celebrated the Eucharist in ways the bishops frowned upon or explicitly forbade. The bishops reacted by stressing their authority, and the Church was plunged into crisis.

Not only the United States, but most of the Catholic world shared this mood. Tension was less in countries like Holland and Canada in which the bishops were more sensitive to the popular pulse, greater in those like Spain and the United States where they feared to relax their traditional grip. As the grass-roots movement blossomed, so did the anguished protests from those elements that had never abandoned their resistance to the teachings of the Council.

These elements continued to polarize, as they had done during the Council, around the Roman Curia, and in particular around the Holy Office. Although shorn of some of its power by Pope Paul at the end of the Council and urged to adopt a new image to match its new title of Congregation for the Doctrine of Faith, it revealed no change of heart. No sooner had the Council disbanded than it embarked on a major effort to reassert its thought control over the Church's theologians. The Congregation sent a letter to each conference of bishops and to the superiors of religious orders listing a litany of beliefs and theories current in the modern world which the authors judged dangerous to faith and morals and asking the recipient to note which of these were widespread among those under his jurisdiction. The errors were substantially the same as those the Holy Office had presented to the Council for condemnation, but which the Council had put aside as irrelevant.

The authors of the letter, which was signed by arch-conservative Cardinal Ottaviani, hoped a correlation of replies from all over the world would persuade the Pope that so many errors were rampant that it would be his duty to issue a new Syllabus of Errors and thus put a stop to what they regarded as the impudent and imprudent efforts of theologians to reformulate old teachings in ways more meaningful to modern man.

Thanks in large part to the press, which quickly published the text of the "secret" communication, the strategy was thwarted. Some conferences did not bother to reply. Others said the questions were meaningless in the context of their situation. Others commented that they knew of some of the errors but believed that only harm could be done by cataloguing and anathematizing them.

Such procedures might once have been valid, but certainly did not fit the needs and realities of the twentieth century. "What is needed is to proclaim the word of God," the French bishops said, "to get the teaching of the Council across to all the people, and to set out precisely the 'fixed points' of the faith, without being afraid to say the good and the bad, the true and the false."

The impact of the communications media has put a world spotlight on the formerly shadowy world of theology. The involvement of the Church in a new era of relating theology to the human condition is a public drama. "I never thought I'd see the day," Bishop Wright told a press conference, "when theology would be the number-one subject at cocktail parties. It's found in the weekly reviews, the *Ladies' Home Journal,* and the Italian publications. With so many amateurs in the field, the pros are nervous."

Pope Paul's decision to summon the Synod to meet in September, 1967, gave the Congregation for the Faith an opportunity to return to the attack a third time. Since the Pope had reserved the drafting of the agenda to himself, it fell to the Curia to determine what were the issues on which the world's bishops should advise the Pope, and how the position papers should formulate these issues.

The Congregation for the Faith clocked in with what proved to be the most important of the five items selected. Under the title "Dangerous Modern Opinions and Atheism," it presented once more its trouble sheet. The other four items on the agenda were reform of Canon Law, updating of seminaries, problems of mixed marriages, and liturgical experimentation.

The position paper on Dangers to the Faith, while striving for balance by pointing out dangers from both reactionary and over-progressive approaches, illustrated a neo-defensiveness. "Institutional absolutism" could crush renewal, it said. At the same time, it emphasized the right of the magisterium or teaching authority of the Church to interpret the deposit of faith. Some twenty contentious points were listed in what the *London Tablet* called "a catalogue of errors." Among them:

Revelation. There are two opposing dangers, one stemming from those who include Sacred Scripture and the latest scientific achievements in their study; the other from those who study Scripture with purely human criteria without attention to the tradition of the Church.

Dogmatic Formulations. It is recognized that many old formulas have changed in present-day language and that at times their translation to other languages is not easy. The opinion that these formulas are dead and surpassed is unacceptable.

Institutions and Charismata. The interest with which lay people, religious, and priests share more actively in the life of the Church is a sign of the times, but this renovation should not develop into a negation of structures and the position of the hierarchy.

Social Morality. It would be wrong to reduce morality to the limits of religious and spiritual life, forgetting that there is a Christian obligation to fight for justice and liberty, but it is also wrong to reduce morality to a purely social ethic.

The Future World. A vision of the future which sees men shut in within themselves and Christianity as the fulfilling of a few rules for individual salvation is unacceptable, but so too is an almost mystical admiration of earthly realities defending "secularisation," which seeks only a love toward the human family based on the so-called "death of God."

The debate on Dangers to the Faith brought into the open the depth of the gulf between the bishops around the world who must deal directly with people in their cultural habitat and the officials of the Curia working in isolation on the basis of theoretical constructions. The intention of the curialists was immediately identified.

"One may presume," a French Catholic periodical summed up, "that if the Synod had approved the position paper, then this document as drawn up by the ex-Holy Office would have served as the starting point for the preparation of a papal statement, almost certainly an encyclical, which would have recalled all too well Pius XI's *Quanta Cura* and its annex, the 'Syllabus of Eighty Erroneous Propositions.'"

Under the rules of procedure, each debate opened with an explanation of the position paper by a spokesman for the curial department responsible for preparing it. Next, one delegate spoke for each national conference of bishops that wished to record its position. Individual members, including those present by virtue of their office and the Pope's nominees, then spoke in their own names, and finally, any who felt the need could offer a rebuttal.

Opening for the Congregation for the Faith on October 4, the 80-year-old Cardinal Michael Browne was the epitome of sweet reasonableness. He assured the Fathers that the Congregation realized that times had changed, that the Church should explore for herself the spiritual culture of the modern world through a dialogue between the center and the periphery, between the Holy See and particular Churches, between pastors and their people. Most of his listeners, however, were not reassured, and they said so in the course of 81 interventions registered between October 4 and October 10.

Cardinal Suenens of Belgium, one of the moderators of the Vatican Council whose influence on Pope Paul has continued to grow, dismissed the document as negative from its title downwards. It made no distinction between real errors and certain loose expressions, and reading it was to get the impression that the Church was a society under siege, he said. Other important prelates, Heenan of England, Leger of Canada, McCann of South Africa, Muñoz Vega of Ecuador, struck the same theme: the Holy Office approach was too negative and academic.

The progressives challenged the basic assumption that a curial congregation could arrogate to itself the magisterium or teaching authority of the Church, as though theologians and the general body of the faithful were not also part of the magisterium. And as they talked, a consensus gradually emerged, a consensus of historic dimensions. The Congregation for the Faith had not merely failed to express the views of the Church. It had shown itself incapable of adjusting its thinking to that of the bishops, thereby forcing the bishops to set up their own commission to formulate their views on the points at issue.

Such is the ultimate meaning of the action taken on October 10, when ballots were distributed for the election of eight members of a committee which the Pope would complete by naming four more.

Spokesmen for the Congregation for the Faith continued to fight bravely to the end. Most of the 16 speakers on October 10 were from their camp, the two keynoters being curial officials, Fathers William Bertrams, S.J., and Louis Ciappi, O.P.

Father Bertrams, a theological adviser during the Vatican Council to a small group of bishops opposed to collegiality,

17

elaborated on the deviations of the theologians and the disrespect for the magisterium. Describing the Church as a supernatural society founded entirely on revealed doctrine objectively indicated, he asserted that the current crisis of "the institutional character of the faith" could be overcome by reestablishing the authority of the magisterium and the value of law.

Father Ciappi, who is remembered principally for the extravagant Marian articles he published in the Vatican newspaper, *L'Osservatore Romano,* deplored the disintegration of the historicity of the Bible at the hands of freewheeling theologians and exegetes. He told theologians that the living magisterium of the Church, the ordinary as well as the infallible magisterium, was for each of them "the proximate and universal norm of truth."

But the voice of the majority was not to be silenced. Cardinal Doepfner of Germany returned to the stand to insist that the Synod should not proclaim the document to the Church. The development of doctrine takes time, he said, and it would be a catastrophe to rule on issues that were not yet ripe. To publish an encyclical or even a list of errors would be most inopportune.

Cardinal Franjo Seper of Yugoslavia supported him, pointing out that it would be a mistake to see the crisis of contemporary man as simply one of doctrine, when his uncertainty spread much wider and included positive elements. In the past, he said, we considered uncertainty to be an imperfection, but today we are learning to realize that our knowledge is limited, so that uncertainty is frequently a proper awareness of our objective situation.

These two interventions acquired an additional significance when the results of the balloting were announced (on the first ballot, no one acquired a majority and on the second, the eight with the highest number of votes won). Cardinal Seper headed the list with 140 votes and Cardinal

Doepfner was in fourth place with 95. With the possible exception of Bishop Carlo Colombo of Milan, reputed to be highly regarded by Pope Paul as a theologian, no supporter of the Congregation for the Faith was elected. Bishop Colombo was in second place with 128 votes and Bishop Wright third with 110. The four others elected were Cardinal Veuillot of France (78), Bishop McGrath of Panama (78), Cardinal Suenens (71), and Archbishop Edelby of Syria (69). The Synod Fathers quietly delivered their final repudiation of the Holy Office mentality: 14 votes for Cardinal Browne.

At the Vatican Council, Pope Paul had always followed a precedent established by Pope John of naming members of the minority to a committee whenever the majority had a clean sweep of the elected members. Now, however, he departed decisively from this compromise procedure. His four nominees did not include a single member of the Curia. Instead, he reached out to Latin America, Africa, and Asia, naming Archbishop Muñoz Vega of Ecuador, Cardinal Paul Zoungrana of Upper Volta, Archbishop Joseph Cordeiro of Pakistan, and Bishop Paul Yoshigoro Taguchi of Japan. In the symbolic language beloved of Rome, it proclaimed the displacement of power that has taken place from the center to the four corners of the globe.

In further acknowledgment of his respect for the collegial judgment of the bishops, the Pope named Cardinal Seper chairman of the committee. As if final confirmation were needed that Pope Paul, so long pictured in mental anguish over what to do, was giving the green light to the progressives, he delivered it a few months after the Synod closed by giving Ottaviani's job to Seper. The 62-year-old Archbishop of Zagreb brought to the Congregation for the Faith an impressive record of seeking and getting an understanding with the Yugoslav Communists, a valuable asset as the Church begins a new opening to the political left. Cardinal

Ottaviani was the epitome of Roman insulation; Seper, well-traveled and open, came onto the post-conciliar, universal scene with progressive ideas that it is better to develop a Christian concern for atheists than to condemn atheism.

The substantial success of the international press in breaking the secrecy in which the proceedings of the Synod were shrouded played a significant part in the progress made by the Fathers. The Pope's curial advisers had learned nothing from their Vatican Council experience with the press. Or possibly they had learned that the opening up of the Council at the second and subsequent sessions had worked against them by rallying world public opinion to the progressive camp. They hoped that the smaller Synod could be held in a vacuum of secrecy. When their intention became known several months before the opening of the Synod, various conferences of bishops protested.

The Canadian bishops, for example, went on record with a strongly worded statement. Since the action of newsmen during Vatican II, they said, "furnished an important dynamism for the life of the Council, we feel it our duty to urge that all facilities be given by the Vatican to the great media of information, so that they can provide the people of God with the services they expect from the press . . . complete and accurate information on all subjects discussed, and also a feedback to the Synod itself of the views formed and discussions provoked by this information among the people of God."

Ignoring this and other protests, the Synod organizers insisted on controls even harsher than those established at the first session of the Vatican Council. Synod members were bound to total secrecy, forbidden even to give press conferences on general issues without advance permission. A daily official release gave brief abstracts of interventions, but without identifying the speakers, and "scrambling" the summaries to complicate the task of determining who had said what. This information would have been practically valueless to the newsmen if they had not been able to establish their own lines of communication into the Hall of Broken Heads.

This was done mainly through the operation of an underground news service, set up in the musty basement of the A.V.E. bookshop down the street from St. Peter's. Through the James Bond tactics of Dubliner John Horgan, religion and education correspondent of the *Irish Times,* the journalists were provided each day with brief summaries of speeches that Horgan obtained from secret sources. A panel of experts, who also had inside knowledge, offered clarifying comments in the manner of the American Bishops' Press Panel during Vatican II.

In mid-afternoon of October 10—the Synod having wound up its daily business at 12:30—the journalists jammed into the basement, their confusion over the Synod compounded by the indignities to which their professional work was daily subjected. Father Lawrence Bright, a British Dominican theologian who has abandoned the Roman collar for contemporary clothing, took his place on the panel and spoke up:

"This unnecessary secrecy should be condemned. It is on the free press of the world that the salvation of the Church depends. We don't know what the national delegations are saying. This is their opportunity to communicate with the world. It's just not true that more important things can be said in secrecy. Washing our dirty linen in public was done at the Council to a very good result. When an elite group talks behind closed doors, this makes the Church seem like a secret society. There is no encouragement for dialogue. There must be open meetings."

Father F. X. Murphy, the American Redemptorist who is widely regarded as being an influential factor in the breakthrough reporting done by the *New Yorker's* "Xavier

Rynne," tried to calm the agitated Bright. "I'm in favor of open debate," Murphy said, "but this debate is not being hampered. The bishops are exchanging differences among themselves and out of this they are growing together and allaying the fear that doctrine is being chipped away. They can thus impress the Holy Father that the problems are not as terrible as the document on doctrine says."

Father Jorge Mejia, a multilingual Argentinian, who was also on the panel, interjected, "They wouldn't describe the state of the Church in their own countries for public knowledge."

"But why not?" asked Bright.

"Mon Dieu!" exclaimed Mejia, slapping his forehead.

It is frequently said that in Rome everything is a mystery and nothing a secret. Cardinal Heenan demonstrated the veracity of this wisecrack. He made a strong speech in the Synod criticizing the document on Dangers to the Faith, and he was eager to let the public know what he had said, as he made clear in a letter to *The Times* of London. Newsmen had been successful in pulling the veil off only a paragraph or two of his speech, and the public was left with a distorted impression, he complained. The result? Despite the Vatican strictures on secrecy, Heenan's full text was published in the *London Tablet* one month after it had been delivered.

Some of the bishops, notably the Canadians, arrived at the Synod with speeches in their pockets to rip open the secrecy rules. But all the progressives quickly saw that a greater issue was at stake. The Synod was an experiment which the Pope desperately wanted to succeed so that collegial government could be started without fractious encounters on the floor that could conceivably end in schisms. Despite the name of the room where the Synod was held, the Pope wanted no broken heads. Synod I had to be a success in order to make a Synod II possible. Without a Synod II and a Synod III to bring this new form of government gradually from consultative to deliberative status, there would be no hope for the final reunion of Rome and the Orthodox.

Caution on the one hand; confusion and distrust on the other. The bishops followed their instincts in supporting Paul's timetable of reform. The progressives reasserted their strength without any blood flowing. And the press survived. As was obvious to the Pope from the start, the substance of the Synod was fully reported. And the Synod Fathers were made aware that the public was watching their action on the crucial document on Dangers to the Faith.

In accordance with standing orders, the Seper committee had to submit its report before the close of the Synod session on October 29, and it beat the deadline by a couple of days. A brief extract will show how different was its approach to current threats to the faith from that of the Congregation for the Faith.

The Congregation's position paper had presented the magisterium in terms of a Church teaching and a Church taught, the former with the direct duty to teach and interpret the deposit of faith, this especially nowadays "because of the trend to challenge everything and to downgrade authority."

The Seper report rejected the dichotomy, insisting that all Christians must cooperate in formulating the faith within the framework of our civilization and the forward movement of culture, and recognizing man's "ever-increasing awareness of the evolution of the universe and of his own life and history." This task, it asserted, "belongs first of all to the bishops, with their helpers in the priesthood, aided also by members of religious orders. But it also belongs to laymen engaged in teaching the faith and in catechizing;

it belongs, in fact, to all the faithful, and in a special way to parents in regard to their children. All the children of the Church, therefore, each according to the charism given him, must be aware of their responsibility for passing on the holy gift of faith to the men of our time."

The Seper group then struck a blow that kept the Catholic revolution on a positive course. Positive ways of setting forth the truth are better than negative condemnations of error, the commission said. "Above all, [bishops] should be aware of how legitimate and even necessary it is for preserving the deposit of faith that there be progress in the understanding that takes into account the progress of the sciences and culture and the ever new questions that face mankind." Therefore, before attempting to teach on new and difficult matters, bishops ought to consult with theologians and seek the prudent advice of their priests and of the laity.

The Seper commission also adopted a proposal which Archbishop Muñoz Vega had made on the opening day of the debate on Dangers to the Faith, a proposal subsequently endorsed by many speakers. It recommended to the Pope the creation of a permanent Theological Commission. Its members, to be named by the Pope from lists prepared by conferences of bishops after consultation with universities and theology faculties, would be "theologians of diverse schools, named for a definite term, of outstanding ability and recognized scholars, living in various parts of both the Western and Eastern Churches." Their function would be, "acting with proper academic freedom, to give their help to the Holy See and especially to the Congregation for the Doctrine of the Faith, principally in regard to questions of major importance."

The Synod itself approved the Seper report, including this recommendation, by an overwhelming majority, thereby committing the Church to something that has been totally lacking from its institutions, a counter-institution able to bring the spotlight of public opinion to bear on any bureaucrat who abuses his authority whether by commission or omission.

In their action on the other four items of the Synod agenda, the bishops similarly showed their determination to remain faithful to the words and spirit of Vatican II, though less dramatically and perhaps less decisively than in their handling of Dangers to the Faith.

This determination came out most clearly in the discussion on reform of Canon Law. All were agreed that major reform was necessary. The Code promulgated in 1917 had been drafted by a small group of canonists working in a strictly legalistic atmosphere and seeking to formulate a series of interlocking, abstract rules capable of resolving all problems. It carried forward the two-class society of the Middle Ages, ignored the change of the world from rural to urban, from illiteracy to universal education, from agricultural to industrial, from isolated parts to unity in religious and cultural pluralism.

Vatican II had made many of its provisions and its total legalistic spirit obsolete, and the curial congregation headed by Cardinal Felici, which prepared the position paper, had tried seriously to take this new reality into account. It proposed the introduction into Church law, for the first time, of some of the legal principles regarded as basic by modern civil society, equality of all before the law, controls on bureaucratic violation of individual rights, public trial, disclosure to an accused of all data charged against him.

While approving this approach, the Fathers urged that it be carried much farther. They found the proposals still unduly legalistic. They urged a massive decentralization of the law-making process, so that the new Code would consist merely of some syntheses of constitutional principles, leaving to the local Churches latitude to express the distinctive spirituality of each. As Cardinal Doepfner put it, the relation of the local churches to the universal Church is different from that of the parts of a state to the state. Each local church is an image of the universal Church and should be free to develop its own character.

The position paper on seminaries had been prepared under the direction of Cardinal Gabriel Garrone of the Congregation of Seminaries and Universities, recently renamed Congregation for Christian Education. As Archbishop of Toulouse, France, he had made a sensational attack on the Congregation of Seminaries at the Council in November, 1964—a condemnation of its outmoded ways that found such universal approval that Pope Paul later called him to Rome to transform the Congregation he had criticized. His position paper followed the lines of reform he had earlier urged and which he was already putting into effect.

The first requirement, he said, was to decentralize the administration, because the bishops of each country were the best judges of the type of education their priests needed. Next, he called for greater confidence in today's young people. "Their qualities and tendencies," he said, "even if they sometimes upset us, are a function of the great changes of our times. . . . Their aspirations express the reality of the world of our times and open it up for us." He expressed his belief that students should play a major part in their own training, living in teams and following courses that would bring them in contact with the world outside the seminary. In all of this, the primary task of his own Congregation in Rome would not be to control or direct, but to serve as a center for the exchange of ideas, and to encourage and inspire local initiatives. Apart from a few curial diehards, the Synod Fathers unanimously approved Cardinal Garrone's position paper and recommended that he continue in the direction in which he was already moving.

The other two agenda items, mixed marriages and liturgical reform, brought into focus the dilemma that has plagued the Church since Pope John's time—how to promote revolutionary change without losing control of the process. The grass-roots response to the Council's directives to advance Christian unity and to find more meaningful ways of worship has brought widespread dissatisfaction with the retention of restrictions which many consider arbitrary or contrary to the mood of the Council.

They see an inconsistency, for example, in the undertaking imposed on the non-Catholic partner to a mixed marriage to raise all children as Catholics, and in the refusal of the Church to recognize as valid the marriage of a Catholic and a Protestant before a Protestant clergyman. Similarly, they urge that much more latitude in liturgical experimentation is essential in order to reach new forms meaningful to modern man, pointing to the several centuries of free experimentation required to produce the Latin liturgy after the change-over from Greek to Latin in the third and fourth centuries.

Faced with these and like issues, in which they considered that their own authority as bishops was immediately involved, the Synod Fathers found themselves unable to reach any logical consensus and settled for largely pragmatic compromise. They voted to retain the principal restrictions presently imposed on mixed marriages, while recommending a wider discretion to bishops to grant dispensations. They also reduced a notch the commitment of the non-Catholic spouse regarding the raising of the children as Catholic. Instead of asking for a promise from the non-Catholic party, if would be enough just to acknowledge the Catholic's intention of raising the children as Catholics.

Regarding the liturgy, the bishops showed a definite wish to continue experimentation, but within a framework of strict controls. The United States bishops were particularly emphatic on this point. Their spokesman, Archbishop John Dearden of Detroit, deplored the many abuses introduced by unauthorized experimenters, asked for a definition of the word *experiment,* and urged that things under study should be "concealed from the public."

As later chapters will document, the battle over the means to implement the Council is here joined. The belief is widespread and growing among priests and laity that the bishops must treat them as adults, acknowledging their freedom to take their own initiatives and trusting their responsible dedication to the Church.

The Pope's health stood up long enough to enable him to give a red-carpet welcome to Orthodox Patriarch Athenagoras, who came to the Vatican to return Paul's visit to Istanbul. But his fever shot up again, forcing him to miss the closing of the Synod. Thus, the Fathers went home without a final word from the Pope, which many were eager to have in order to contrast it with Paul's opening address which had not at all encouraged the progressives.

Many observers have been exasperated by the frequent refusal of Pope Paul to declare himself on controverted issues. They see him as waiting on the sidelines for a consensus to develop rather than providing the dynamic leadership that clarifies issues and produces a consensus. I think, however, that such critics fail to appreciate Paul's style. He is not Pope John, and a comparison of the men is unreasonable. It is not simply that he lacks the all-embracing benevolence that made John unique, but that his role is totally different. John launched the Church into revolutionary orbit, whereas Paul is concerned with the intricate and unglamorous task of a safe re-entry. For a revolution to succeed, the innovator must give way to the consolidator.

And consolidation is the correct way to describe the Pope's subtle but decisive subordinating of the Congregation for the Faith to the Synod of Bishops.

Paul is clearly trying to be a bridge between the progressives and the traditionalists. His speeches are filled with warnings to avoid extreme positions in theological, liturgical, and disciplinary areas. But his actions reveal his intentions of restructuring the government of the Church in the Vatican as the surest way to make Vatican II a permanent reality. In fact, it is only a reform of the Roman Curia that can give a credibility to the lofty desires of the Council.

Paul is a gentle, kind man, unable to hurt, much less fire, anyone. He exercised the Roman virtue of patience in waiting for some resignations of aged officials who had held power for a long time. Their replacements, in many cases, were men from outside Italy. He took his time sweeping out the papal court, cutting back on titles and eliminating the hereditary rights of the Roman aristocracy.

Internationalizing the Curia and adding bishop-consultants from around the world was a major move. Under new rules that went into effect in 1968, the senior officials can only hold one job (instead of being an interlocking directorate as previously), their terms are limited to five years, and on the death of a pope their office is automatically terminated; moreover, the new pope is now compelled to wait three months before making any appointments.

Of course, the game of chess goes on in the Vatican. The liberals take a step forward; the conservatives sidestep. A permanent Synod is urgently needed to assure co-responsibility.

Even after the Synod, curial congregations tried to block liturgical experimentation and to cramp the renewal of the sisterhoods. The old guard, astute to the end, knows how to use new names as a smoke screen for their continued intransigence. But thanks to the continuing momentum of reform, sustained by the Synod, such regressive actions are vociferously opposed by public opinion. Repressiveness has not yet been eliminated from the Roman heights—the Pope still moves cautiously—but the revolution makes a deepening imprint on the timeless façade with each passing month.

Though the first Synod did not touch on the burning issues of birth control and celibacy, it demonstrated that the paralysis that keeps the Church from moving forward on vital topics can be lifted through a collegial form of government that will in time be made compatible with the authority of the Pope. This progress is doubtless not fast enough to catch up to the needs of modern man in the secular city. But, given the defensive mentality that anchored the Church in the Middle Ages while a new world was being born, it is as fast as the Church is able to move without plunging everyone into chaos.

Chaos, however, has proved inescapable as the reformers press forward more boldly only to encounter the stiffening theological conservatism of Pope Paul. The battle lines of the reformers versus the Pope have tightened as Paul, once more cut off from developing theological thought, relies increasingly on papal authority to govern. His jealous retention of the birth control and celibacy issues for his own personal decision reflect his nagging fears of a complete break with the past. The ambiguities within him allowed him to introduce the Synod, but not to trust it completely. He raises hopes of a new style of government—but only for tomorrow.

CHAPTER 2

A New Mankind—Today

Midnight had come and gone in Rome, and the lights still burned in the Palazzo Pio, an auditorium a few hundred yards from the Hall of Broken Heads where another meeting was in progress that would provide a far sharper jolt to the ecclesiastical serenity of the Vatican than the Synod of Bishops.

From a hundred nations of the five continents, 3,300 actively committed Catholics and nearly a hundred observers from other Christian bodies had gathered for a week-long World Congress for the Lay Apostolate. The contrast between the Synod's interior concentration on Church renewal and the Congress' exterior vision of religious reform was the talk of the town.

Another moment of historical significance in the Catholic revolution was approaching as the heads of the national delegations struggled through the first hours of October 18, 1967, to formulate a vote that would tell the hierarchy what the laity really thinks about the great questions facing the Church. And the issue at this particular moment, with everyone tired, tempers edgy, and the translators gone home, was the subject that chills the hearts of the hierarchy because it is so directly connected to their authority—birth control.

Organization of the laity is a 20th-century phenomenon

in the Catholic Church. The temerity of the 16th-century Reformers in stressing a common priesthood of all believers and an active role in Church government for the layman had driven Catholicism further along the road—on which the medieval culture had started it—of a two-class society in which clerics had rights and the laity had duties. By the 20th century, however, it had become evident that the increasing socialization of life called for active involvement on a scale beyond the resources of the clergy. They accordingly enlisted the laity in organizations of Catholic Action, to work as enlisted men under their clerical officers, to constitute the presence of the Church in a hostile world, to carry out obediently and unquestioningly the policy conceived behind the closed doors of the Vatican and of diocesan chanceries.

The system worked fine at first. The previously ignored lay men and women were flattered by their new importance. The "Father-knows-best" mentality, which long instilling had made second nature, enabled them to execute faithfully policies which their experience and judgment told them were irrelevant or stupid. With the sophistication of expanded higher education and the breakdown of the ghetto mentality, however, rumblings grew louder.

Starting with France in the years following World War II, the ranks of Catholic Action were shaken by revolts that resulted in mass defections of members to found their own unapproved organizations, or the withdrawal by the bishops of the "mandate" or authorization which was the seal of official approval—the mark regarded as making an activity part of the Catholic apostolate.

Life was quieter in the United States because the bishops and priests entrusted only marginal activities—bingo, building drives, rubber-stamping approval of episcopal proclamations on issues of Catholic concern—to the official organizations, with the result that a growing number of educated

Catholics drifted away from them as a waste of time and effort.

Vatican II initiated a revolutionary transformation of this as of so many areas of Catholic life and practice. It proclaimed, in agreement with the 16th-century Reformers, that the Catholic in the pew shares a common priesthood with bishops and priests by virtue of his incorporation in Christ through baptism. It insisted that he was to assume his own initiative and accept his own responsibility, not only in his secular work, but in his apostolic undertakings. It told him not to imagine "that his pastors are always such experts that to every problem that arises, however complicated, they can readily give him a concrete solution, or that such is their mission"; but that rather he should make his own decisions "enlightened by Christian wisdom and giving close attention to the teaching authority of the Church."

This was heady wine, indeed, for people long restricted to grape juice. As we shall see in subsequent chapters, it immediately provoked a stampede of enthusiasts and zealots in all directions, to the consternation of the bishops who had proclaimed the good news, and to the confusion of the many traditional Catholics to whom their bishops and priests had neglected to explain either the fact that they had changed some of the rules or the reason for the switch.

As far as Catholic lay organizations were concerned, however, it had produced little significant change. If the subject was raised, the answer was usually that nothing should be done until the World Congress took a global look at the situation. And certainly nobody expected any revolutionary impetus from this Congress (two previous ones had been held in 1951 and 1957). Its constitution provided that the national delegations should be named by the bishops or by bodies chosen by the bishops in each country, and the international delegations came from international Catholic organizations chartered by the Holy See and carefully screened by the Roman Curia. Each national delegation was headed by a bishop and had one or more priests as advisers. Six members could be "non-lay," priests, seminarians, religious men or women, with the result that laity actually formed a minority on a handful of delegations. In addition, some lay delegates were employees of bishops or so long involved in official movements as to be steeped in clerical thinking.

It all added up to something far short of a true cross-section of contemporary thinking of Catholic lay people around the world, and this magnifies the significance of the bombshell it exploded in Rome. For these delegates revealed from the first day of their brief deliberations a dynamism and a world-embracing concern similar to that which the Vatican Council had developed only through several years of effort and reflection.

As I met these people in informal gatherings and listened to them in workshops and meetings, I recognized a leadership now coming to the forefront of the Church, thanks to Vatican II. The American contingent of 30 delegates and 20 experts (median age: 55) had a particularly interesting cross-section of laity.

There was Daniel Meaney, an engineer from Corpus Christi who had sent advance word that "I'm not traveling from Texas to Rome if the report's already written"; Angela Harper, a stunningly beautiful mother of six children from Washington, D.C., and a Doctor of Philosophy who warns that one-way communication in the Church is producing "de-institutionalized" Catholics faster than the hierarchy realizes; Tom Cornell, a product of the Catholic Worker movement and the father of two small children who faced imprisonment for his dedication to the Catholic Peace Fellowship movement that led him to burn publicly his draft card; George E. Heneghan of St. Louis, a veteran of

St. Vincent de Paul charity work who jumped up at every opportunity to protest against any lay infringement on the rights of the bishops; John Cort, a former official in the Peace Corps who struggled in vain for the beginning of a real dialogue between the Americans at the Congress and the American bishops at the Synod; Lucy Nevels of Lincoln, Nebraska, a Negro university graduate who has given up the possibility of full-time work now that her family is grown so that she can spend her time in volunteer community service; and Nunzio Giambalvo, head of the delegation, a Chicago lawyer whose tigerish tactics with the laity quickly yield to the traditional deference in the presence of bishops.

If the Congress delegates arrived in Rome wary of the polite ecclesiastical speeches of former congresses, Thom Kerstiens of Holland, general secretary of the International Christian Union of Business Executives, quickly set a postconciliar tone in his keynote address on the Congress theme, "God's People on Man's Journey." Christians must concentrate on the problems of men today, he said. "Questions about war and peace, about a world divided into a small, opulent part and a vast part wallowing in misery, about the increasing alienation of men in an economy of abundance, about racial prejudice and the absence of solidarity, about the behavior of a youth which is not given worthwhile enough causes to fight for." Modern man wants to understand a God seen through his daily existence. "If we do not attempt to answer those questions, then we must not be amazed if humanity considers us laymen as useful as hippies and our clerics as interesting as the bird in the cuckoo clock."

The delegates fanned out throughout Rome into dozens of multilingual workshops where they dwelled on the problems of building up the underdeveloped countries, racism, birth control, and democracy within the Church.

At previous lay congresses, the style had been to spend most of the time pondering the role of the laity within the Church and then to take a hurried look at the outside world. The change this time to a compelling concern for the world was startling. For all the conservative background of its members, the Congress was totally committed to contemporary problems and needs, acutely conscious of the urgency of man's situation: millions of people, mostly nonwhites, who have no jobs, no homes worthy of the name, not enough to eat, and, worst of all, no hope.

The delegates zeroed in on these red-hot issues which the institutional Church has been fielding with a virtuosity that has promised much and delivered little since the Council. And by doing this, they formulated right in the heart of Rome and presented directly to the Pope and his advisers the current dilemma of the Church—the conflict between an institution that proclaims its desire to change while insisting on a tempo of forward movement in keeping with its venerable age and constant tradition, and a charismatic grass-roots revolutionary drive that threatens to explode.

The Lay Congress and the Synod of Bishops coexisting in Rome at the same time, with only the most formal and symbolic of contacts between them, provided a perfect example of the conflict that has developed in the Church since Vatican II.

It is a conflict between those committed to "ecclesiastical" reform and those committed to "religious" reform. The first group, as personified in the Synod, looks inward to the institution and is concerned with bureaucracy; the second, as reflected in the Lay Congress, looks outward so that the spontaneous and creative powers of Christianity can somehow be made to help man in his misery—today.

There are many Christians who think that the institutional Church, so enmeshed in forms and formulas, has fallen so far behind modern thinking that it is already out of the race with Dietrich Bonhoeffer's "religionless Christianity," which makes more converts every day. The issue is not black-and-white. The institutional Church *is* concerned with improving the human lot of mankind, however slow its advance into the modern world may be. On the other hand, the bulk of individual Christians are still blissfully unaware of the social implications of their beliefs. It would be an error to think that the Catholic laity in their homes around the world are as zealous for social reform as their representatives at the World Congress.

Nonetheless, the distinction between these two styles of Church life, the one inward-centered and the other outward-directed, is valid. And a developing trend of the laity and many of the younger clergy to bypass the institution in carrying out the challenges of Christ's Sermon on the Mount is unmistakable.

It was precisely this trend that Pope Paul strove to head off during his only appearance before the delegates. It was a Sunday-morning Mass for Peace, the traditional liturgical spectacular in St. Peter's, during which the Pope was wildly cheered by the throngs as he sat waving from a portable throne carried by young men in red silk breeches and long flowing arm capes.

Near the great high altar, the entourage stopped and for a brief moment an unforgettable scene filled the eye: standing next to each other were the American astronaut, Colonel James McDivitt, and a member of the Swiss Guard, dressed in a wild array of red and yellow and blue, his lance at the ready. The contrast between the man of space and the man of medieval times was startling. And as the 261st successor of St. Peter hovered above them, the organ at a crescendo, a multitude of tongues singing out, "Praise to the Lord Almighty the King of Creation," the red light glowing on

37

a television camera, the religious pilgrimage of twenty centuries came into focus and the Catholic Church shone as a Church for all people for all time.

Deep lines of fatigue and pain creased Paul's face. And when he had finished concelebrating the Mass with 24 other high-ranking prelates, he appeared near exhaustion. He began his 28-minute address himself, but three cardinals took turns reading parts of it in different languages.

The laity's role in the Church, he said, is not only one of membership, but also of apostolate. The documents of Vatican II had fittingly proclaimed his dignity. The Church looks to the layman for improvement of the temporal order, for the infusion of a Christian spirit into the world. Then the Pope struck a theme that spoke directly to the issue of two organizations ("two parallel hierarchies," as he called them) existing side by side. This would be to forget how Christ had set up the Church, he said. "Certainly the People of God, filled with graces and gifts, marching toward salvation, present a magnificent spectacle. But does it follow that the People of God are their own interpreters of God's word and ministers of His grace? . . . That they can boldly turn aside from tradition and emancipate themselves from the magisterium?" The Pope went on, in his key paragraph: "Indeed, no one can take it amiss that the normal instrumental cause of the divine designs is the hierarchy, or that, in the Church, efficacy is proportional to one's adherence to those whom Christ 'has made guardians, to feed the Church of the Lord.' Anyone who attempts to act without the hierarchy, or against it, in the field of the Father of the family, could be compared to the branch which atrophies because it is no longer connected with the stem which provides its sap. As history has shown, such a one would only be a trickle of water, cutting itself off from the great mainstream, and ending miserably by sinking into the sands."

This comment was widely read at the time as a warning

that the laity should remember their lower status. But another interpretation was offered by Congress officials, that the Pope was thinking ahead to the day when one great Synod could be called, in which the representatives of all the People of God could sit together.

The Congress' Assembly of the Heads of Delegations, rejecting conventional greetings, had previously sent a strongly worded message to the Synod of Bishops calling for representative structures so that the laity could function side by side with the clergy in the Church. Starting from an observation of Kerstiens on modern man's search for a theology in which all can participate actively, they invited a dialogue in the terms advocated by the Vatican Council texts. "The hour has come to associate the laity effectively in the process of decision-making on which Church government rests."

The Council of the Laity, a hand-picked team of professional Catholics operating in Rome under the watchful eye of the Curia, was not enough, the Congress declared. What was needed was the creation of representative structures animated by a spirit of total openness and mutual confidence, with free elections at all levels.

In other words, the Congress struggled not to go its own way in the Church as laity but to get an integrated structure started, a single structure in which all the elements in the Church would be fairly represented. The very thing the Pope was trying to avoid—"parallel hierarchies"—was precisely what the public observed as the Synod and the Lay Congress each went its own way. Many of the Congress delegates were offended at the "clubhouse" attitude of the bishops who did, it is true, come to the Congress' closing session but left *en masse* half way because they had a meeting of their own.

The failure of bishops to grasp the urgency of opening up a frank dialogue with the laity was brought home to me graphically near the end of the Congress. Three of the four American bishops elected to the Synod—Cardinal Shehan, Archbishop Dearden and Bishop Wright—came to a meeting of the American delegation to the Congress, held in the basement of the USO, beside the Palazzo Pio. After a deferential address of welcome by Nunzio Giambalvo, the three prelates spoke in turn.

A short man with rimless glasses and a delicate air, Cardinal Shehan gave the keynote talk. It lasted two minutes and added up to one concept: he was glad to be present.

Archbishop Dearden, president of the United States Conference of Bishops, was somewhat more meaty. A tall man, soft-spoken and with a determined look on his honest, open face, he offered a half-joking, wholly earnest criticism of the press coverage of the Lay Congress.

Bishop Wright, with chubby face and rolling eyes, also found the occasion appropriate for some witticisms at the expense of the press. Apologizing for the absence of Cardinal John J. Krol, he said the cardinal had just held one press conference and had now entrusted to him the task of "throwing the newsmen off the scent."

By this time, I could sense a growing restlessness among the delegates, a realization that their valuable time was being wasted in futilities.

John Cort attempted to get down to business. "Could we not read for the information of the bishops the resolution formulated by the U.S. delegation on dialogue in the Church?" he asked Giambalvo.

Sorry, the chairman said as he smiled weakly, he didn't seem to have his copy around, and he quickly added that the coffee and cakes were ready.

If the Lay Congress delegates had restricted themselves to discussing representative organization, one might have interpreted their concern as primarily a change in the balance of power within the Church, an effort to upgrade the layman within the institution. The rest of their program, however, showed that nothing was farther from their minds than power for its own sake. If they sought change of structure, it was as a means to an end. And the end was clearly spelled out: a Church of missionary effort and witness, seeking to alleviate the social injustices afflicting the mass of mankind; a Church dedicated to the pursuit of peace, of human dignity, of racial equality; a Church sensitive to the distress of its members, its friends, its enemies, and the indifferent alike.

"A little patience, please," boomed the big man with the brooding face in the chairman's seat. "Everything comes in good time. It took me nine months to be born." The voice belonged to a 42-year-old Canadian trade unionist and veteran social action leader—Romeo Maione—whom the Congress had elected President of the Assembly of Heads of Delegations.

The Assembly became the sovereign body at the Congress, charged with formulating in a democratic manner texts, resolutions, and motions. And now the moment of demonstrating post-conciliar lay integrity and responsible collaboration had come. All afternoon and through the evening and into a new day, the Assembly had been debating resolutions.

Everyone knew that birth control, a subject that Pope Paul had not even let be debated at the Council or Synod, would be the real test of the laity's newfound determination to speak out. The Palazzo Pio was charged with the electricity generated by opposing forces. Maione, a veteran of the World Congress of 1957, tried to calm the atmosphere. Sitting coatless at the microphone, switching easily back and forth from French to English, he was the ideal image of the new layman in the Church; knowledgeable, determined, fair, and not a man to be pushed around.

Since the applause had been immediate and thunderous any time a speaker in a general assembly had urged reform in the birth-control law, it was foreseen that this request would work its way through the workshops and resolutions committee to Maione's Assembly. And it did, in frank language, in a draft resolution, No. 32.

The resolution said: "As laymen, we are convinced that responsible family planning is necessary to guarantee the integrity of matrimonial love and of the family institution, in a world where the total population is growing with such an accelerated rhythm. In the line of this unambiguously moral and Christian perspective, we are of the opinion that the choice of means to prevent a new conception should be left to the conscience of the married couple, with due consideration of medical, psychological, economic and sociological insights."

A minority in both the workshop and resolutions committee had opposed the resolution, arguing that the laity should, with patience and confidence, await a papal ruling. A substantial majority, nevertheless, insisted that it was the duty of the laity to express what was on their minds. They were stating their opinion, not invading the field of theology. It was well known that Pope Paul had consulted experts in so many fields in his long and tortured process of making up his mind on whether or not the Church's traditional ban on artificial contraception would stand that the laity felt they would be remiss in their duty if they kept silent. After all, as the great theologians keep saying, theology is not formed in a vacuum, but is arrived at through the study of God's revelation in the light of the human condition.

With exhaustion setting in and the Congress' wind-up session only a few hours away, Maione saw that he could not get to No. 32 before dawn and decided to make the test case of the Congress' will resolution No. 22 on Development. This was a statement that took a sweeping look at

42

the needs of humanity, fitting in family planning as one of the necessary aids to the promotion of social justice.

It called for "a radical transformation of the world economy" because of the "growing gap between rich and poor nations," a gap which "traditional attitudes toward investment and trade cannot lessen." It urged developed countries to give more government aid, "free from political and economic conditions leading to a new form of alienation on the part of the young nations."

Following United Nations guidelines, it asked that the level be raised quickly to one percent of gross national product "in genuine capital assistance." It proposed to Christians and the Church a deep theological reflection on creation, on Christ's role in creation, and on the new creation. The laity, it said, should participate not only in spreading the Church's social doctrine, but in developing it in accordance with their technical competence and experience. The Church should seek a spirituality calculated to inspire Christians to struggle for development and for the necessary change of social structures. It should play a prophetic role in man's efforts to achieve international and social justice, eliminating contrasts of wealth and poverty within its own body, renouncing a standard of living that is often a countersign, working cooperatively with other Christians, and creating structures calculated to form a real People of God through "participation and democratic representation of the masses who play a leading role in development."

Family planning was discussed in a section on population growth. The section reminds states that their demographic policies should be both realistic and respectful of the responsible freedom of parents, that they should exclude the geopolitical intervention of the great powers, and that they should be neither an excuse for delaying development nor a substitute for efforts to realize it.

The resolution then went on to recall "the very strong

feeling among Christian lay people that there is need for a clear stand by the teaching authorities of the Church which would focus on fundamental moral and spiritual values, while leaving the choice of scientific and technical means for achieving responsible parenthood to parents acting in accordance with their Christian faith and on the basis of medical and scientific consultation." Here, as in the other resolution, the message was clear and to the point. For the Lay Congress, the question of means was primarily a medical and scientific one.

The Assembly instinctively sensed the power of this resolution, for it put the laity out ahead of the hierarchy in meeting head-on the problems of development—not only in principles but in practicalities. A delegate tried a parliamentary maneuver to head off a vote. Another stormed out, shouting that his conscience had been violated. A confused, indecisive vote followed, and Maione called for a second ballot, section by section in the auditorium, first on the controversial family-planning paragraph and then on the whole resolution. The resolution carried, 67 for, 21 against, and 10 abstaining. A reporter noted the hour and said to a colleague, "This is an historic moment in the life of the Church."

It was not a moment of rebellion against the Pope, nor was it an attempt to proclaim new Catholic teaching. But it was a testimony, as the Vatican Council had urged the laity to give, of their own experiences and insights—in this case insights into the realities of married life and their informed Christian sense of right and wrong.

As Father John Reedy, C.S.C., editor of the Catholic weekly, *Ave Maria,* put it, "In effect, these well-educated, thoroughly committed Catholic laymen—from all parts of the world—were looking up the street toward the Holy Father and the Synod of Bishops and they were saying: 'You must hear the shared viewpoint which we have discovered to be present among ourselves. We state this awareness with respect for the teaching authority, but also with respect for the dignity of our own Christian responsibility.' "

Although some prelates in Rome immediately tried to downplay the significance of the birth-control vote, it was clearly a major step in the Catholic revolution. For, as we have seen by now, the revolution embraces not only those who want to find their way in life without the institutional Church, but also those growing numbers of Catholics who want the Church to respond sensitively to the needs of contemporary man. The direction of history and quite possibly the survival of civilization is at stake. The birth-control statement, then, is particularly significant in this light.

There is no doubt that the attitudes and practices of married Catholics of childbearing ages regarding the use of means to prevent an unwanted pregnancy have changed significantly since World War II. The official teaching of the Church has similarly changed significantly regarding the obligation of parents to limit the size of their families, whether for such personal reasons as the physical or mental health of the mother or the well-being of the children already born, or for such social reasons as an excess of population in relation to a nation's ability to feed its people.

The official Church, however, has avoided a clear withdrawal from the position formulated by Popes Pius XI and XII, namely, that the only licit means to achieve this purpose is rhythm—the exercise of marital rights only during the sterile period in the woman's monthly cycle. Originally hailed by Catholics as a breakthrough, rhythm is increasingly recognized as not a satisfactory solution for the majority of people, in part because of the education level required to practice it, in part because of the emotional conflicts it can create and the high percentage of failure accompanying its use.

In consequence, as is generally agreed, a big and growing number of Catholic couples are using other contraceptive methods. There are few statistics to determine just how many, but it is frequently asserted that in the United States and most of the industrialized countries of the world, the percentage of Catholics is rapidly approaching the general average for all citizens.

A survey in the United States showed that in the five years from 1960 to 1965, the percentage of U.S. college-educated women favoring birth control rose from 39 to 67, with "a substantial shift" from exclusive endorsement of rhythm to a general endorsement of fertility control. A poll by *Newsweek* magazine found that one-third of adult American Catholics, including 60 percent of those under 35, use a birth-control pill or other artificial device. A large majority, 73 percent, favor a change in birth-control regulations.

At the Vatican Council many bishops from around the world were convinced that something would have to give. The Council, however, refused to face the issue directly. Fearing the confusion that would result from the overruling by a Council of a decision made by several pontiffs, Pope Paul asked it to leave further action to him, and the Council agreed. But it did provide some small new opening by refusing to confirm the previous rulings.

As Pope Paul continued to postpone a decision, the laity assumed the active role to which the Council had called them, challenging the traditional theological conclusions in the light of today's knowledge of human nature, of the natural law, and of the cultural assumptions and encrustations that had been regarded as theological principles.*

Evidence poured in to show that theology as seen in a context of human reality is quite different from theology

* Pope Paul's encyclical of July 25, 1968, *Humanae Vitae*, restating the Church's traditional teaching, is discussed in an Afterword at the back of this book.

practiced in a vacuum. For one thing, it became clear that the Church's failure to evaluate properly the rights of woman as an equal member of the human race had played a significant part in leading theologians into their blind alley.

The reevaluation of the historical factors brought out the part played by St. Augustine, the theologian who carried over from his youth as a Manichaean the atmosphere of a heresy which proclaimed all marriage sinful. Then came the medieval attitudes to marriage, largely conditioned by the low esteem in which society held women. The philosophers doubted that woman had a soul. The theologians stressed Eve's role as the temptress who caused Adam's downfall. Sex was seen as a concession to weakness, an animal action necessary to maintain the species, yet dragging man down close to the level of the beast. In such a context, it was logical to see the marital act as justifiable only for the maintenance of the race, making any use which excluded its reproductive capacity a grave sin against the natural law.

Once woman is recognized as a person endowed with equal rights and capable of equal intellectual and emotional development, such an interpretation of marriage can no longer be sustained. In addition, the development of the life sciences has shown, from a new viewpoint, how right Christ was when he stressed love as the supreme virtue. It is now recognized that love between man and woman is supremely ennobling, and that it is eminently expressed in the act by which they give themselves to each other in marriage. A reason quite distinct from the maintenance of the species is thus identified for the marital act.

Concurrent advances in the biological sciences have shown that the old theologians were wrong in regarding reproduction as the "natural" result of the marital act. This act is now scientifically established to be a random one, the effect of which is occasionally to cause fertilization and the

47

production of new life. The biology hitherto used to condemn interference with the reproductive possibility of the marital act thus turns out to be as inadequate as the cosmogony on the basis of which theologians condemned Galileo in 1633 for asserting that the earth moves.

What is revolutionary in all of this is not only the initiative taken by the laity in challenging the traditional views of theologians and of the institutional Church, but the expression of the conclusions in everyday life without waiting for the clarification that Pope Paul had promised but continued to postpone.

This trend to a personal judgment of the licity of the means flows logically from the proclamation of the Vatican Council that the layman should make his own decisions "enlightened by Christian wisdom and giving close attention to the teaching authority of the Church." Many theologians and confessors accept this viewpoint, no longer regarding the use of contraceptives as excluding Catholic spouses from reception of the sacraments.

By relating the issue to that of world development, the Congress wanted to insist that its concern was not only for the personal anguish of those involved, but for the forward and upward struggle of mankind.

The emphasis on racial justice in this same resolution on world development is a further demonstration of the thrust of the Lay Congress, its concern with what Vatican II had called "the joys and the hopes, the griefs and the anxieties of the men of this age, especially those who are poor or in any way afflicted."

Through the vagaries of history, helped no doubt by a narrowness of outlook on the part of its leaders, the Catholic Church is no longer the church of the slaves and the outcast, as was the Christian Church in the first centuries of its existence. Instead, it is distinctively today the preserve of middle-class members of the white race. The missionary efforts of the 19th and 20th centuries won some millions of adherents in Asia and many millions in Africa. Until quite recently, however, these new churches were regarded as in a state of tutelage, not strong enough in the faith to be entrusted to their own leaders, and the upgrading to full equality is still far from complete.

Nowhere is the identification of the Church with the white middle-class more complete than in the United States. Negroes constitute 12 percent of the population of the United States, but only 1.7 percent of the Catholic population; and most Catholic Negroes are in parishes that continue to be *de facto* segregated. The typical suburban Catholic, the son or grandson of immigrants and still only a few rungs up the social ladder, is bitterly opposed to open housing. If his town has a Negro ghetto, as most of them now do for the domestic help and semi-skilled labor, it is seldom that he welcomes those who live there to the Catholic Church, the school, or the parish societies. The middle-class white suburbanite regards people like Father Groppi, the crusading demonstrator, as renegades to their own people for espousing the Negro cause. In this case, where one's own vested interests are challenged, the teaching of Vatican II has not penetrated very deeply as yet into the Catholic body. For this reason, the Congress made a double request: the Church should continue to make clear "without equivocation" that racism is contrary to all human value and to the Christian faith; Christians all over the world should put into practice this teaching.

A workshop charged with studying obstacles to peace came up with a resolution touching many of the same points. It condemned racial discrimination, urged support of the peace-making activities of Pope Paul and U.N. Secretary General U Thant, and called for studies of ways to change the economic system that is widening the gap between rich and poor. In an obvious reference to Vietnam, it deplored "the scandal of all wars at present in progress" and urged "all possible steps" to end them. In an equally obvious reference to China, it called on lay people everywhere to foster all efforts "to achieve a truly universal participation in the United Nations."

Dramatizing its concern to end another form of discrimination—the discrimination against women which is traditional within the Catholic Church itself—the Congress sent Mrs. John D. Shields, president of the United States Council of Catholic Women, to carry its message to the Synod of Bishops. Wearing a black dress and gray veil, this pleasant-faced, gray-haired lady trooped into the Hall of Broken Heads with Maione, Vittorino Veronese, and a handful of other Congress officials for the only formal encounter of the Synod and the Congress.

The delegates (Veronese, long the leading Catholic layman in Italy, dressed formally for the occasion) were seated beneath the three-president podium. The cameras flashed as Maione presented a formally inscribed message to Cardinal Conway who, choosing humor as befitting the historic encounter of laity and bishops, replied in Gaelic.

"The hour has come," Mrs. Shields told the bishops, "for the laity to be more effectively associated with the decision-making processes on which the Church government rests. Lines of communication within the Church call for extension and strengthening. . . . We desire to develop dialogue essential to the Church's life at every level."

The Synod of Bishops, though neglected for many centuries in the Church of the West, is a venerable institution in the Church, and this was undoubtedly the first time in history that a woman had lectured the Synod Fathers.

"I was in a trauma," Mrs. Shields afterwards confided.

The Lay Congress also struggled with Vatican officials over the place of women in the liturgy. At the last moment a monsignor tried to change the program of the Mass arranged in St. Peter's.

"The Secretariat for State forbids women to act as readers in liturgical services," he said. "You must substitute men at this point where you have a group of women leading the recitation of a series of prayers."

The Congress officials stood up to him. "Let us see the prohibition in writing," they said. The monsignor went off, and that was the last heard of him.

The Congress spelled out the same view of women expressed in these and similar actions. A resolution recorded its view that baptism not only incorporates all who receive it in Christ, but makes them "persons" on a footing of total equality in the Church. Women's concrete place in the Church, it noted, depends on social and cultural circumstances, and since the status of woman in most countries is evolving toward complete equality of rights between man and woman, her place in the Church should change accordingly.

The Congress asked "that women be granted by the Church full rights and responsibilities as Christians, and a serious doctrinal study be undertaken into the place of women within the sacramental order and within the Church." It further asked that "qualified women" be consulted on the revision of canons (of the Code of Canon Law) which affect women, "and that competent women be included in all pontifical commissions."

Perhaps the most insistent of the themes of the Lay Congress was that the Church should recognize the progress made by the modern world by drawing all the governed more closely into the processes of government through democratic institutions. Its final resolution returned to this point.

Earlier in the year the Vatican had set up a new section, a Council of the Laity headed by Cardinal Maurice Roy of Quebec, a move that reflected the new importance of the laity in the Church as a result of Vatican II. The Lay Congress resolution urged the Pope to enlarge the membership of this Council "in accordance with democratic processes so that it may become truly representative of the multiple cultures, organizations, and forms of the Lay Apostolate in all parts of the world, taking into account a just geographical representation." It called on the Council, when so enlarged, to "accelerate the democratic establishment of structures of the laity at all levels across the world," and it directed its own members to undertake the same task in their respective countries on their return home.

Not a few of the members of the Congress, in both formal and informal discussion, had been critical of the Council of the Laity and of another Vatican section created at the same time and also headed by Cardinal Roy—the Justice and Peace Commission for world development. They doubted that these bodies as curial units with nominated members could achieve a truly representational quality or remain long free from institutional commitments. The majority, however, preferred to welcome the initiatives as being in the right direction, while stressing that they still fell short of expectations because they lacked democratic structures and because the membership was not sufficiently representative.

Criticism was also tempered by the first steps taken by the Justice and Peace Commission, steps taken with a rapidity that shook lethargic Rome. The reasons for this change of pace were clearly evident when I visited the Commission's offices on the Piazza San Calisto. They were its soft-spoken but hard-driving secretary, Monsignor Joseph Gremillion of Alexandria, Louisiana, and his personal assistant, the English missiologist and demographer, Father Arthur McCormack. While most Vatican offices are deserted in the afternoon or consigned to a doorman who has no idea when or if anyone will be back later, these two and their staff were going full speed. The offices were modern by Roman standards, with bare walls, functional desks, tape recorders and other similar equipment, a striking contrast to the typical baroque splendor of Vatican offices, which prize neatness and dignity above productivity.

The Commission had quickly established a clear line of policy and action. Starting from Pope Paul's declaration to the United Nations that development is the new name for peace, it is working to arouse the Christian conscience to the growing disequilibrium of the world, and to channel the moral force of Christianity into a concerted effort to create the conditions for peace by developing the economic and human resources of the poor nations. "We are not interested in building a bureaucratic structure or regime here," was the way Father McCormack explained it to me. "Rather, we want to marry the moral concern of the Church to the realities of economics, to spread the teaching of *Populorum Progressio,* and especially to see that it is implemented everywhere."

As they travel around the world, helping national justice and peace commissions to get rolling, the message of McCormack, Gremillion, Cardinal Roy, and Barbara Ward, the famous British economist, is the same: Christians have a moral responsibility to work for the development of all men. It is no longer enough to be charitable to the oppressed. Kindness without a remedy merely covers up the illness. The remedy is the extension of economic justice to halt the growing gulf between the rapidly advancing (and nominally Christian) nations of the West and the poor nations of the underdeveloped world.

Through technology, the world is becoming unified physically. The absence of an accompanying moral unity is, as Barbara Ward says, "a recipe for total disaster." Peace will be an unattainable goal as the millions in the Third World exercise their rightful indignation at starvation all around them while the Western nations become more affluent. Not only the question of social justice for its own sake is involved here; the world is rapidly falling into despair in the midst of the arms race, increasing violence, and mounting racial discrimination.

The Justice and Peace Commission does not rest its case on idealism. Rather, through developing education programs, the Commission is trying to make Christians understand that they must be involved in the technicalities. Countries must adopt the same kind of *international* development policies as they have for *national* development. This means taxation specifically for international development, rather than the yearly pleas in national governments for "foreign aid." More equitable trade policies must be established, because unfavorable trade balances in key primary commodities (such as sugar and coffee) wipe out foreign aid benefits.

The 2.5 percent annual population increase in the developing countries means that current food production will have to treble by the year 2000. And it clearly will not do that unless there is an agricultural revolution brought on by an annual $6-billion capital investment in developing agriculture. Yet the sum of all foreign aid from the rich nations to the poor nations totals only $6 billion, and the aid is now starting to go down. Leading economists and demographers are agreed that massive famine is on the horizon.

"The world," says Cardinal Roy, "is sick. And the prognosis is higher fevers, greater pain, and more convulsions—unless drastic remedies are brought to bear."

By the mid-1970s, at least $16 billion in investment and assistance will be needed in the developing countries. This sum will represent less than 2 percent of the gross national product of the Atlantic nations by 1975. If governments accept the target of 1 percent of G.N.P. in genuine aid, and public and private investment reaches another 1 percent, the impending calamities could be averted. These measures can hardly be said to be too difficult in light of the fact that the Atlantic nations are today adding $60 billion yearly to their production—a figure equivalent to the whole income of Latin America and twice as great as the incomes of either India or Africa.

The special Christian contribution in these complexities, the Justice and Peace Commission maintains, is to project a vision of justice, to give governments the backing they need to mount such a campaign. Christians must face the fact that in a world made every day more abundant in science and technology, millions of people are denied the food, clothing, shelter, and literacy they need for full human development. Developed nations spend $150 billion a year on arms, $50 billion a year on tobacco and alcohol. It is not, therefore, lack of resources, but lack of will to improve the human condition that plagues the world.

All these were ringing themes at the Lay Congress. "We must take up the duty of creation," Barbara Ward declared in the jammed Palazzo Pio, "and hold out to the world the duty of faith and hope and willingness to create this kind of world. If we don't see this, we deserve to be thrown into the privy."

It is significant that I found in the Justice and Peace Commission the same views on birth control as the Congress had expressed. "It is certainly one of the keys to development," Father McCormack told me. "To plug it as the total solution while neglecting positive action is, of course, phony and selfish on the part of the rich nations. But runaway increase of population negates other efforts and can lead only to starvation."

He is optimistic that the Church is seeing all of this in a more realistic framework. "It is our function at the Commission to present this picture to the Pope in its correct perspectives. When birth control was first proposed, it appeared as an attack on marriage and the family, a means to permit free love without responsibility. Today, on the contrary, big families become a threat to the values of marriage, and it is the duty of the Church to defend marriage against this attack, just as it was earlier her duty to defend it against the other."

At noon on the final day of the Congress, I encountered Maione, rested and in high spirits, walking down the Via della Conciliazione on his way to the Vatican radio station where he had been invited to give his impressions of the Congress. He still had an hour or so before his appointment, and we ducked into a side street and found a restaurant with some tables in a quiet garden at the rear.

Maione was ravenous after a week of little sleep and irregular meals, and as he consumed *pasta* and chicken, he reflected on the astounding difference in the demeanor of the laity in 1957 and 1967.

"Then we had to listen to a lot of set speeches," he said. "When we wanted to talk about the world first and then about the Church, we were accused of heresy, and we could do nothing about it because there was total control of our structures from the top down. This time, we insisted on free election of the president of the Assembly of Heads of Delegations, and from that point onward, we had effective control of our destiny."

But there's far more at stake than just the interaction of various bodies within the Church, Maione insisted. "We live in an alienated world. People don't feel like people. The job of the Church is to try to save these people, to bring them love, to share with Christ living in their neighbor. I'm not interested in just sitting down to have a cup of tea with the bishops. I want to tell them that I know a 22-year-old foundry worker who's asking, 'Is it possible to love in this modern world?' "

He talked of the need for experimentation in the building of new structures in the Church, lest by jumping too
quickly from one "permanent" way of acting to a new
"permanent" way the Church be left behind once more in
a constantly changing world. Then he looked up from his
plate. "You know what the real issue is today? It's how to
live a spiritual life in a highly complex technical society.
Faith has got to be a continual growth. But when I look at
organizations within the Church, I don't see a growth in
faith. There's fraternal and human growth, but there's no
searching for spiritual growth. Most Catholics in these associations have the religious culture of a fourteen-year-old."

With the Synod of Bishops and the Lay Congress having
completed their sessions, I returned to North America to
examine the Church at an entirely different level—the world
of ordinary people caught up in the revolution of ideas,
practices, and styles.

The image of the Synod, as I have said, was one of internal Church questions, while the image of the Lay Congress
was a driving concern for humanity. It would be wrong to
infer that the ecclesiastical side of the Church is concerned
only with internal balances, while the laity are doing the
job of saving mankind. There are bishops leading social
reform, and there are vast numbers of laity who still see no
reason for projecting their religion out of the sanctuary.
In fact, 57 percent of U.S. Catholics, according to a 1968
Gallup poll, hold that the Church should not be involved
in political and social issues.

Although younger people tend to see more clearly the
relationship between religion and life in the world, the bulk
of Catholics feel that the first duty of religion is to comfort
the individual, that priests do not have the training needed
to deal with social and political problems, and that churches
should concentrate on raising the level of religious belief

and practice. The Catholic parishes' long preoccupation with a narrow theology of sin and personal salvation to the exclusion of much concern for love, the community, and Christian witness has come home to roost.

Had the Gallup survey been taken a decade ago, the percentage of Catholics believing in non-involvement would undoubtedly have been much higher. But the major social encyclicals of Popes John and Paul, notably *Mater et Magistra, Pacem in Terris,* and *Populorum Progressio,* combined with the Vatican Council's Constitution on the Church in the Modern World, have begun to change the climate of thinking.

What the Lay Congress established is that the social teaching of the Church, which has been on the books for a long time, has at last taken hold in the lay leaders of the world, who are now running faster than the institutional Church. The urgencies of the world condition, the multiple educational programs around the globe, and the building of a new social concern into the catechisms and the seminary systems will produce in the next decade a much greater number of socially committed Catholics. This advance, linked with the Council's insistence on equality of baptism and co-responsibility in the Church, has already started to break down the artificial barriers that previously existed between the different classes in the Church.

Thus, I found in my journey that the only meaningful distinction in the Church today is between those who are involved in expressing Christ's love for all mankind and those who are not. Both groups include bishops, priests, nuns, and laity. The tensions and eruptions in the post-conciliar Church are not between classes of people as such, but between those who want to plunge a remodeled Church into the cascading mainstream and those who want the Church to be a refuge from the secular city.

In the United States, this cleavage shows up dramatically in the two overriding social issues of our time—race and peace.

When Martin Luther King was murdered, Catholic leaders went into a state of shock. In the instant of a single bullet cutting down the apostle of militant non-violence, the Church bolted into a new state of consciousness about its responsibilities for racial justice.

Archbishop Dearden of Detroit set a standard for other dioceses by pledging the major portion of Detroit's annual archdiocesan fund—from $1 million to $1.5 million—to programs to eradicate racism and aid ghetto residents.

"May God forgive me," Cardinal Richard Cushing of Boston publicly prayed, "and all peoples identified with me who have been hesitating about the practical application of human right for human beings, irrespective of their race, creed, or color." He asked his people to back him in giving "everything that the Catholic Church has to give under my jurisdiction" for the Negro community.

In Newark, where Catholics had joined in the white rush to buy guns following the summer riots of 1967, 25,000 people joined in a Palm Sunday "Walk for Understanding" past the ramshackle tenements of the Central Ward ghetto.

The American bishops, assembling in St. Louis less than a month after the funeral of Martin Luther King, Jr., made an unprecedented public confession of failure in changing the racist attitudes of many Catholics.

"In the name of God, our Father—and we do not lightly invoke his name—let us prove to all men that we are truly aware that we are a single human family."

The bishops moved on to set up an "urban task force" to coordinate work for the Negroes. On the surface, the response did not seem impressive, but a program outlined by the bishops' social action department contains the seeds of long-term gains. Catholic schools serving ghetto areas must stay open (200 had been closed in the past few years); investments in buildings should not be made before deciding how the same money could be used to help the urban poor; correct teaching on the immorality of racial discrimination should be built into the Catholic curriculum, instead of being merely an adjunct to the traditional teaching on morality.

The effectiveness of the bishops' response cannot be measured for some time to come, but they have made clear that, at last, the priorities of Church work are undergoing a profound change. From an age of building Catholic institutions to serve Catholics, the more enlightened bishops have shifted into a new era of committing Catholic resources to the social betterment of the community.

In similar outpourings of guilt across the country, Catholics *reacted* to the King slaying. They had never before *acted* with such Christian concern for the education, housing, and jobs that are barred to Negroes.

Nothing more clearly illustrates Catholics' long-standing lethargy on social issues than the race question. Aside from a handful of priests and sisters who devoted their lives to the Negro apostolate, the record of the Catholic Church's rejection of a commitment to the black man is grim. White racism infected the Catholic Church as much as it did the Christian Churches generally.

The American hierarchy condemned racism as a moral evil in 1958. Some bishops, such as the late Cardinal Joseph Ritter of St. Louis, led in desegregating institutions, and Catholic interracial councils developed north and south, but for the most part, racial justice has been on the far fringe of the Church's concerns. Racial justice could not be put anywhere near the Church's teaching on obscenity, birth control, anti-Communism, and the need for Catholic schools, as subjects repeatedly emphasized in sermons since World War II.

Even after the shock of the 1967 riots, recalcitrant Detroit pastors were still opposing open housing legislation. Dearden's Department of Community Relations sent a sermon outline promoting open housing to pastors and then followed up with a survey.

"Don't send us any more of those sermons," one pastor in a white suburb insisted. "They antagonize the people and divide the parish. There were arguments and hard feelings after the Masses. And a number of people have stopped contributing to the Church as a result."

Another pastor in a changing neighborhood was hostile. "We're a dying parish," he said, "and the parishioners are blaming both the city officials and the Church agencies like yours for fostering all this help for the Negro, who will never show his appreciation. More should be done to safeguard the homes of those who poured life savings into these homes and have been paying taxes and costly improvements for many years—only to see it all going down the drain."

"Go easy on the pressure," a third pastor cautioned. "Many people feel that this is a political issue and should be left to the politicians."

Many pastors, of course, supported the moral stance of the Church in behalf of open housing. Archbishop Dearden himself had spoken out strongly in favor of the Michigan legislation. Nonetheless, the bill went down to defeat, 55–47.

The Detroit Archdiocesan Department of Community Affairs, headed by Father James Sheehan, is the closest to a model organization for U.S. dioceses. It functions as a central agency of the Church, rather than on the periphery. The fact that even this advanced body makes only a mild impact on Catholics testifies to the residue of indifference that lies deep inside the Church because of the ambivalences of the past. Everywhere in America, the Church has been part of the social system that developed with the black man on the outside looking in. Since Negroes form such a small part of Catholic Church membership, Catholics deluded themselves for years by assuming that race was not a "Catholic" problem.

Thus, the advances of the Negro people through the 1950s in education and voting rights were made despite Christian indifference toward them. The Church followed, not led, the state in ending outright discrimination. Because Catholics were indistinguishable from the rest of the middle-class white population in running to the suburbs, *de facto* segregation in Catholic Churches and schools actually increased.

When the 1960s saw mounting Negro drives for housing and jobs, and the rise of Dr. King's militant non-violence as a means to obtaining them, the moral power of the institutional Church was again absent. A number of priests, nuns, and laity began marching and linking arms with ministers and rabbis in a common religious cause; Father Groppi became the supreme example of white Catholic militancy for Negro rights as he led marches in Milwaukee night after night. But the activity of the few contrasted all the more starkly with the millions in the Church—of high and low station—who turned their backs on the Negro cause.

"Here you find a theological ambiguity," says Dr. William A. Osborne, a sociologist at St. John's University, who has done a pioneering study of race relations in the Church. "A tremendous proportion of the Catholic population still believes in the Mass and frequent attendance at the sacraments as the principal means of salvation. A smaller number of Catholics say that true Christian belief requires involvement and commitment to moral problems of race, poverty, war, and peace. Both kinds attend the same Church. And in any institution, the momentum is toward advancing its own welfare first."

As urban riots began to threaten the viability of the philosophy of non-violence, more Catholic consciences awakened, although there was still a "suspicious disdain" in the Church toward black militancy, a caucus of Negro priests in Chicago charged. Crash programs were started in several cities to improve Negro conditions. A dozen of the 200 American bishops attending the annual meeting of the hierarchy in Washington, D.C., went to the Catholic University of America one evening to participate in an inter-faith rally for poverty legislation then before Congress. But the most acid non-comment on the extent of Christian churches' involvement with the Negro was in the U.S. Riot Commission report, which had virtually nothing to say about the Christian churches—Catholic and Protestant—in its 608 pages.

Then came the Memphis bullet. Too late, Catholic leaders realized that had Martin Luther King received the full and unequivocal support of the 47-million-member Church in the pursuit of his dream of the promised land, America might well have escaped its new civil war. Catholic leaders who had never marched with King in life now trailed behind the mule-drawn coffin. *Reaction,* not *action.*

The King tragedy was a turning point for the Church, as well as for the nation. It suddenly sent gushing through the Church a new will to help the blacks, a will that had only slowly been coming to maturity ever since the Council had underlined the need for Christian involvement with the modern world. The new conscience brought into the forefront long-standing interracial work that had previously been relegated to the shadows.

The leading Catholic organization in this area is the National Catholic Conference for Interracial Justice, which operates out of an office in the near-slum of South Wabash Avenue in Chicago. Its director, Mathew Ahmann, invited me to spend a day (several months before the King shoot-

63

ing) at a staff meeting to get an overview of the Conference's work. The Conference began in 1961 on what Ahmann calls "a shoestring budget." Since then it has developed field services that help Negroes get education, health, and employment opportunities.

The program that has won the most attention is Project Equality, an interdenominational effort to use the purchasing power of the churches exclusively with businesses that maintain fair employment practices. Although directing the financial power of the Church in a way that helps to produce jobs for Negroes would seem to be an elementary step, only 22 of the 154 Catholic dioceses in the country had joined Project Equality at the time of my visit. As I listened to the staff members giving their reports, I could not escape the impression that they spent a good deal of their time in the elementary task of trying to convince Catholic leaders of the need for racial action.

The painful history of Christian non-involvement with Negroes colliding with the explosive force of black power now raises the crucial question: will the Church spend its moral prestige for black housing, black jobs, and black education in continuing *active* programs? Or will the conscience-stricken *reaction* to the King murder, impressive as it was, give way to the traditional "prudence" in contentious questions?

"No large city will be able to solve its housing and related problems," Ahmann says, "if the Catholic Church is not actively involved in seeking and working for the solution. For no other 'white' institution is still so rooted in the life of our cities. If, as was true in some dioceses, some Catholic parishes could help buy houses to keep Negroes out of the parish neighborhood, now we must be as imaginative in developing ways of helping Negroes into our neighborhoods." Since racial equality deals with the basic life of the Church—the indivisibility of human nature and the great commandment of the New Testament—no renewal in the Church can be genuine that does not face up to the racial crisis.

If the Catholic revolution is to succeed, the Church must regain the moral initiative in racial equality, an initiative it has willingly allowed the Federal government to exercise. If the Church does not continually assert its moral commitment, it will be written off as moribund by the new forces shaping society. But for the Church to lead, rather than follow, the state puts it in an exposed position, which until now most bishops have wanted to avoid. To prove its Americanism, the Church has always wanted to be part of the scenery, not standing alone like a mountain towering over the forest.

This determination to be American has also kept the Church mute on the morality of the Vietnam war. The peace movement had to forge its uphill battle without institutional Church support, despite Pope Paul's repeated condemnation of the immorality of the war and the Vatican Council's assertion that the concept of the "just war" is dangerously outmoded.

"My country, right or wrong"—Cardinal Spellman's catchword—made bishops wince, but only a handful of them spoke out forcefully against continuing the war, and then only when public opinion had begun to turn against American involvement.

The civil rights and peace movements have a similarity in that both required civil disobedience in order to polarize the issues in public opinion. Martin Luther King and his comrades were willing to go to jail for their cause. So were the anti-Vietnam protesters who burned their draft cards. Civil rightists and Christian pacifists have had to go it alone, earning the scorn of the institution before they could hope for its understanding and eventually its support. The vocation for equality and the vocation for peace have required a charismatic heroism that stands out against institutional conformity.

The Vatican Council pulled away from the old idea that all leadership has to come from the top; but the Church is not yet used to the new idea that moral leadership frequently involves demonstrations and disobedience of unjust laws. Thus, in order for the Church to take its rightful place in the transcending issues of our time, bishops, priests, and nuns, as well as the laity, must be free to follow the dictates of their consciences. In a new age of Christian enlightenment, this is bound to identify the Church increasingly with the civil rights and peace movements. As Dr. Osborne points out, "This will bring the right wing into the fray, thus polarizing the two extremes, already quite dynamic."

The turbulence the Church has already passed through since the Council is mild compared with what lies ahead if the leadership of the socially committed—bishops, priests, nuns, and laity alike—is to advance the Church over the protests of those who still want their religion to be a comfort to them. If this advance is not pursued at an accelerating rate of speed, then all hope for making the Church a credible and relevant servant of modern man, and particularly the developing millions in the Third World, will be lost. The delegates to the Lay Congress in Rome seemed to sense this imperative intuitively.

The progress made in Rome by Catholic lay leaders grappling with the major issues in the world was a stimulant for more home effort, Dan Meaney, the independent-minded engineer from Corpus Christi, Texas, told me several months after the Congress ended. "After twenty-five years of lay activity in the Church, I had just about come to the conclusion that I'm not the lay apostle type. The action was elsewhere." But the Lay Congress demonstrated a new maturity, he said, which was characterized by a deep longing to be *with* the hierarchy, not *against* them.

"Now I think we just might be able to make something out of the lay apostolate," Meaney said. "It may well be worth our time and talents as adult Christians, and joint owners and full partners in the people of God."

CHAPTER 3

The Post-conciliar Sheen

The effect, as I stood looking at the magazines clamoring for attention on a newsstand, was intriguing. The cover of *Ramparts,* an intellectually racy monthly that began as a Catholic exponent of the left and graduated into a slick mudslinger, featured four pictures under the title "Left Wing Catholics." Father James Groppi, the courageous demonstrator for Negro housing, was one. Father William DuBay, who captured national attention by trying to organize a priests' union, was another. They clearly belonged in this category. Then there was Jesus Christ, and it took only a second's reflection to say why not; Christ was the greatest reformer who ever lived. But the fourth member of this team—Bishop Fulton J. Sheen?

For three decades, Sheen has been a household word throughout America. He is a radio and television star (his "Life Is Worth Living" series was carried on 123 TV and 300 radio stations at its peak), and such giants of the entertainment world as Jackie Gleason and Johnny Carson can be sure of extra attention when they lure him onto their programs. Sheen is an author (a dozen major books) whose speciality has been comforting people in a confused world. Sheen is a convert-maker; the illustrious Clare Boothe Luce, Heywood Broun, and Henry Ford II entered the Catholic

Church under his direction. Through the years he has fought Communism and collected money for the missions with undivided zeal. Equally at ease in the salons of Vatican aristocracy or eating dinner with a beggar, Sheen has long since reached that pinnacle denied to all but a handful of mortals—he is a living legend.

Among his pursuits, he was for fifteen years one of the auxiliary bishops to the late Cardinal Francis Spellman. While Sheen's national work doubtless kept him close to his own office several blocks away from Spellman's New York powerhouse on Madison Avenue, the fact that Sheen stayed under his episcopal boss for so long indicates either that he has been a very patient man or a very obedient one, or that he was not particularly upset by the Spellman brand of religious conservatism which so strongly influenced the American hierarchy.

Because Sheen, ardent actionist that he has been, was considered a solid member of the institutional establishment, it came all the more as a shock to observe his grass-roots breakthrough once he was named, on October 28, 1966, Bishop of Rochester, N.Y.

The people of Rochester, Catholic and non-Catholic, could scarcely believe their luck, and many wrote directly to Pope Paul thanking him for his generosity in giving them one of the great figures of the Church. The Catholics were grateful because they felt singularly blessed, the Chamber of Commerce because they had an international newsmaker in their domain. Rochester, the epitome of middle-class America, was in awe when Sheen arrived.

The media pictured and described the flashing, magnetic eyes, his overpowering characteristic. The silver wavy hair, the slender frame, the expressive hands all received attention. And the city basked in his accomplishments: his boyhood in Peoria, Illinois, preparing the scholar who would race through the Catholic University of America, Louvain, the Sorbonne, Angelicum, emerging in 1925 at the age of 30 with a collection of degrees capped by the distinction of being an *Agrégé en Philosophe* at Louvain. And all of this preparatory to a spectacular ecclesiastical career.

The television lights (it was amusingly revealed by insiders that Sheen himself had aided in their placement) bathed the sanctuary of Sacred Heart Cathedral for the traditional installation of a new bishop, a ceremony that did not disappoint those who relish the triumphalism of such occasions. With the eyes of Rochester fixed on a 71-year-old man, dressed in the white, gold, and purple robes of the medieval age, being led to his throne in the measured strides of an authority figure, the idea of grouping him with revolutionary figures on a magazine cover would have appeared ludicrous to some people.

Yet within the year, Sheen would earn that selection. And the city that was his upon entry would be bitterly divided over him.

The issue was the reality of the Second Vatican Council. In every action that he took, Sheen revealed an intense commitment to conciliar thought as formulated in the sixteen Council documents. Sheen determined to make the Council come alive in Rochester, but the Catholics didn't know what it was all about, and the city began to reel under a new kind of episcopal influence. The conciliar revolution, launched by Pope John, was brought down to earth and planted in local soil by Fulton Sheen. I decided to go and see for myself.

My visit to Rochester provided some of the greatest contrasts I observed in the 35,000 miles of my search for the meaning of the Catholic revolution. There was evidence all around of what conciliar supporters were calling the Sheen "miracle." He had not come with a blueprint. He was not always sure that his decisions were correct in his zeal to bring about needed reforms in his diocese. But, unlike

70

many younger men who had spoken more loudly during the Council session in Rome, he did not content himself with naming study committees and talking vague generalities. He began to experiment immediately. He started to listen to his people, to involve them, to provide openings for those who wanted to move ahead.

On the other hand, it was shocking to listen to the response of many priests. "He is not going to get away with it," a monsignor occupying a key post in the diocese told me, in effect, as we had lunch one day. "We have only to stall him off for four years until he reaches retirement age. Then the whole nonsense will be quickly forgotten, and we'll get back to the tried and trusted methods that always served us well." When this monsignor said "we," he was referring to a small but influential bloc of priests and lay people, mostly over 50.

They wanted no change in the power structures, and Vatican II was an episode they were convinced they could erase from the records and relegate to the status of a bad dream. What surprised me especially was the cynicism with which they tossed aside the clearly expressed will of the Church they purported to serve and the specific instructions of their bishop. It is amazing to observe intelligent people so obsessed by their own interests as to be incapable of reading the most obvious signs of the times. Thought control of the kind they once exercised is no longer possible in today's climate of instantaneous and total communication.

What, concretely, has Bishop Sheen done to earn so violent a reaction? The answer is simple. He has questioned everything that the institutional Church had previously been doing by measuring each existing procedure, attitude, and presumption against Vatican II standards. He did this with rigorous objectivity and a directness that was no respecter of persons. And he did it with a rapidity shocking in an ecclesiastical world noted for its slow tread and solemn mien. There is no doubt that Bishop Sheen is in a hurry. He has only a few years. But in his projection, the shortness of the time for reform seems to be less related to his own age than to the urgency of the situation. That is where he differs with his opponents. That is why he is in a hurry.

We don't need conjecture and circumstantial evidence to establish Bishop Sheen's master plan. Just eight months after his arrival on the scene, he issued a detailed analysis of the situation and a progress report. It tells precisely what he is doing, and why. Undoubtedly the most radical departure and most determinative factor was the summons to the entire body of Rochester Catholics, priests and people, to participate actively in the decision-making process.

In principle, it is now widely agreed that the concept of collegiality applies not only to the relations of pope and bishops in top-level decisions, but to those of bishop and priests at the diocesan level, and to pastor and people at the parish level, and more broadly, to the whole people of God in the total life of the Church. The principle is being translated into practice in different ways and to different degrees throughout the world. The most sophisticated and advanced implementation is in Holland, where a national pastoral council held its first plenary meeting in January, 1968. Of its 109 voting members (44 laymen, 28 laywomen, 37 priests and bishops), 70 had been elected by universal suffrage, and the others represented religious orders and other special groups. Its agenda reflected the work of thousands of study groups distilled over two years. The consensus of observers was that the entire body of the faithful is now actively involved in the decision-making process in the Church in Holland.

In the United States and Canada, many dioceses have established assemblies of the clergy and the laity, with varying authority and effectiveness, depending on the judgment or innovative ability of the bishop and other local conditions.

Sheen started informal consultations as soon as he arrived in Rochester. He picked four churches in different parts of the diocese and visited each for an afternoon, from 3 o'clock to 7:30, exchanging ideas with all comers. Simultaneously, he began an organized effort to reach directly every member of the clergy and as many as possible of the 362,000 Catholics in the diocese. His notification to the priests that he would hold elections for a senate or council of priests to help him in governing the diocese is dated January 27, 1967, six weeks after his installation as bishop. This short letter (500 words) tells a lot about its author and his program. It starts with his reason for taking a step that will provide "the first opportunity given to priests to be co-workers with the bishop in the government of the diocese." His reason is simply that Vatican II had ordered every bishop to create such a body to operate "in a manner adapted to modern circumstances and needs, and have a form and norms to be determined by law."

The letter next informed the priests that the voting procedures had not been established by the bishop arbitrarily, but followed the recommendations of his existing board of consultors. They provided for the election of twelve priests, one for each age group from the youngest to the oldest, with freedom to the bishop to add "a few others, including religious," to a total not to exceed twenty. The first business of the Council would be to draw up its own constitution, deciding length of service, future voting procedures, and other issues.

Finally, the letter assured the recipients that the Council would be no rubber stamp, but a participator in the government of the diocese. "I can foresee that such problems will be discussed as parish boundaries, appointments (both parochial and supra-parochial), length of tenure of a pastor

73

or curate in one place, etc. It is, therefore, important that with prayer to the Holy Spirit you choose a priest of your age group who is walking worthily in his vocation."

In this same spirit, Sheen sought the widest possible consultation on all decisions. He visited every part of the diocese in his first eight months there, preaching more than 400 sermons and talking to as many priests and lay people as possible. He asked all priests to list the fellow priests they considered most representative and named Monsignor Dennis Hickey, who headed the list, as his vicar general, the top official of the diocese under the bishop. Hickey was subsequently selected by Sheen as one of two auxiliary bishops.

Sheen changed the name of the central diocesan administration from Chancery, a word with strong legal overtones, to Pastoral Office. Decisions were no longer to be made by the bishop alone, but through what he calls "corporate wisdom," resulting from discussion and dialogue with the officials of the Pastoral Office.

Within a month of his installation he took a step that gravely upset some of the older priests. He transferred the financial affairs of the diocese to laymen who would be responsible only to himself. John Ritzenthaler was named comptroller, charged with setting up the diocesan operation on a business basis, and a three-man advisory board—a banker, a lawyer, and a certified public accountant—was formed to advise him. A uniform system of bookkeeping was introduced in all parishes, and Mr. Ritzenthaler was instructed to visit each parish in order "to supervise budgets, examine the financial books, and urge practices of economy."

Concrete changes include new provisions to increase the aid of rich parishes to poor ones, a purpose further promoted by coordination of parishes in the run-down central sector of Rochester under a central administration which will permit an intensified apostolate.

74

Limits of expenditure have been imposed on the building of churches, rectories, convents, schools, and other diocesan buildings. One reason offered by Sheen for this policy is the folly of pouring a lot of money into a building which, because of the rising mobility of Americans, may have no congregation in 25 years. Meanwhile, he constantly calls attention to the need for rich Christians to dramatize by concrete acts their concern for the world's poor. We must share our prosperity and progress, he has declared, "with the poor of the diocese and of the world."

He has, accordingly, imposed a progressive tax, rising to 3 percent where the amount involved exceeds $500,000, on all new construction, the proceeds to be paid to the poor of the Inner City and the poor of the world. Its purpose "is not only to cut down on extravagance in building, but also to make the local Church conscious that it is part of the Mystical Body throughout the world." A percentage of the diocesan Development Fund has been allocated for the same purposes.

Pastors of the wealthy parishes could not work up much enthusiasm for this proposal. Moreover, they were still smarting from a directive stating that henceforth the Christmas collection could no longer be considered a gift to the pastor, but would have to be put in parish funds. This was tempered by news that a more realistic salary scale would be started. But to some pastors, accustomed to five, six, and seven thousand dollars in Christmas collections, a salary increase of a thousand dollars was not enticing.

As head of the national organization for the Society for the Propagation of the Faith, Bishop Sheen had been uniquely successful in getting middle-class American Catholics to contribute to the world missions. To do this, he had not found it necessary to challenge the power structures of a Church whose policies and attitudes had long been dominated by that middle class. On the contrary, he was able to achieve his fund-raising objectives by a form of appeal that ultimately strengthened this group in its complacent satisfaction by making it feel it is concerned to the point of generosity with the sufferings of the less worthy.

As chief pastor of the diocese of Rochester, however, the bishop quickly injected a further dimension that sent immediate rumblings of dissension among the relatively small group of priests and lay people who had hitherto constituted the "conscience" of the diocese.

"He got the message across right away," was how one priest put it to me, "that he was not prepared to be bishop of *some* of the Catholics of Rochester. He was the pastor of his entire flock."

Within a week of taking over, Sheen exploded his first bombshell by plunging into a sizzling civil rights dispute. The immediate issue was between a militant civil rights organization called FIGHT (Freedom, Integration, God, Honor, Today) and Eastman Kodak, a company so important to the economy of Rochester that the city is commonly described as a Kodak company town. In late December, 1966, Kodak announced it would not honor an agreement reached with FIGHT by one of its executives, an agreement stipulating that Kodak would hire and train a specified number of unemployed Negroes. Kodak claimed that the executive had exceeded his authority. FIGHT charged that it had been doublecrossed.

Without mentioning Kodak explicitly, Sheen showed where his sympathies lay. He visited the Church of the Immaculate Conception on Plymouth Avenue, in Rochester's Third Ward ghetto, then followed up the visit by appointing Father David Finks, the church's 36-year-old assistant pastor, as episcopal vicar in charge of the Inner City problems.

The appointment was significant for many reasons. It was Bishop Sheen's first in his diocese. It was made under a

Vatican II decree authorizing bishops to delegate some of their powers for the better performance of their tasks. It was the first appointment of an episcopal vicar for Inner City problems in the United States, giving Finks responsibility not only for housing, education, employment, and health, but also for "social justice, equality, and the sharing of the common heritages of American well-being and Christian civilization." Finally, Finks was a leading member of FIGHT. His choice could only be interpreted, as it in fact was, as an endorsement by the bishop of the things FIGHT was striving for.

If further endorsement was needed, the bishop added it when he addressed a dinner meeting of the Chamber of Commerce. Speaking of the race situation in Rochester, he compared the town to a beautiful woman with a pimple on her nose. It was a particularly apt comparison, and it hurt all the more for being so apt. With today's know-how, there is no more justification for a modern city living with a suppurating slum area than for a beautiful woman allowing a pimple to mar her perfection. The Rochester Establishment has never forgiven Sheen for the "pimple-on-your-nose" speech.

In the light of the U.S. Riot Commission's indictment of white racism infecting America, Sheen's rebuke was only a wrist-tap. His sense of dramatic impact impelling him on, he subsequently offered the site of St. Bridget's church and school in a Negro and Puerto Rican slum area as a gift to the Federal government to be used for a housing development. But his sense of timing was off, and the gesture backfired. Unknown to even the pastor of St. Bridget's, Sheen had been quietly dealing with Robert C. Weaver, Secretary of Housing and Urban Development, to make what the bishop called "a sacrificial gift in order that the diocese might alleviate the plight of the needy."

The parishioners rebelled at the loss of their $680,000

property, the pastor said that the Church would be destroying its greatest witness—the school—and 123 priests signed a letter protesting both the action and the fact that they had not been consulted. Sheen was left alone with his grand gesture, and he quickly rescinded the offer.

By declaring that an acre and a half of land was hardly enough to solve the housing crisis, Sheen's critics missed the point he was trying to establish: in order for the Church to make sense to the poor of the world, the institution must sublimate its own interests so that "a socially disenfranchised people might have roofs over their heads." Had Sheen gone through the arduous and lengthy process of discussing big changes slowly with his people (and officials), he might have been able to win their support. In this case, impulsiveness won out over Sheen's declared intentions to consult with his people on matters affecting the diocese. As it was, the noble idea turned out to be a lesson in collegiality: bishops can no longer take it for granted that unilateral action will be followed by support from the troops.

While Sheen insisted repeatedly that his approaches to problems were experimental and consequently always subject to revision in the light of results, the individual initiatives quickly revealed an organic unity because of the basic inspiration provided by the spirit and directives of the Vatican Council.

Thus, the support of FIGHT and the naming of Father Finks to deal with the problems of the Inner City brought him the immediate sympathy and moral support of the Rochester Council of Churches, the coordinating body for the major Protestant denominations. It had been under heavy fire from the conservative elements in the city, and it was elated at this support from an unexpected quarter.

"Instead of the personable, dynamic religious conservative we expected, we got a man infused with the whole spirit of Christian ecumenism," said Richard Hughes, its execu-

78

tive director. "Bishop Sheen has become an exciting presence in this town."

The bishop, for his part, welcomed the reaction, publicly urging that Catholics and Protestants pool both manpower and facilities in attacking the problems of the ghettoes in the Third and Seventh Wards. Teams of students from his diocesan seminary joined Protestant seminarians from Colgate Rochester Divinity School in social work in the slums in summer 1967, as a first step toward a broad cooperation in the training of future priests and ministers for urban work.

From such beginnings the ecumenical movement, blessed by the Vatican Council, went forward in Rochester by leaps and bounds. Sheen took the initiative for joint prayer services with Protestants, for mutual visitation of Protestant and Catholic churches by their respective congregations, for monthly meetings with associations of clergymen. He not only spoke in Protestant pulpits, but set all Rochester agog by speaking in synagogues.

More than 2,300 persons, standing in the aisles and overflowing into the auditorium, packed Temple B'rith Kodesh for his first appearance there in January, 1967.

Rabbi Herbert Bronstein told them he had to go back to the fourth century, when St. Jerome came to the synagogue to consult rabbinical scholars about his translation of the Bible into Latin, for a precedent.

Bishop Sheen said he felt like St. Paul at Ephesus, where "he used to go to the synagogue and speak confidently, holding discussions." Nor did he confine himself to polite generalities. In the same synagogue, he subsequently discussed with Rabbi Marc H. Tannenbaum the relationships between the faith of Jews and that of Christians. Christian faith and practice, he emphasized, is rooted in Jewish faith and practice. "To deny this heritage and this background would be to deny our own parentage. . . . In this synagogue,

God is worshipped by right, by a reading and a law which God himself gave."

Many of Sheen's actions indicate a belief that the role of separate Catholic education is destined to decline. It is a conviction that is becoming more widespread among American Catholics in general. When he created the new post of Episcopal Vicar for Religious Education, he stressed three things: the importance of religious instruction to Catholics in teaching institutions other than Catholic schools, the importance of cooperation with other Christian denominations in teaching religion, and the importance of developing courses of religious information in public schools.

His comment on the final point is particularly interesting. The new office, he said, "should cooperate with all educational agencies which seek to introduce objective courses on religion in elementary schools in accordance with the decision of Justice Clark who wrote concerning the Abington School Case: 'Nothing we have said indicated that such a study of the Bible or religion, when presented as part of the secular program of education, may not be effected and be consistent with the First Amendment.'"

I have earlier indicated the opposition to what by now clearly reveals itself as not merely a series of changes, but a complete pattern of change—something calculated to alter the traditional power structures in the Church and to formulate different value standards for Catholic life and activity. That some of Sheen's actions would hurt some people is not surprising. The business community was shocked by his identification with the have-nots.

"The old crowd who surrounded the previous bishop are now out in right field," was how one priest, a member of Sheen's team, expressed it to me. "They don't like him, because he is shoving their ingrained materialism down their throats, examining their consciences in public."

Some of them called for an economic boycott to let him

see how dependent he is on their goodwill. But the challenge didn't frighten Sheen. And there is at least some evidence that, even if they have the big money, he has the masses. The Mission Sunday Collection in 1967 was twice as big as that of a year earlier.

Many of the Catholic upper crust were chagrined that Sheen did not establish a big residence in the customary style of bishops. But Sheen underlined his concern for the poor by residing in a tastefully furnished but modest apartment two floors below his office in the downtown Columbus Civic Centre. A red leather desk in a combination study-living room is the focal point of the carpeted suite. There is an abundance of dictaphones, telephones, books, and framed photographs of the bishop's famous friends (Jackie Gleason has a place of prominence). A TV set is located at the foot of the bishop's bed.

Bishop Sheen is, of course, aware of the opposition, but it doesn't seem to upset him. And it certainly does not deflect him. "I was sent here to do a job," he said at an early stage. "If some people don't like it, they will like it less as time goes on."

What I consider significant is the emphasis on long-term projects, especially the seminary. Bishop Sheen has long projected the image of a man seeking spectacular effects. Here, on the contrary, he is quietly laying a foundation on which it will fall to other bishops to build.

The Rochester diocese has three seminaries, a high school for boys aged 12 to 16 studying toward the priesthood, a college teaching philosophy for students between 16 and 20, and a school of theology for philosophy graduates aged 20 to 24. During his first months in the city, Sheen had each of these institutions reviewed in the light of the Vatican Council instructions on the training of candidates for the priesthood. The consequent changes already introduced are quite startling.

First of all, it was established that only 10 percent of those enrolled in the high school survived to ordination and that, in addition, some of the high school graduates exhibited emotional instability when they moved up to the study of philosophy and theology. The decision was to deemphasize the traditional seminary character of the institution in two important respects, making the regime more like that of a typical American high school. The first step is to make the school coeducational by enrolling girls who are thinking of becoming nuns or of engaging in some Church-related work. The other is to put a layman in charge of discipline with instructions to find "a golden mean between a false conception of clerically imposed authority on the one hand, and permissiveness on the other."

For the philosophy and theology schools, Sheen has outlined significant new approaches. The Vatican Council asked for an integration of philosophy and theology, which will require a change in the present system. More generally, updating is envisaged in the four major areas of spiritual, intellectual, pastoral, and psychological formation. The seminary "is not to be a copy of a monastery, nor is it to be a secular college." There is to be freedom, but not without responsibility. Authority will be exercised in a climate of dialogue. A lay review board of seven members will help the bishop and the seminary authorities to decide on the suitability of candidates for ordination to the priesthood.

The aim of instruction is described as "the combining of the knowledge of the Christian heritage and the contemporary world." As a first step, a layman was named to the faculty to start the integration of philosophy and theology. An expert on Teilhard de Chardin, he will teach a course on the philosophical backgrounds of dogma, contrasting the traditional scholastic and the Teilhardian background of dogmatic truths.

The overall thrust of this and other changes in the curriculum is described as follows by the bishop. "The great defect in theological education," he says, "has been its piecemeal, unrelated, 'jump-through-the-hoop' transmission of knowledge, thus leaving little time for the seminarian to develop his skills and to prepare him for a ministry where he never ceases to be a student. Textbooks which give the student the impression of a 'summa' of knowledge too often become a *terminus* of knowledge, and not an incitement. Collateral reading will prepare an 'open end' to learning and for the entirety of the priestly ministry."

Even more radical are the changes Sheen has introduced in the pastoral training of the seminarians. Instead of learning from books how to deal with people, as was the past practice, they will now learn principally by doing. Under the direction of a priest experienced in the problems of the Inner City, they will work in slum parishes. Another priest will develop programs to involve them with prisons, hospitals, and other social agencies. A professor of Colgate Rochester Divinity School will introduce them to "the problems of contemporary society in the midst of changing world structures," particularly as these problems are related to or flow from urbanization. Specialists will also train them in leadership, group formation for apostolic purposes, the utilization of existing structures and institutions to promote their objectives, and preaching.

Several other innovations indicate the same impetus toward opening up the seminary to the world. Seminarians from other dioceses and from religious orders are now admitted, and nuns and laymen can also study at the seminary. The new faculty members include lay specialists, Protestant ministers, and members of religious orders. And under active discussion is a project to join the seminary with Colgate Rochester Divinity School and the Episcopalian Bexley Hall, an affiliate of Kenyon College in Gambier, Ohio. Colgate Rochester, one of the oldest theology schools in America, was founded by the Baptists and currently prepares ministers for 15 Protestant denominations.

Sheen has expressed his approval of the proposal by saying that "the needless multiplication of faculties, the need of dialogue, the recognition of sharing God's work, and the common resolve to be a spiritual leaven in the mass of society have prompted this move to a coalition."

"Careful inquiry should be made concerning the rightness of the seminarian's intention and the freedom of his choice, the aptness of his bodily and mental health, and any tendencies he might have inherited from his family." This quotation from the Vatican Council was used by Bishop Sheen to introduce his program for determining and protecting the mental and emotional health of his seminarians, an area in which the traditional seminary regime has tended to be grossly remiss.

To reinforce the point, he quoted also at some length from the encyclical in which Pope Paul in June, 1967, reaffirmed the long-standing discipline of celibacy for priests of the Latin rite. "The responsibility for defection falls not on consecrated celibacy in itself, but on the judgment of fitness of the candidate for the priesthood. . . . It is also necessary that exact account be taken of the biological and psychological status of the candidate in order to guide and orient him toward the priestly ideal. These conditions should be ascertained as soon as the signs of his holy vocation are first indicated; not hastily or superficially, but carefully, with the assistance and aid of a doctor and a competent psychologist. A serious investigation of hereditary factors should not be omitted. Those who are discovered to be unfit—either for physical, psychological or moral reasons—should be quickly removed from the path of the priesthood. Let educators appreciate that this is one of their grave duties."

As preacher, lecturer, and writer, Sheen has always shown

little sympathy for Freudianism, but he has taken quite literally the instructions of the Council and of Pope Paul on the mental health of seminarians. He has directed the seminary to establish psychological testing and to introduce courses on the "mature man," to treat development, motivation, emotion, personality, maturity, and basic drives with particular reference to the priest. Further attention will be given to the study of mental illness, drugs, addiction, children, adolescence, alcoholism, counseling. These courses will be taught by highly qualified professors, one of them the senior psychologist of the Rochester Mental Health Center. Theory will be supplemented by field work in a mental hospital to teach the seminarians to distinguish between mental conditions in the province of the priest and those requiring a psychiatrist.

This is how Bishop Sheen has summed up the purpose of his broad program of seminary reform. "The laity are not the servants of the priests, the priests are servants of the people. The authority which the priest exercises is service. The tradition of servanthood was revived in its purest form by Pope John XXIII and the Vatican Council, and with the help of God's redeeming grace, we hope to infuse it into every seminarian in the new and renovated seminary of St. Bernard's."

Many of the changes introduced in Rochester are being duplicated elsewhere in the United States, and at least some of them have became commonplace. I have described the Rochester experience in some detail, nevertheless, because I think it has characteristics that make it a test case for the survival of the institutional Catholic Church, for its ability to change quickly enough to satisfy the progressives, while making the alterations sufficiently understood by the mass of the relatively uninvolved and the congenitally conservative to carry along all but a fringe group of dyed-in-the-wool reactionaries.

One very significant element is the rapidity with which change has been effected in a situation that had been rigidly static. Sheen was installed in Rochester in December, 1966. His predecessor had left behind him a machine built on personal loyalties and incarnating the essence of paternalism.

"The former bishop had a personal contact with several generations of Catholics," as one priest describes it. "He ordained most of the priests. He went to practically every dogfight in the diocese. He both blessed the cornerstone and dedicated the completed structure. At the start of the school year, he would make the rounds of the schools to celebrate the Mass of the Holy Spirit. At the end of the school year, he would award the diplomas. . . ."

Within a few months, the placid ways of the past had given way to the dynamism of a new era. In spite of the opinion of the monsignor whom I quoted earlier to the effect that he and his kind can survive underground for a few years until Sheen's retirement and then re-emerge in possession, it seems perfectly clear that an irreversible shift of the center of power has taken place.

The young priests have been given a decisive voice in decision-making in the elected Council of Priests. The laity have been installed in key positions in relation to diocesan finances. The planned reform of lay organizations will give the laity a progressively larger role in formulating and implementing policy. In fact, the opening up of so many areas to public scrutiny is already creating an informed public opinion. Finally, the involvement of the seminarians in the social problems of the community, combined with the psychological testing and other new techniques for weeding out misfits, is going to produce a type of priest who could not and would not function within the old-style paternalistic structures.

There is, consequently, no going back. The opposition to progress has already been overcome, even if the battle scars are not yet fully healed. A particularly significant indication of the way the wind is blowing is the fact that the priests of the diocese have launched their own organization, not as a union to bargain with the bishop, but as a voluntary organization to promote liturgical celebrations, catechetical programs, ecumenical relations, practical cooperative programs for the poor, and help for old and sick priests—all objectives fully in line with their bishop's programs. About a quarter of the approximately 400 diocesan priests were founding members, and membership grew to about 200 in six months. Intransigents there still are, and they will continue to criticize, to impute motives. But time will take care of them, and rather quickly.

That Sheen also had his eyes fastened on an outer world that cares little about the restructuring of the diocese of Rochester was highlighted by a bold step he took that made the liberals of the land perk up their ears. Speaking at a Day of Prayer for racial peace in July, 1967, Sheen staked out a specific position on the Vietnam war that broke with the vagueness of a previous collective statement of the American hierarchy. His message was clear: the U.S. should get out of Vietnam.

"May I speak only as a Christian," he told the parishioners in his cathedral, "and humbly ask the President to announce, 'In the name of God who bade us love our neighbor with our whole heart and soul and mind, for the sake of reconciliation I shall withdraw all our forces immediately from Southern Vietnam.' Is this reconciliation to be limited only to our own citizens? Could we not also be reconciled with our brother in Vietnam? May we plead only for reconciliation between black and white, and not also between black and white and yellow?" Stressing that he wished to disassociate himself "from those who would carry placards instead of a cross," he said that Christians must not only be concerned with reconciliation within the nation, but also seek reconciliation at the international level.

Sheen's dovish stand was a great contrast to his own previous anti-Communist writings and also to the overflowing patriotism of his old boss, Cardinal Spellman, who had maintained the holy nature of U.S. fighting in Vietnam.

At the time, public reaction to Sheen's statement reflected the split in the country: doves praised it; hawks opposed it. But shortly afterward, a small number of individual Catholic bishops began to call for immediate negotiation. At their fall meeting, the Catholic hierarchy did not go beyond urging the U.S. on to negotiation. However, mounting public opposition to continuing the war, dramatized by the opening stages of the 1968 Presidential campaign, was foreshadowed by Sheen's solitary call.

Shortly after his Vietnam speech, Sheen was named by Pope Paul to the Synod of Bishops which was then about to open in Rome. Though most of the delegates to the worldwide Synod were elected by the national hierarchies, a small number were personal appointees of the Pope. Whether Sheen was specially designated because of his striking post-conciliar work in Rochester or because the Pope wanted to throw a further world spotlight on a U.S. prelate who had stood up to his own government on the most pressing moral problem of the time was not, of course, revealed. But in the symbolic ways in which the Vatican operates, it was noted that the pictures taken at the opening of the Synod showed Pope Paul in animated conversation with Sheen. The four elected Americans were not observable.

Much discussion has centered on Bishop Sheen's motives for what he has accomplished in Rochester. There is no doubt that the vigor and extent of his reform surprised admirers and critics alike. Warren Hinckle, editor of *Ramparts* and a self-described former Catholic, has synthesized all the hostile interpretations in his magazine. For him,

Sheen always was and still is an actor, an actor now playing the toughest role in his long theatrical career. Like an old caterpillar, says Hinckle, he "has metamorphosed, at age 71, from a fundamentalist anti-communist and modernist-baiter to the social butterfly of the Renewal Movement." He saw "the Catholic left" as the coming thing, and he not only joined it, he proceeded to lead it.

This, in Hinckle's view, is why Sheen supported a Council of Priests, why he involved laymen in administration of his diocese, why he named Father Finks as "Vicar of the Poor," why he urged President Johnson to get out of Vietnam.

While most individuals would express themselves more moderately, not a few people are in basic sympathy with the Hinckle interpretation, at least to the extent that they regard Sheen as a man influenced more in his actions by a sense of the dramatic impact than by internal conviction and intellectual consistency.

I think the Hinckle interpretation is totally unjustified. Sheen can no more quash his sense of drama than a sportsman his love of the game. The evidence is present to support the view that Sheen, deeply affected by the impact of Vatican II, is that rare development—a charismatic ecclesiastic. He is conscious, as he told me, of a double spirit moving through the Church—the Holy Spirit and the spirit from below. They are meeting at this moment in history. "The Holy Spirit," Sheen says, "will renovate us and we will get back the Christ on the Cross instead of a plastic Christ on a plastic Cross."

My discussions with priests and laymen close to him in Rochester have confirmed this interpretation. Even those who least like him recognize his saintliness, idealism, and devotion. Those who approve of what he is doing, and in my judgment they are the majority, entertain no doubts about his sincerity. It is significant that he constantly refers to the decrees of Vatican II, quoting the specific pertinent passages, as the justification and reason for the changes he makes. If Sheen was formerly a conservative and is now a progressive, if he was happy in the Church as it was before Pope John and now wants to reform it, it is perfectly clear that he has effected basic structural changes at revolutionary speed without shattering the institution.

The question that is still not fully answered is whether Sheen is advancing fast enough for the leading edge of the progressives, whether he is, in fact, in the picturesque words of Hinckle, leading the Catholic Left. Actually, Rochester has had little involvement in the ferment of religious experimentation among Catholics that has mushroomed in many parts of the United States in recent years, as I shall describe in the next chapter.

An experimental group that developed in Sheen's first year produced a potential area of conflict and was regarded by Rochester liberals as a real test of Sheen's permissiveness. Approximately 50 Catholics established what they called an apostolic group with the title of Servants of God. It evolved from several study groups moderated by a Rochester priest, Raymond Kenny, for 19 years a seminary professor and now assistant pastor of a parish.

In June, 1967, they asked Bishop Sheen to establish them as a non-territorial parish. This would give the group its own pastor, permit it to draw members from existing territorial parishes, and exempt these members from the jurisdiction of the pastor of the place in which they live.

The concept is not new. Members of the armed forces belong to what are, in effect, non-territorial parishes under the jurisdiction of their chaplains and the Military Bishop. Many parts of the United States have non-territorial parishes for members of minority language groups, such as Poles and Italians. The reasons given by the Servants of God for their request were those which various spokesmen of progressive groups have been urging as justification for the downgrading and ultimate elimination of the traditional parish based on geographic division of the diocese and the substitution of groupings of people based on common tastes, interests, and objectives.

"We are trying to develop a sense of community and find it hard to do this in our ordinary parishes," they told the bishop. "We seek to integrate our liturgical life and our formal Christian activities with our life in the world."

Bishop Sheen refused to grant their request, but did not ask the group to disband. It continued to meet once a week for a community Mass and to plan apostolic activities in the area of social action, an area in which many of the members are already involved as individuals, working in the Inner City or promoting better race relations. "The community Mass," according to Father Kenny, "provides a maximum of participation and permits some liturgical experimentation within the guidelines of established directives."

A moment of considerable tension occurred while Bishop Sheen was in Rome at the Synod of Bishops. The Servants of God publicly announced an ecumenical service to be held in a Presbyterian church, the ceremony to include a Mass celebrated by Father Kenny. When the news reached the Pastoral Office, the officials there notified the group that even the most recent decrees from Rome did not permit the celebration of a Catholic Mass in a Protestant church.

The program was immediately rescheduled and held in a Catholic church with considerable numbers of Protestants participating as well as Catholics. The newspapers the following day stressed that Protestants and Catholics alike had received the Eucharist at the Mass. Father Kenny, however, quickly pointed out that he had made it quite clear that he was not encouraging inter-communion, but did not feel it appropriate to ask each worshipper what his religion was when he approached to receive the consecrated wafer.

A few days later, Kenny and three members of the group met Vicar General Hickey in an air-clearing meeting. Monsignor Hickey later reported all-round agreement on the issues and willingness on the part of the group to observe Rome's instructions.

"I was impressed with the spirit of the delegation," he said. "They seem to be Catholics concerned for a fuller liturgical life and anxious to be apostolic. We don't want to discourage people with such goals."

The vicar general was understandably anxious to avoid a showdown in the absence of the bishop in Rome and, equally understandably, Sheen did not reopen the matter on his return. The eventual resolution of the Servants of God issue will in all probability turn on the direction taken by the broader movement of Christian experimentation which is affecting the Catholic Church across the United States and around the world.

The Sheen impact on contemporary Rochester is one of the beacons of the post-conciliar age. The effect for the future cannot be estimated, because of the conflicting forces in the modern world that emphasize in ever sharper tones the discrepancy between what modern man needs and what the institutional Church is able to provide.

At the moment, Sheen's work has the exciting coloration of a pioneering enterprise. But the skepticism that has swept the younger generation with the force of a tidal wave may render the Rochester breakthrough, in the final analysis, as a patchwork on a fading quilt. Rochester may eventually be a determining proof of what many today already suspect—that wholly new concepts of program and style must shape the Church of the future.

Hardly anyone in the Church is yet willing to face up to the realization that old skins will not hold new wine. This thought was driven forcibly into my mind on my final night in Rochester. I went to St. John Fisher College to hear a student-faculty panel on pacifism and was invited to dine with the participants. My dinner companion was a 20-year-old senior, tall, articulate, and possessed of that precocious omniscience that marks the campus progressive. After several subjects had been depleted, I asked him what he thought of Bishop Sheen.

"Well, he's doing a lot of interesting things," my friend admitted, "and maybe there's hope for the Church yet." Then he added, as we made our way across the campus, "You know, if Sheen were here right now, I'd say to him, 'Keep it up, Bish, but if you don't, we'll turn you off.'" The remark, half-jesting, half-earnest, was more chilling than the night air.

CHAPTER 4

The Experimental Church

In St. Louis, Jean and Joe Walsh invited me to their home not far from Forest Park. They were celebrating their twenty-second wedding anniversary, and the other guests were members of a group of fellow-Catholics with whom they have been developing an experimental liturgy. It is in this area of worship that the most obvious change has occurred in Catholic attitudes and practices since the Vatican Council.

All over the world, the formerly popular "devotions"—the Rosary, the Holy Hour, the Miraculous Medal Novena, the Way of the Cross—if they have not disappeared, attract a diminishing handful of devotees. Attention is centered instead on the Eucharist as a commemoration and renewal of Christ's Last Supper. But with the new interest has come a dissatisfaction with the rites of the Mass as rigidly formalized for centuries.

The official Church has recognized and approved this dissatisfaction, introducing through legislation at the Vatican Council procedures more in keeping with the concepts and spiritual needs of contemporary man. Jean and Joe Walsh, however, find the official changes quite inadequate, and so do millions of others among the clergy and laity. They are plunging ahead on their own, producing what is becoming widely known as the Underground Church.

We were thirteen people, including three priests, who gathered in the Walsh living room. We sat and chatted for a while, as one does while a party is gaining momentum, covering the usual topics—where one has been, last evening's TV spectacular, the report cards of the respective children, somebody's new job or sprained ankle.

Joe looked around to check to see whether all had come. "Shall we begin?" he asked.

A young woman produced mimeographed sheets with Mass prayers and hymns. We passed them from hand to hand.

The three priests, dressed in black suits, continued to sit informally in the places they had found as members of the group. We began to sing.

> Shout from the highest mountain the glory
> of the Lord,
> Let all men rejoice in him.
> Sing from the highest mountain the
> praises of the Lord.
> Let all men know the wonders of our God.

The opening prayer was from Psalm 92, read in unison by all in a measured voice.

> It is good to give thanks to Yahweh,
> to play in honor of your name, Most High,
> to proclaim your love at daybreak
> and your faithfulness all through the night
> to the music of zither and lyre,
> to the rippling of the harp....

"Lord, have mercy," said the priest who was to be the principal celebrant of the Mass. "Christ, have mercy," came the response. "Lord, have mercy," the priest repeated, then called on all to join him in a Prayer of the Assembly, taken this time from Psalm 150.

> Praise God in his temple on earth, . . .
> Praise him for his transcendent greatness. . . .
> Praise him with drums and dancing. . . .
> Let everything that breathes praise
> Yahweh. Alleluia.

Instead of the reading from Scripture prescribed in the Missal for this day, three members of the group read aloud a short passage each had selected as appropriate to the occasion. The first was not even taken from the Bible, though related to it. It came from the Dutch Catechism and told how the Old Testament had developed and refined the human concept of marriage, preparing the way for Christ to make it a sacrament. After these readings, the Bible was handed to the celebrant, who—still seated—read a passage from the Gospel. It was a short selection from St. Matthew, in which Christ told his followers that they were to be the salt of the earth and the light of the world.

Closing the book, the priest began in a conversational voice to open up a discussion. He spoke for perhaps a minute, touching on the meaning of married life, the commitment of the family unit to society, the commitment of every individual to society. His exposition was a question rather than a statement. The host took it up. Lighting a cigarette, he talked for several minutes about his own experience and that of his wife in trying to make their family a unit in society. Others chipped in with their experiences and ideas. The conversation flowed in an atmosphere marked by frankness, searching, and concern. The priests contributed on a level of equality with the others, while stressing that on the particular subject of family life they have more to learn than to teach.

The discussion continued for about half an hour, and we then moved on to the celebration of the Eucharist, singing a song of offering as we walked to the dining room and took our seats around the table.

The celebrant robed himself in the Mass vestments (I discovered that the group doesn't usually bother with vestments, but in this case the pastor had been invited) and took his seat at the head of the table. In front of him was a loaf of French bread, baked that day by one of the girls in the group, and a bottle of red wine, Saint-Emilion 1964. The priest poured half the wine into a chalice and added a few drops of water from a goblet. After the prayers of offering, he stood to recite the Preface and continued with the Canon of the Mass in the approved English translation of the text in the Roman Missal. He spoke very softly but audibly, as if still in conversation with the others, who remained seated around the table while he consecrated the bread and wine and completed the prayers of the Canon. Still seated, we joined hands to recite the Our Father, then passed the Kiss of Peace from the celebrant all around the table, each in turn wishing the one next to him or her the peace of Christ and exchanging a brief kiss.

When the moment for Communion arrived, the priest broke the consecrated bread into pieces and passed the tray around for each to take some. While all of us held the bread in our hands, he recited the prayer, "Behold the Lamb of God," and all partook together.

He then passed the chalice from hand to hand, so that each might drink, waiting until last for his own turn. As the chalice moved round the table, a hymn was sung which by its words and the expression of the singers filled the room with an atmosphere of joy and happiness.

"We are one in the Spirit. . . . We are one in the Lord. . . . We will work with each other. . . . We will walk hand in hand. . . . And they'll know we are Christians by our love, by our love. Yes, they'll know we are Christians by our love."

It was a statement, a commitment, a challenge. The priest resumed it in his closing words. "Go, this is the end of the Mass," he said. "Go and give witness to it."

The informal conversation started up again. We greeted each other with a new awareness of brotherhood. We thanked the priest for having come to make Christ present to us. As we sat around the living room, relaxing and laughing, someone remembered that we hadn't taken up a collection.

"How about two dollars from everyone for Senator McCarthy's campaign for the Presidency?" a girl suggested. We tossed the bills in a pile on the rug.

Such a ceremony could hardly be held in public anywhere in North America. Many Catholics would regard it as shocking. Most bishops and chancery officials would doubtless hold that some of its elements go beyond the kind of experimentation a bishop is today authorized by Rome to permit in his discretion. But approved or not, it is a spreading phenomenon. In fact, it is far more conservative than many of the current experiments.

A frequent characteristic of the "underground churches," for example, is a fraternization of Catholics with other Christians in worship. This includes a sharing in the Eucharistic celebration, or inter-communion, that is not authorized by Catholic Church authorities.

The facts about the Servants of God in Rochester, as related in the last chapter, indicate that at least some members of that affiliation find no difficulty in inter-communion. The trend in many quarters is to celebrate the Eucharist in a much more informal manner than the St. Louis group whose service I have just described. Modern Catholics feel the desire to improvise rather than repeat the same fixed prayers each time. They are influenced by the practice of the Protestants among them and seek consciously to adjust to the ways of their guests as a gesture of friendship and as a breaking down of what they see as arbitrary and meaningless walls.

Experimental groups include crackpots, malcontents, and misfits, of course. But this is certainly not their characteristic. On the contrary, what is significant almost everywhere is the leadership provided by priests and nuns. They are intelligent and committed individuals, highly respected by those who know them, and they risk the wrath of their superiors and lead a double life because they find a spiritual satisfaction in their clandestine worship. They also believe it is their duty to give guidance and support to fellow Christians whose emotional and spiritual needs are unfulfilled by the existing institutional forms.

The nucleus of the lay membership also tends to consist of educated and well-instructed Catholics who got to know one another through some parish activity, such as the Christian Family Movement or an evening education program, and who discovered that deep down they shared a common dissatisfaction with the religious life they led.

Interestingly enough, it was the recognition by the Vatican Council that the Mass in Latin had no meaning for most of those who attended it regularly each Sunday that stirred these people to an awareness of their own problems and needs. Previously, they had gone faithfully each Sunday and achieved a silent and numb semi-participation out of a sense of duty. The partial substitution of English for Latin and the call to join in the prayers and singing brought a gratified response at first—a response which soon, however, changed to disillusionment as they faced the weekly gulf between promise and delivery.

The pressure of the intransigents in high places restricted the first phase of the liturgical reform to a translation of the introductory and final parts of the Mass, leaving the central, solemn element, the Canon, during which the bread and wine are consecrated, in Latin, to be recited by the priest in a low tone as though it was no business of the rest of the group.

The utter illogicality of that decision has now been recognized, so that in the United States and Canada, and increasingly throughout the world, the entire service is in the language of the people. But for many, the delay has proved fatal, because of its combination with the rest of the reality of Sunday Mass in a typical American spiritual supermarket. The great concrete edifice will be steam-heated in winter and air-cooled in summer, but its creature comfort gives them no compensation for its repelling atmosphere.

They had come to recognize that they were strangers among strangers. They got no uplift from bad music played by squeaking organs at funereal tempos. They grew tired of platitudinous sermons about renewal from preachers who had little understanding and often little wish to comprehend what the word meant. And so they came together in suburban homes or in meeting halls in the Inner City, or wherever. They came seeking brotherhood, human comfort, a sense of belonging and fulfillment.

What started for most of the participants as a search for a more meaningful form of worship, and specifically for a more meaningful Mass, inevitably has brought them to a total reevaluation of their beliefs, of their understanding of the Church and of their own relationship to it. It was in the nature of things. It flowed directly from the previous training—indoctrination, if you like—of Catholics.

They had been taught that everything commanded or forbidden by the Church imposed an equal obligation on their consciences. It was a sin not to genuflect in honor of the Blessed Sacrament when entering and leaving a church. It was a sin to touch the consecrated host or even the chalice into which the wine would be poured at Mass. It was a sin to eat meat on Friday, to miss Mass on Sunday, to neglect one's prayers morning and night. It was a sin to deny the existence of God or the divinity of Christ.

Catholics heard plenty about a hierarchy of government of the Church, with a pope at the pinnacle, passing the word to the bishops, from the bishops to the priests, from the priests to the "common" faithful. But they knew little or nothing of a hierarchy of values or a hierarchy of truths.

To join an underground group in an experimental liturgy, however, involves a total reformulation of belief for the traditional Catholic. He may not realize this, at first, but if he is a reflective type, as are many of the experimenters, he will soon see it for himself.

How can I justify the use of ordinary bread in the Mass, when the regulations insist upon unleavened bread? he will ask himself. How can I take the consecrated wine from the chalice, when the current discipline of the Church permits this only to the priest, with a few carefully guarded exceptions?

Once he asks himself such elementary questions and finds in his conscience a justification for violating an official instruction of the Church because, in his opinion, it is arbitrary and restricting, he is no longer a Catholic in the old sense. Here, I think, lies the essence of the revolution. The "underground church" as a loose union of liturgical experimenters, no matter how far out, is only a phenomenon. The underlying reality is the change of attitude toward the institution, the altered concept of what it means to be a Catholic.

How far have they gone in their establishment of a hierarchy of values or truths of faith? Many of them have not progressed very far, because it is human to be inconsistent, and most people take a long time to follow completely the logic of their principles. But the direction of movement cannot be denied, and it is hard to say where it will stop.

Jack M. Bickham, managing editor of the Oklahoma

Courier, a Catholic diocesan newspaper, has made a national survey of the phenomenon, and his conclusion is forthright. "I suspect," he writes, "that most members of the Underground everywhere ignore the institution's regulations on birth control, don't really believe in papal infallibility, openly question the dogma of the Virgin Birth, aren't at all sure where they stand on abortion and euthanasia, and couldn't care less about pronouncements that come periodically from the Roman Curia and from the Pope himself about keeping the faith 'pure.'"

Donald J. Thorman, publisher of the *National Catholic Reporter,* and an exceptionally well-informed commentator, has put his finger on a key element in the new wave of experimentation. "There have been innumerable unofficial movements within the Church before," he says, "but they came and went rapidly because they lacked the unifying factor of a priesthood and a liturgy of their own. In the past, the clergy has generally felt a superior loyalty to the universal Church, their bishop or their religious superior. Now, an increasing number of priests tell me they feel a personal obligation to a higher authority—to Christ, to the Christian community wherever they find it, and to the demands of their conscience. They have suddenly discovered something bigger than the institutional Church—Christianity—and it has changed their lives."

Nevertheless, as Bickham also points out, these people—both the priests and the laity among them—think of themselves as Catholics and have not given up hope that the institution will follow far enough in the direction in which they have led to permit some kind of *modus vivendi.* In addition, "these people meet here and there and everywhere, all over the nation, and try to love one another, and celebrate a Eucharist."

I talked at length about all these ferments to a brilliant, progressive, open member of the American hierarchy—47-

year-old Auxiliary Bishop James P. Shannon, of the St. Paul and Minneapolis diocese. It is instructive to see how it all looks to one directly involved in the institutional Church. Our talk ranged over broader issues than simply why people join the liturgical underground and whether or not membership in this underground is compatible with good standing in the Church. But I think what Bishop Shannon told me helps to bring these issues into their proper perspective.

Bishop Shannon traces the present ferment directly to the Vatican Council, on the ground that it inaugurated a new era for the intellectual in the Church. "The emphasis for centuries on a narrow pietistic tradition had cast a cloud of suspicion on speculation and on intellectuals," he said. "The prominent role given to the *periti* [experts] at the Council, especially in the construction of the major documents, reassured them and reassured the world intellectual community that the bishops did not rely on their own resources but looked to the scholars for the real leadership. There has been some subsequent retrenchment. The *periti* were not given the same role at the Synod of Bishops in October, 1967, for example. But the mandate of the Council and the directives of its decrees point to a new era for the intellectual or expert, for the professional, in the Church. They provide a role previously lacking for the inductive and behavioral sciences."

To call the resulting changes a revolution creates no problem for Bishop Shannon. "The transformation going on in the Church is so profound that any lesser term is inadequate to describe it. It operates at all levels, and that is really why it is a revolution. It is not just a change of leadership or a movement from one level to another. It is going on through the whole body. The Council established what I call a principle of trust among all who constitute the people of God. The Constitution on the Church spells out collegiality, which is in essence a principle whereby the

Holy Father extends greater trust and confidence to the consensus of the bishops of the world.

"The Decree on the Pastoral Office of Bishops applies the same principle to the relationship of the bishop with his priests, calling for a senate of priests to enable the bishop to ascertain the consensus of his priests in administering the diocese. The Decree on the Laity calls for a council in a diocese in which lay people will participate with the priests in advising the bishop on policy, which is an extension of trust from the clergy to the laity.

"This same concept underlies another theme of the Council documents, namely, a greater reliance on the democratic process and a greater trust in the pluralistic system, a readiness to admit that the Holy Spirit works in the people, speaking not just through the structures but through the consensus. A right understanding and application of these principles must bring a drastic qualification of the traditional style of Church administration. Even an advisory senate qualifies a bishop's administration. Once the priests formulate a consensus, how can he in practice go against it without at least offering some explanation of his decision?"

Bishop Shannon then touched on a point which I think has a direct bearing on the status of and prospects for the Underground Church. When I asked him if he thought the institution could be reformed fast enough to hold the interest and activity of the generation now coming into adulthood, he said he was afraid not. "Part of the answer is future tense, a guess; but part of it is past history. I think we have lost a portion of these people already. I can't give statistics, but the number of college people, youngsters with better educations, young intellectuals, young married couples who have left the institutional Church—not only the Catholic Church—in recent decades is large and growing.

"It is a touching experience to talk to such people in a situation in which they will candidly confide their moral anguish. Most were reared in orthodox Christian homes—Catholic or Protestant—successful in their careers as scientists, researchers, or members of the business community, maintaining the rapid pace of the culture in which they live.

"I know from substantial experience that such people have a common denominator. They have made valiant and repeated efforts within their lights, trying to resolve their differences with an institutional Church which they think is not speaking to the issues that are of paramount importance in their eyes. They are concerned with the issues raised by recent popes in *Pacem in Terris, Mater et Magistra* and *Populorum Progressio,* the issues of war, peace, freedom, and progress.

"They see the validity of these principles as they operate in their secular life. They have demonstrable evidence, for example, of the success of the principle of freedom as applied in the world in which they live—freedom of knowledge, freedom of investigation, the democratic process. They have seen the companies for which they work or the universities in which they conduct research projects move ahead by the application of these principles. Then they see that the Church does not apply these principles. It talks about piety and about petty issues unrelated to their lives.

"One of the great sources of anguish for such people is that they continue to believe in God, to have a Christian response to society, but can find no Church that shares their concern in a way meaningful to them. Even if not numerically numerous, they are influential people. As they grow in numbers, they begin to link arms and exchange telephone numbers, and next thing they are ready to elect a chairman. . . . You asked me if we can move fast enough for such people. I hope so, but I fear we are not now moving fast enough."

It is my belief, from my observation and enquiry, that the kind of people Bishop Shannon is here describing are precisely those who form the nucleus of the Underground Church. Before the Council, they simply drifted away from all association with organized religion. Now, in the conciliar atmosphere, they have this intermediate state, a state so vaguely defined that Catholics and Protestants can worship together without either feeling the need to challenge the beliefs of the other. In some instances, these people are so loosely structured as to welcome Jews and humanists also to the brotherhood. The willingness of priests to participate in unconventional experiments and sponsor unpopular causes in a way unthinkable for Catholics ten years ago has given new impetus to "hanging loose." Such names as Father DuBay in Los Angeles, Father Groppi in Milwaukee, and the Berrigan brothers instantly leap to the mind. Bishop Shannon had interesting observations on this phenomenon, too.

"You must recognize in such priests," he said, "very concerned Christians who cannot reconcile their consciences with the normal ground rules expected within the administrative Church. This is just as much a problem for the Church as it is for the Berrigans, DuBay, and Groppi. We can't resolve it simplistically by saying they have to change. The Church must take into consideration the fact that these men are operating in great part from Christian principles. (I leave here some latitude for personal differences between DuBay and Cardinal McIntyre, because I have a theory that the one is the other's intellectual grandfather, the DuBays of this world making the conservative bishops more conservative.) We have here examples of men who follow their conscience to the ultimate, come what may in the society in which they live, and come what may in the Church. They are willing to accept the consequences of their action.

"Such a phenomenon is rare in the recent history of the Church. Yet I think these men have a mandate—or at least an opening or endorsement—from the Council in its document on freedom of conscience and religious liberty. That is a very revolutionary declaration, even implicitly allowing a man to pursue his convictions as an atheist. The Western World had already subscribed politically to that principle, but here we have it in a statement of the Church. This freedom of conscience endorsed by the Council is one source of encouragement to those with an honest conflict between what their conscience dictates and what either society or the Church authority as traditionally patterned expects of them."

Looking at all these developments from a sociological viewpoint, Dr. William A. Osborne, Associate Professor of Sociology at St. John's University, New York, distinguishes between changes in the hierarchical and bureaucratic structures on the one hand, and religious reform (which he defines as changes in the norms, values, and behavior of individuals) on the other hand. While structures are capable of modifying themselves rapidly and thus minimizing conflict, as is occurring in Holland, Dr. Osborne's research—and this is universally agreed—indicates that the same is not happening in the United States. Meanwhile, the religious reform, the changes in the norms, values, and behavior of individuals as described above, is progressing rapidly and "almost independently."

Dr. Osborne offers two possible solutions. The mounting conflict, he says, may be institutionalized by the emergence of "participants or antagonists from and by each opposing group," leading either to a disruptive tension or a dialectic resolution of the conflict in a new equilibrium. Alternatively, the parties may refuse to recognize each other, so that each goes its own way, running "the risk of alienating those involved or inducing an 'underground schism.' "

There is another theoretically possible solution to the conflict. It is the one implicit in a stream of statements emanating from Rome ever since the end of the Vatican

Council, statements echoed by many of the American bishops individually and by the entire hierarchy in a collective pastoral issued in January, 1968. The characteristic of these statements is an alarm at the way in which so many Catholics are following their own insights in interpreting the Council's call to renewal and reform, an insistence on submission to authority understood in a pre-conciliar juridical sense as a prerogative of the pope and bishops to be exercised in their exclusive wisdom, and an assurance that all will again be well if only the simple faithful will renew their trust in their leaders.

Acceptance of this approach would undoubtedly resolve the existing tension. Dr. Osborne considers, however, that it is sociologically unviable. Not only do I agree with him, but I do not see how it could be reconciled theologically with the teaching of Vatican II.

"Those changes are already under way, irreversible, and beyond the control of the official Church," says Dr. Osborne. His reason for regarding them as irreversible is that "norms, values and ritual are central or essential to any religious institution." Since these have already changed for the members of the Underground Church, the only alternative to disruption is for the structures to change "in order to establish equilibrium and become functional."

As is clear from Bishop Shannon's views presented above, some recognition exists among the American bishops of the constructive potential of the current grass-roots ferment. Here, as in all human affairs, one finds a gradation of positions. A considerable number of the bishops will look the other way, permitting a broad range of experimentation as long as it is not brought to their official notice or presented in a sufficiently ambiguous perspective. Others are promoting or permitting a change of structures in ways intended to meet at least some of the demands of the underground experimenters.

Among the most advanced of such authorized innovations I encountered in my travels is the John XXIII Community in Oklahoma City. The initiative in this case came from a priest, Father William Nerin. Aged 42, with black hair and sharp features, he projects sincerity and confidence. I saw him going about in a yellow sports shirt at a symposium of the Chicago Association of Priests. Such garb for such a place and occasion would be regarded by many people as an act of defiance or the expression of an immature personality. As a matter of actual fact, Father Nerin was simply presenting himself as an individual human being exercising his inalienable right of freedom of dress and action.

During several years as adviser to a Christian Family Movement group in Oklahoma City, a role for which he had prepared by obtaining a Master's degree in Marriage and Family Life from Columbia's Teachers College, he became friend and confidant of many unhappy Catholics. They had a common problem, which one of them put succinctly in words. "The religiosity of our parish turns me off. It is a Mickey Mouse approach to the world."

In June, 1966, he linked forces with Paul Sprehe, a 37-year-old consultant engineer, father of seven children, and a close friend from the Christian Family Movement. "Let's start our own parish," he urged Paul. The idea was that Nerin would bring his pastoral experience and philosophy to the union, while Paul would contribute his knowledge of the world and his managerial expertise. Since the community would be what Nerin calls "secularly marked"—an association of people located in time and space to perform specified human tasks—it was decided that the layman would act as director of the enterprise, while the priest would serve as professional consultant insofar as those activities have a religious finality.

The principle is revolutionary in the perspective of the long-standing parish structures of canon law and Catholic

Church practice, but Bishop Victor J. Reed gave approval for a two-year experiment. "I don't know if it will work or not," the bishop said at the end of a three-hour discussion. "There's only one way to find out."

He set up the John XXIII Community as a non-territorial parish, with Father Nerin as administrator. The laymen wanted at first to carve a territory out of other parishes for the experiment, but Bishop Reed decided they could achieve their objectives better without a territory and without any fixed property. Membership is open, the only condition being a willingness and ability to interrelate with the founding group, which embraces a wide social range of poor and middle-class families.

The community quickly grew to 40 families and 20 unmarried members, forcing it to move from its original location in the YWCA, in a Negro section of town, to bigger rented quarters where eight unwed mothers, who are members, can live in. The Community is run on democratic lines with an elected chairman and board. Father Nerin is a paid employee, with one vote in ten on the board. Like any employee, he can be dismissed if his employer becomes dissatisfied with him. The community can ask the bishop for another priest who will be able to relate satisfactorily to it. Nerin has neither stipends nor stole fees, and he can live where he wants to. Actually, he lives in a furnished apartment. The lady who rented it to him said, seeing the Roman collar, "You must be an Episcopalian." When he said he was a Roman Catholic, she asked in astonishment, "What are you doing out in the world?"

The Community has a strong social orientation. In addition to helping the unwed mothers who are members, it runs a Montessori Day Care Center in Oklahoma City and has adopted a poverty center in South America. When the Vista Volunteers first moved into Oklahoma City, it acquainted them with the local problems. It holds only one meeting a week, on Sunday morning from 9:30 to 11:45, usually in a high school. The meeting starts with a discussion or "dialogue homily," and the agenda is mailed out in advance so that people can come prepared. The favorite topics are social issues and pressing questions, like the war in Vietnam.

"When we first talked about Vietnam," Nerin told me, "we were equally divided between hawks and doves. After three or four discussions, only 12 percent were for involvement and escalation, and 45 percent were for de-escalation."

Open housing is another frequent topic, leading to a general evaluation of racial issues. "We usually get a consensus on the moral duty of the Christian to promote full racial equality," says Nerin. At the end of the first year, they held a "Faith-In" to evaluate the maturation of their views from membership in the Community.

"Most members felt that their ideas had changed on God and Christ and the Church and the goals of life," Nerin reported.

He sees as one of the major benefits of the experiment the fact that people acquire a better understanding of their own role in their religious life as compared with that of the priest.

"Only twice have I talked more than ten minutes, once on the concepts of abortion, and the other on the concepts of faith," he said. "My influence is thus quite indirect. They realize that the priest has no corner on telling people how to live, that it is a fallacy to imagine that he can spout wisdom from the pulpit."

The celebration of the Eucharist follows and grows out of the group discussion. "The people are sort of warmed up," says Nerin. "There is a spontaneous feeling. We have all come alive. We are full of life. On Palm Sunday, for example, I remember the young people had made banners and were singing crazy songs. They formed their own procession through the group. It meant something. We have an agnostic with us and a near-atheist, and we have learned mutual respect of conscience.

"I think that Christ is acquiring a significant meaning for the agnostic as a result of his association with us. And that is how it should be. When Christians get together, that meeting is itself a sacrament, a holy thing, a maker of holiness. It is not only the bread and wine that constitute a sign of what the people are. Every meeting should constantly announce the Christian message through the interaction of the people present."

Other places in which experimental non-territorial parishes have been formed with Church approval are Tulsa, Oklahoma (also in Bishop Reed's diocese); Pueblo, Colorado, a diocese headed by Bishop Charles A. Buswell; and Atlanta, Georgia.

Bishop Charles J. Helmsing of Kansas City has approved a slightly different kind of experiment, the creation of an ecumenical parish as a joint undertaking with the Episcopal Church, the Presbyterian Church, and the United Church of Christ. Except for worship, to be held in the same building but at separate times, the parish will have a totally unified life, to include integrated parish activities and joint religious instruction.

In other areas, however, the hierarchy is cracking down on the experimenters without offering alternatives. Bishop George W. Ahr of Trenton suspended Father George J. Hafner of Toms River, New Jersey, for continuing home celebration of the Eucharist for a group of about 40 people, after the bishop had told him to stop.

Bishop Thomas K. Gorman of Dallas, Texas, ousted four Paulist priests from a parish in a Dallas suburb. The bishop said they weren't doing enough Newman Club work on neighboring college campuses. A petition signed by 2,500 parishioners indicated that his real objection was to the progressive nature of their parish apostolate.

Cardinal Patrick O'Boyle, of Washington, D.C., ignoring the written plea of 35 of his priests, halted the weekly liturgical celebrations of a floating, non-territorial group of about 450 (known as The People), calling it "destructive of the concept of the parish" and engaged in efforts to avoid "ecclesiastical supervision." He ordered a halt to "any kind of personal innovation" in the liturgy and threatened with suspension any priest who did not "conform unfailingly."

One evening, I sat in a living room in suburban Virginia, listening to some members of The People express their astonishment at the cavalier treatment they had received at the hands of Cardinal O'Boyle.

"We had a Mass that people could sing without being embarrassed," said a mother whose baby was sleeping in the next room. "We were drawn together through our social concerns, not out of any thrill in operating 'underground.' "

Another mother said, "It was nice to give money at The People Mass and have it sent to relief agencies in Vietnam."

Her husband added, "The people who came to these Masses were those who were alienated from the parish, but who wanted to fulfill the obligation of Mass."

The first mother spoke again: "The bishops see experimentation as a threat against their total control."

The group, which numbered six or seven couples, was unanimous in declaring that, since the Vatican Council, the bishops have reflected a "bankruptcy in leadership." This statement, although it reflects a prevailing mood among the Christian experimenters, is not totally correct.

The late Archbishop of Atlanta, Paul J. Hallinan, tried to light a crusade among the American hierarchy to recognize the wisdom of those who would create new forms. "Those who feel the strong desire to create have only a limited interest in dusty sacramentaries," he said. "The great issue in today's pastoral worship is, how best will God be praised in the accents of our society, how best will this vast, impatient, ailing body be served?"

But Hallinan was a prelate ahead of his time. The majority of the hierarchy feel that the liturgical changes already introduced are quite enough for a while, that the vast body of Catholics are confused, and that the experimenters are out in left field.

Although sinking under the weight of severe illness that had plagued him for five years and would take his life in the spring of 1968, Hallinan went before his fellow bishops at their annual meeting in Washington, D.C., in November, 1967, and pleaded with them for six hours to give order and guidance to experimentation and thus rid it of its clandestine murkiness. "Thousands upon thousands who love the Church are convinced that the time is now," he said.

But the best that Hallinan could win was approval to ask the Vatican to authorize three or four Catholic universities as centers for further experimentation in the liturgy, and some experimentation without prior examination by Rome. Although universities provide a setting far different from the parochial life of the masses, there is some merit in carrying out experiments where they can be measured. Nonetheless, the choice of universities was viewed by many as a repudiation of the Liturgical Conference, a national body founded in 1940 and numbering 7,000, which strongly favors unstinting experimentation and has been goading the bishops for more updating. Moreover, the frugality of the bishops' concession to the increasing hunger for new forms amounted to a virtual condemnation of most of the liturgical experimentation already in progress.

Small as the American hierarchy's request was, even more astonishing was the answer sent back by the Congregation of Rites and the post-conciliar Liturgical Consilium: *No.* The two offices, headed by Cardinal Benno Gut, a 71-year-old Benedictine advocate of Gregorian chant, would permit the substitution of some hymns at Benediction, new translations, and musical instruments other than the organ. But it was made clear that liturgical changes should come from Rome to the grass roots, not the other way around.

Other national hierarchies, notably the Dutch and Canadian, conscious of the liturgical reactionaries reasserting their strength in Rome, have stopped asking for permission for each and every change. Playing the Roman game, the Canadian bishops, for example, avoided the word "experimentation" and set up a number of "adaptation" centers where new forms can be quietly tried out.

I sat alone with the courageous Hallinan in his hotel room after his two days of stormy meetings. He was tired and depressed. Though eager to talk about the liturgical developments, he was faithful to his orders not to discuss the request to Rome (even though the press knew about it), and our conversation stayed on a higher level than the current in-fighting. Just a few words, uttered while he slumped in a chair, indicated why Hallinan commanded such respect among Christian reformers.

"I have none of the fears that some men have in changing the Church," he said. "We have a tremendous number of maturing Catholics. As for the bishops, we are moving through a transition stage. Formerly, we were the kingpins, we had the costumes and salutations of court etiquette, but the Council made it clear that the only title worthy of a bishop is that of service. We still have the image of an earlier style, but a number of the younger bishops are aware of the human condition and want to help people and are thus developing a new style."

In his final speech and press interview, Hallinan made another plea for experimentation. Lamenting that only thirty to forty of the 220 active American bishops could be considered "top-rate modern renewal men," he said that

the American Church was in danger of creating a generation of disobedient priests because of episcopal rigidity.
Without a creative spirit, "we will lapse into a new system
of rubrics as rigid as the old. This would not only be prema-
ture but death-dealing to the spirit of the liturgy."

The questioning attitude of the experimenters, who
won't take no for an answer, brings into sharp focus the
crisis of authority in the post-conciliar Church. The more
the bishops are pushed to change, the more rigid many of
them become. Yet to believe that experimentation can be
stopped (Father Nerin is in demand as a speechmaker all
over North America) is wishful thinking.

Following the November meeting of the American
bishops, the Liturgical Conference charged the hierarchy
with failure to provide "open, creative and vigorous leadership" in reform, and warned that disregard for hierarchical
authority would become even more widespread "if the
quality of episcopal leadership were not upgraded."

The Liturgical Conference holds that the bishops are
more interested in censuring experimenters than those who,
despite the Council's statements, refuse to budge a liturgical
inch. Authorized liturgical changes are too little and too
late, the conference warns. But most bishops don't like these
dire warnings.

In addition to the opposition from the traditionalists and
from Church authorities, the experimental liturgy has been
coming under increasing criticism in the United States from
a very different viewpoint. During and immediately after
the Council, it was fashionable to present liturgical reform
as a cure for all the ills of religion in our society. Experience has shown that it falls short of its billing. Guitars will
bring the young, but guitars by themselves won't hold them.
Liturgy is meant to be an expression of the community,
but in isolation has proved inadequate to create a commu-

nity, and the typical North American congregation is no longer a community in any significant sense.

This new challenge to the primacy of the liturgy was placed formally on the record by Daniel Callahan in the *National Catholic Reporter* in August, 1967. An editor of *Commonweal*, lecturer and author of such books as *Honesty in the Church* and *The Mind of the Catholic Layman*, Callahan is, at 37, one of the most talented, vocal, and respected critics of the Catholic Church as institutionalized in the United States.

Far from the liturgy being the center and the source of Christian life, as claimed by the Council, Callahan argued that "the primacy of place accorded to liturgy is one of the most important hidden sources of the Church's failure to carry out its Christian work and witness in the world."

Among the unexpected problems that have arisen since the Council, he presents as the most important "that even a reformed liturgy has not yet begun to bear out the Council's confident claim that 'the liturgy in its turn inspires the faithful to become of one heart in love.' For all the changes introduced into the Mass, there is not much evidence to support the Council's statement that 'the renewal in the Eucharist of the covenant between Lord and man draws the faithful into the compelling love of Christ and sets them afire.' Nor is there much evidence to suggest that a richer, more intelligible liturgy impels people to move beyond the walls of the Church toward greater service in the world."

To illustrate his point, Callahan suggested that the archdiocese of Chicago cancel its $250-million Operation Renewal, aimed primarily at constructing new facilities, and instead guarantee food to the same value over a few years to the starving people of Bihar, India. "A proposal like this assumes that the needs of the poor and starving and downtrodden are more important than the need to build more and better churches for American Catholics to worship in."

Cries of anguish from the liturgical reformers at this dagger in the back while they were battling entrenched reaction quickly yielded to a recognition of the substantial validity of the Callahan thesis. The John XXIII Community in Oklahoma City, for example, thinks along the same lines.

"When a community of Christians get together, they come not merely to pray but to serve man," is how Father Nerin expressed it to me. "We have to downgrade cultic activity, which the New Testament deliberately avoided. Christ came for the needs of man. While offering us a meal, he reminded us that if we bring a gift to the altar without forgiving our neighbor first, we had better forget the gift. There must be service outside the community. I am wary of inward-oriented groups. A couple of dozen couples can meet with their pastor and get their spiritual kicks out of an underground liturgy. But if an experiment like that doesn't serve the world, it will die."

A similar awareness of the need for a total involvement as a worshipping group in the world was evident in a Detroit group, called the Cardinal Leger Community, which for some time had been negotiating with Archbishop John F. Dearden for recognition as an experimental community when I visited them.

It was a Sunday afternoon, and the families were pouring into the basement of the Visitation Church in the heart of the Negro section still wearing the brutal scars of the previous summer's riots. They carried with them baskets of food, soft drinks, and coffee. Most of them knew one another and exchanged affectionate greetings. As the group grew, each was given a name tag to facilitate the incorporation of the newcomers.

A girl began to practice the guitar. The mothers assembled the food. Jim Shaughnessy rang a bell, called for volunteer teenagers to baby-sit. We took places at the tables and opened up the baskets of food. My neighbor was Doug Wree, a 31-year-old insurance adjuster. As he opened a Coke, it fizzed and spilled over the chicken lunch he had brought. "I'd rather come fifteen miles and feel that I worship," he confided to me, "than go to a huge parish and come up with a big empty feeling again."

Jim Shaughnessy banged on the table for silence. "Who wants to go to the rec center for a party, a movie, some games?" The invitation was directed to the little ones. The baby-sitters took the hint, and while the tables were being cleared, about 60 children were hustled off. One 10-year-old girl stayed to be with a retarded child in a wheelchair.

The setting was still informal, but I could sense a certain spirit of anticipation developing in the thirty couples now left in the hall. Doug Wree turned to me again. "I hope through a thing like this," he said, "that my kids will grow up thinking Christians really love one another."

I felt that he spoke for them all and that he embraced them all in his words—the market researcher at Ford, the engineer at Fisher, the quality-control man, the special education teacher, the construction engineer, the apprentice electrician, the plumbing contractor, the truck driver, the two or three Negroes who were not bunched together but distributed randomly among the whites.

"What is a community?" the chairman asked, starting an informal exchange. "Is it an exclusive group willing to go the extra mile, or should we be home in our own churches?"

"If you stay in the churches in the parishes, you can't influence them," a mother observed rather sadly, "and that's the real dilemma, because if we come out and begin our own community, we can't influence them either. As I see community, it is an effort to be with others and influence the world. We here want to serve the community, and that's not a bad starting point. We should keep in mind the dangers involved in withdrawing."

119

"To belong to this community is to accept each member as he or she is," another mother interjected. "We share what we have, and we are happy to do so."

Such was the beginning of ninety minutes of real soul-searching on the basic issue of whether or not they were justified in breaking away from the parish structures, whether their motivations were selfish and exclusivist, or whether by the finding of themselves they could hope ultimately to contribute to the welfare of the others they were temporarily leaving behind. As the conversation ebbed and flowed, a highlight would suddenly sparkle here and there. Gradually I could see a consensus developing.

A man: "We are trying to show the archbishop that we can break with the traditional parish successfully, that we can establish effective interpersonal relationships in spite of our diverse backgrounds."

A woman: "There is more than liturgical worship to this. We can as a community become an agent of social reform. We can lobby for legislation. We can do a lot of things."

A Negro girl reporter: "We have to replace the Sunday charade. We need a place to be educated and to worship."

A man: "The parish obstructs Christian growth in the community. We are here because we have suffered institutional anguish, because we are horribly frustrated at the obstructionism against Vatican II. If we don't have something like this, we'll just walk away."

From various points around the room came a soft, soul-filled "Amen." The Spirit had moved. The consensus was achieved.

We collected the children from the rec room and all went up to the church vestibule. Father Dick Fournier was already vested for Mass.

"I'm ready when you are," he called out.

Two or three guitar players strummed a few chords. "Here we are," we sang as we walked up the church to take our places informally around the altar. "Here we are joined together. . . . Shout the joys of freedom everywhere. . . . Happy is the man who does his best to free the troubled world of all its pain . . ."

The lector, a blond woman, went to the pulpit. A little girl wandered over and stood beside her. The beat of the guitars came through loud and clear. "Join we with that man and free the world . . ."

After he had read the Gospel, Father Fournier continued where we had left off downstairs. "You were probing your consciences down there," he said, "struggling to communicate, trying to understand each other's hopes and sorrows. I suffer as you do. You ask what it means to be lay people. I ask what it means to be a priest. Won't you tell me what you expect of your priest?"

The answers came quickly and spontaneously.

A woman: "I expect a priest to be another Christ."

A man: "The priest should lead us."

Another man: "Maybe we'll find a new role for the priest. We may find he doesn't have to be a financial genius."

A Negro girl: "I don't expect anything different from you than from other Christians. But we should take away the unnecessary duties from you. As for us, we haven't been living up to our responsibilities. The Mass you celebrate is the only distinction I see between the priest and the layman."

Father Fournier nodded agreement. "I have been to community Masses," he said, "where people placed their hands on the altar during the consecration to show they share in the priesthood. My role is the same as yours, except that I can make Christ present through sacramental action."

As they pressed close at the moment of consecration of the bread and wine, I could see that all were recalling what Father Fournier had said. The children were almost on top of him, their noses jutting over the edge of the altar. Later, when the people shook hands with each other at the Kiss of Peace, I noticed a husband kiss his wife tenderly. As the priest began to distribute the Communion, a father perched his restless child on his shoulders. The guitars strummed. The words of *Sons of God* rose merrily: ". . . and we'll sing a song of love: Allelu, Allelu, Allelu, Alleluia!"

A sensation of happiness pervaded the community. The happening had happened. Spontaneously, a woman started to sing "The Impossible Dream." Everyone joined in the glowing reprise.

The priest was smiling as he said, "Thank you, Lord, for the opportunity of coming together in you. The Mass is ended. Go forth and witness to it."

CHAPTER 5

A Time to Know and Grow

About a year and a half after the Second Vatican Council ended, the Secretariat for Promoting Christian Unity issued a set of directives that told Catholics how to proceed in this new ecumenical age. The Secretariat, which rose to prominence during Vatican II under a kindly German Cardinal, Augustin Bea, has been one of the chief symbols of the new openness in the Catholic Church.

More than one battle was joined by two antagonists, the Bea universalists versus the Ottaviani immobilists. Respect for other Christian Churches written into the Council's legislation, the Ecumenical Directory was awaited with considerable impatience around the world because, while nearly everyone favors the ideal of Christian unity, not many comprehend the do's and don'ts. After exhorting the faithful to "change of heart and holiness of life" as the soul of the ecumenical movement, the directory set out certain ground rules in Paragraph 59.

"Catholics," it said, "may be allowed to attend occasionally the liturgical services of other brethren if they have reasonable ground, e.g., arising out of public office or function, blood relationship or friendship, desire to be better informed, an ecumenical gathering, etc. In these cases... there is nothing against Catholics taking some part in the common responses, hymns, and actions of the community of which they are guests—so long as they are not at variance with Catholic faith. The same principles govern the manner in which our separated brethren may assist at services in Catholic churches. This participation, from which reception of the Eucharist is always excluded, should lead the participants to esteem the spiritual riches we have in common and at the same time make them more aware of the gravity of our separation."

Not long after the Directory was published, I spent an afternoon with two women, a Catholic and a Protestant, calling on Negro families in riot-torn Detroit. The two women were part of a community-action team finding new accommodations for riot victims, jobs for deserted mothers, and nurseries for the children. We went up and down filthy stairways in stinking tenements, searching for families, and in some cases partial families, who had seemingly evaporated into the faceless ghetto.

I remember one call particularly. A Negro mother and her four children, one of them with third-degree burns on her leg, had been burned out in the riots and were living in a cramped one-bedroom apartment in a decrepit building. The two women callers took down sizes of the children's clothing, checked welfare payments, and outlined job prospects for the mother, giving her the friendly encouragement so obviously needed. Afterwards, in the car, we talked about how the Churches can help such families, and then the conversation drifted to how little denominational differences count in the face of such gigantic human problems.

"If you believe in God and Christ and baptism, I don't see why we have to get hung up on all this other frilly stuff," said the Catholic.

"Yes," said the Protestant, "so you've got a Pope and we

don't, so who cares? You've got seven sacraments, and we've got two. What's the difference?"

"Let's just be Christians, for God's sake," replied the Catholic, as she tramped down on the gas.

In yet another field, we see the conflict and the paradox of the Catholic revolution. Cautious explorations forward by the Secretariat for Promoting Christian Unity; a carefree dash past the crumbling barriers by the advance wing of Catholic actionists. The Catholic woman's gay dismissal of institutional regulations guiding an ordered development of the ecumenical movement brings out all the tenseness and rigidity never far from the surface of the hierarchy, who fear widespread theological indifferentism. On the other side of the coin, the control exercised by the hierarchy over what can prudently be done in the name of Christian unity seems far too short-sighted to those who perceive the disastrous effects of a fractured Christianity on the modern world in which two-thirds of the people don't even know the name of Christ.

The issue can be summarized in "spiritual ecumenism" and "secular ecumenism"—not that they must necessarily be opposed. Spiritual ecumenism, as the Secretariat notes, stresses prayer, public and private, as the route to unity. Secular ecumenism views man in his human condition and through the joint activity of men of goodwill promotes his betterment. In the process, those who have labored for social progress find out, most often unwittingly, how much they have in common theologically. The bonds of union, sociologically if not theologically, are quickly forged.

The distinction, while valid, does not mean that the institutional Church stands opposed to secular ecumenism, or that the charismatic elements in the People of God fail to support the work of spiritual ecumenism. There are cross-sections of viewpoints. Indeed, the importance of Christians working together in the world was underlined by the Vatican Council's Constitution on the Church in the Modern World after it had already been stressed in the Decree on Ecumenism.

That decree asked, for example, for cooperative efforts of Christians to contribute "a just appreciation of the dignity of the human person, the promotion of the blessings of peace . . . to relieve the afflictions of our times, such as famine and natural disasters, illiteracy and poverty, lack of housing and the unequal distribution of wealth." A common effort by Christians for these ends "vividly expresses that bond which already unites them and . . . sets in clearer relief the features of Christ the Servant."

The harmonizing of the spiritual and secular approaches is one of the great challenges facing ecumenism today. For what can be stated with certainty is that there is a deepening yearning throughout the Catholic Church both to improve relations with other Christians and non-Christians and also to serve God by putting the Church at the service of man. As a result, even though there are the customary yellow caution lights signaling amid the confusion, the ecumenical field has largely escaped the deeper conflicts which in other areas have produced such phenomena as the "underground" worship groups and the splits over contraception, celibacy, and authority.

The quick turnabout in the official and publicly stated Catholic position on ecumenism is attributable directly to Pope John. In fact, it was one of the very few things on which he was specific when he announced his plans for a Council. One of its main purposes, he said repeatedly, would be to prepare the way for the reunion of Christians.

Presented in such broad terms, the proposal created no problem. Unity of his followers had been Christ's dying wish. "That they may be one," he prayed his Father at his last meal with his disciples. Unity of Christians had been the objective of many councils—Lyons, Florence, Trent.

Pius IX had not only reaffirmed the objective when summoning the first Vatican Council in 1869; he had formulated the procedures. Unity, he said, was to be brought about by the return of "Protestants and other non-Catholics" to the one true fold of Christ, namely, the Roman Catholic Church.

Understandably, the response was totally negative, but the only immediate effect of the rejection by the Orthodox, the Anglicans, and the Protestants of reunion on the basis of total surrender was to harden the Catholic position. When a unity movement among Protestants themselves began in the early years of the 20th century, Catholics generally interpreted it as evidence of a decline of belief among the Churches that resulted from the Reformation, a subordination of dogma to expediency. The adherence of the principal Orthodox Churches to the World Council of Churches under a formula that fully protected their dogmatic positions did not change the Catholic viewpoint. That way, Catholics insinuated, lay not unity but religious indifferentism.

A rigid censorship of Catholic theologians by the Holy Office prevented any public expression of the dissident viewpoints that developed within the Catholic Church on this issue, particularly in Europe during the Nazi regime and World War II, when Catholics, Protestants, and Jews found in prison camps and on battlefields the strength that came from their common sharing of basic religious beliefs. What the Second Vatican Council did was to reveal how widespread among Catholics was an ecumenical attitude totally at variance with official professions and practices. Not only many theologians and bishops but Catholics at all levels had come to realize the sterility of the position they had been forced to defend, its lack of humility, its misunderstanding of the basic teaching of Christ. They knew that Catholics shared the blame for division, that they had much to learn from other Christians, and even from those who were not Christians.

As happened with every major issue treated by the Second Vatican Council, an intransigent minority opposed the new ecumenical vision of the majority. Entrenched in the central organs of the Church, it exercised considerable control over the Council's outdated machinery and introduced ambiguities and vacillations into the documents which at the time seemed unimportant, but which are responsible for today's growing tension as some individuals press ahead and others hold back.

Pope John anticipated much of what has since happened by stressing the importance of living and working together. He invited observers from the Christian Churches to the Council, opening up its secrets to them, even at a time when the press was excluded as an enemy. They received all documents, were provided simultaneous translations of the discussions, informed of the range of theological and emotional conflict, and invited to help behind the scenes to find solutions. Their presence forced speakers to be honest and realistic.

The results can be seen in every one of the Council's sixteen documents, and not only in the Decree on Ecumenism —the one devoted directly to the issue. The Constitution on the Liturgy, the first to be discussed and approved, foreshadowed what would follow. In small but significant ways, it agreed with principles and practices of the Reformers that Catholics had previously resisted—the use of the vernacular in the Mass, the active participation of all in worship, greater stress on Scripture, approval in principle of reception of the Eucharist under both types—bread and wine— wider use of community singing, adaptation of the liturgy to the culture of each country, de-emphasizing of the veneration of statues, and other practices which might "create confusion among the Christian people and promote a faulty sense of devotion."

The Constitution on the Church was even more significant. It shifted the emphasis from a legalistic concept of the hierarchy to the spiritual unity of the members of the Church. It proclaimed that God makes use of other Churches as a means of salvation and that those who are not Christians are also related to the People of God and play a part in promoting the kingdom of Christ.

The teaching on the collegiality of bishops as co-rulers with the pope provided an opening for an understanding of papal infallibility less shocking to the Orthodox and Protestants than the previous Catholic understanding of the definition of the First Vatican Council. The upgrading of the laity as full members of the People of God and the express affirmation of their common priesthood in baptism also served to meet legitimate criticism advanced four centuries ago by the Reformers.

By the time they reached the Decree on Ecumenism, the Council Fathers were ready to endorse views that were not even discussed publicly when the Council opened, as Protestant observer Robert McAfee Brown put it. They agreed that the Catholic Church as an institution here on earth is not perfect, that on the contrary Christ summons it "to continual reformation." They identified the Protestant bodies as "Churches and ecclesial communities" through which the grace of Christ flows to their members. "Some, even very many, of the most significant elements or endowments which together go to build up and give life to the Church herself can exist outside the visible boundaries of the Catholic Church: the written word of God; the life of grace; faith, hope and charity, along with other interior gifts of the Holy Spirit and visible elements. All of these, which come from Christ and lead back to Him, belong by right to the one Church of Christ. The brethren divided from us also carry out many of the sacred actions of the Christian religion. Undoubtedly, in ways that vary according to the condition of each Church or community, these actions can truly engender a life of grace and can be rightly described as capable of providing salvation."

The recognition that a Church not in formal communion with Rome could be a channel of grace for its members and could possess "most of the significant elements and endowments" that give life to the Church herself immediately raised the issue of worship in common. It was an issue on which the Catholic position seemed irrevocably fixed. The Code of Canon Law is absolutely explicit: "The faithful are not allowed to assist actively in any way or to take active part in the religious services of non-Catholics." According to the recognized commentators, the prohibition was "founded in the natural and the divine positive law." Concrete rulings of the Holy Office had entered into such detail as to forbid Catholics to play the organ or sing in connection with the religious services of non-Catholics.

The Council simply swept away this rule of Canon Law and nearly all the theological fences erected to protect it. Dealing first with the Orthodox Churches, it said that they "possess true sacraments, and above all, by apostolic succession, the priesthood and the Eucharist, whereby they are linked with us in closest intimacy. Therefore some worship in common *(communicatio in sacris)*, given suitable circumstances and the approval of Church authority, is not merely possible but to be encouraged."

The Secretariat for Promoting Christian Unity stated that this common worship can extend to celebration of the Eucharist, with the agreement of the Orthodox authorities. When Patriarch Athenagoras visited Pope Paul at the end of the 1967 Synod of Bishops, the common prayer service did not include celebration of the Eucharist. It is generally believed that Athenagoras would himself welcome a eucharistic liturgy. Not all the Orthodox Churches, however, are in agreement, and Athenagoras is extremely careful to avoid offending any of his sister Churches while he pursues his efforts to draw them all with him into closer relations with Rome.

The Council's approval of common worship with Protestants was more limited, though it did break decisively with the older position. Worship in common, it said, is a witness to the unity of the Church and a sharing in the means of grace. Insofar as it is a witness to unity, it cannot be permitted between those who, in fact, are not united; but insofar as it is a sharing in the means of grace, it may at times be commended. Thus, the Secretariat for Unity authorized the giving of the Catholic sacraments of the Eucharist, Penance, and Anointing of the Sick to "a separated brother" for adequate reasons, such as danger of death, during persecutions, or in prison. It added that a Catholic in similar circumstances may not ask for these sacraments except from a minister who has been validly ordained, but without any attempt to determine which Protestant ministers are validly ordained.

In the course of preparing this book, I attended services in many different Christian Churches as well as specific unity services often held on neutral ground, such as auditoriums. With each service, particularly as I became aware of a common stress on the Gospel, I became more convinced of the practicability of the often-heard (but long sidestepped by Rome) slogan, "Diversity in Unity." While there are many Christian Churches, other than Catholic, steeped in their own traditions and protective of their way of worshipping the Lord, there is a discernible pattern emerging of a common groping toward a new kind of diverse worship befitting the pilgrimage toward unity, the outline of which is still over the horizon.

Just when the faithful are getting used to the idea of

common worship, the advance sections in all the Churches are raising new questions. They recognize that such new expressions of friendship as pulpit-exchanges are healthy, but wonder whether polite camaraderie makes any real imprint on modern man. Friendship is a welcome progression from outdated polemics, yet does it really come to grips with the key problem facing all the Christian Churches today—the credibility of their role as instruments not only for personal worship of God but vehicles for the mobilizing of Christ's love for all mankind, especially the poor and downtrodden and all those consigned by unjust social systems to continuing affliction?

Christians are praying together more and enjoying it more, yes. The linking of the Vatican and the World Council of Churches in social work reflects a growing concern for combining resources to complement common prayer, yes. Nonetheless, Churches have not yet learned how to work together in the political, economic, and social arenas where secular man makes the important decisions about how life can be improved. Many Christians rejoice in the new commingling as a sort of revolution, if not a miracle. But the greater revolution is a technologically oriented society sweeping past a religion weighed down by divisions over theological constructs nobody cares about any more and by styles and rituals that speak of cultures long dead.

It is obvious that Christianity, if unified, can be heard better in the world. But the legalities of union are so protracted that no one dares to hope that unity can be accomplished in the foreseeable future. And it is the foreseeable future that modern man cares about.

"The Pope cannot afford to compromise his position; I understand that better than his most conservative advisers," Dr. Eugene Carson Blake, General Secretary of the World Council of Churches, said as he sat, urbane and distinguished, holding a press conference following a lecture in

132

Rome's Gregorian University, a time-honored citadel of Vaticanology.

The Secretariat for Unity's Directory, while treading delicately through fields not yet cleared of all the mines, seemed to anticipate closer future spiritual collaboration. One of the Secretariat's stars, Father Thomas Stransky, an American Paulist, conceding that Catholic participation in ecumenism is a bit like a clumsy elephant sniffing at a cultivated garden, has set down a working principle: Churches should do everything together except what conscience tells us to do separately. This is a big step forward from the traditional Christian position of doing everything separately, unless the world said to do it together.

All of these problems and currents of progress came sharply into focus for me during the most memorable of all the Christian unity services I attended. The delegates to the World Congress for the Lay Apostolate at Rome came in the late afternoon to St. Paul's Outside the Walls, a basilica containing the tomb of St. Paul and a jewel second only to St. Peter's in Rome's ecclesial firmament.

The hundred or so official delegates from other Churches were given places of prominence by the colonnades that support the high altar. Cardinal Bea, stooped with age but with alert eyes, took his place with the congregation. Candles flickered in the dim light as the representatives of various denominations took turns in leading the prayers. With each hymn, the voices became stronger, until the Church was filled with a resounding praise, "Hosanna in Excelsis," chanted by a universal chorus: African, Asian, Latin American, North American, British, French, German, Spanish, black, yellow, white, Protestant, Anglican, Orthodox, Catholic. Unity in diversity.

The looseness of structure of Protestant Churches, as contrasted with the centralized organization of Catholicism, was in the past a major obstacle to determining precisely what are the objective denominational differences. In the new spirit of confidence and openness, rapid progress is being made in distinguishing the basic from the merely verbal issues.

In the United States, for example, a joint Anglican-Roman Catholic theological commission has been meeting regularly since 1965. It achieved a major breakthrough in 1967 when it decided that the two Churches are in basic agreement on the Eucharist as sacrifice. This had been regarded as one of the major points of tension. "It is clear to us," the participants said, "that the findings of modern biblical, theological and liturgical studies have transcended many of the polemical formulations of an earlier period."

The issue of Anglican orders still remains, but it is no longer regarded as insuperable. Although Pope Leo XIII said that his statement in 1896 declaring Anglican orders to be invalid was a final pronouncement, Catholic theologians are today questioning that decision and the evidence on which it was based.

Lutheran and Roman Catholic theologians in the United States are also engaged in an evaluation of their respective beliefs, and they have issued an important statement on the Eucharist. Following an intensive study of the Eucharist as sacrifice and of the presence of Christ in the Lord's Supper, they declared that "we are no longer able to regard ourselves as divided in the one, holy, catholic, and apostolic faith on these two points." Any consensus on inter-communion, however, must await deeper study.

In a talk to 28 Roman Catholic bishops, Dr. George Lindbeck of the Yale Divinity School, a member of this group, said it had now conducted intensive discussions of faith and baptism, as well as of the Eucharist as sacrament and the Eucharist as sacrifice, and that it was the consensus of its twenty members that there was no important difference in either theology or doctrine between the Lutherans and the Roman Catholics on any of them.

The discussions of Catholic theologians with their Anglican and Lutheran counterparts have the official sanction of the Catholic bishops who have arranged for bilateral talks of this kind with at least six Protestant communities through the Commission on Ecumenical and Interreligious Affairs of the National Conference of Catholic Bishops. The National Council of Churches has set up a joint working group with the National Conference of Catholic Bishops, paralleling the liaison arrangements made between the World Council of Churches and the Vatican.

At a more popular level, the National Council of Churches is working with the Paulist Fathers to develop Christian ecumenical leadership. Directly involved are Father William B. Greenspun, C.S.P., Dr. William A. Norgren, and Cynthia Wedel of the NCC. Their *Living Room Dialogues* (more than 125,000 copies have been sold) are carried on by several thousand groups across the United States. More or less closely related with these are a multiplicity of local arrangements, ranging from open houses to ecumenical lecture series in summer schools and Lenten ecumenical discussions.

On the practical level, these initiatives are being translated into such things as the development of common facilities for worship, fellowship, and study. One such program is St. Mark's Church in Kansas City, Missouri. Here two Protestant bodies, the United Presbyterian Church and the United Church of Christ, pulled down an outmoded and inadequate church structure to make way for a new, functional one. They have been joined in the new center by the Episcopal Church and the Roman Catholic diocese in a cooperative ministry to Inner City residents. Lutherans, Methodists, Presbyterians, and Catholics have agreed to establish a single center for worship and educational facilities in the new city of Columbia being constructed in Maryland, halfway between Baltimore and Washington, D.C.

Nowhere is the thrust toward Christian unity more in evidence than on college and university campuses, and this is the area in which one can see plain evidence of pressures tending to sweep the movement forward to experimentation that takes little account of the officially imposed limitations. Typical of today's atmosphere on campus was a gesture made by eleven Protestant Churches in Minnesota in October, 1967. To celebrate the 450th anniversary of the Reformation, they made a joint contribution toward the erection of an institute for ecumenical and cultural research at a Catholic institution of higher learning, St. John's Abbey and University, Collegeville, Minnesota. The gift was handed over at an interdenominational service at St. John's on Reformation Sunday.

The institute will be a residential center on the Catholic campus, where ten Protestant, Orthodox, and Jewish scholars will live with their families while engaging in ecumenical study and dialogue. Such exchange of theologians among Catholic, Protestant, and Jewish seminaries and schools of theology has become commonplace in the United States in the past few years, as has the creation of joint courses and unified schools of theology. The Graduate Theological Union in California has incorporated units directed by Jesuits and Dominicans, and there is similar cooperation in New York between the Union Theological Seminary and Fordham University.

Many of those who become involved in such exchanges quickly develop the view that the theoretical issues of belief are not the sole or even the main obstacle. Catholics and Protestants have institutionalized the expression of their beliefs and religious life so differently that it seems impossible to get adjustment by each side to the specifications of

136

the other on the level of the general body of worshippers. Here, of course, the official line is to urge patience, to wait for a gradual growing together over an indefinitely long period, just as it took centuries to grow apart.

For an increasing number of those most immediately involved, however, the solution is to be found in common sharing of the Eucharist. One expert who believes this is Jesuit Father David J. Bowman, who joined the Faith and Order Division of the National Council of Churches in 1966 as the first Roman Catholic staff member of that body.

"Among theologians and others who are struggling with the intellectual issues that divide Christians," he told me, "a great feeling for the discriminating use of the Eucharist as a means toward unity is developing. This has been encouraged by the ruling of the Vatican Secretariat for Unity to allow such inter-communion in a few exceptional cases, such as danger of death."

Father Bowman confirmed for me what I had learned from other sources, namely, that inter-communion far beyond that allowed by the Secretariat for Unity rules is occurring throughout the United States, particularly in college communities. During the Liturgical Week in Kansas City in August, 1967, after two papers on the subject had been presented, the participants broke up into small groups to discuss their contents.

"I was one of a group of eighteen," Father Bowman informed me. "When we were asked if we knew of concrete instances of communion in which Roman Catholics had taken part across denominational lines, fourteen of the eighteen said they did. Some of them had participated themselves, and the others knew for certain of the fact, the most frequent location being a public university. I think the proportion was about the same in the other groups."

Dr. Philip Hefner, a Lutheran theologian who read a

paper at the same Liturgical Week in Kansas City, confirmed the existence of this trend. "We all know," he said, "that present practice does not conform to the explicit teaching of our Churches. There is inter-communion between us, and it is fairly common and widespread. In some cases, this practice is to be lamented as irresponsible and misguided. But in other cases it is a sound instinct, that the sacrament and the power of Christ that is in it will not be bound. There is a unity in our community together, even when our institutional arrangements cannot and ought not recognize unity. Inter-communion may well be the expression of that unity. As such, it ought to be welcomed as God's gift to his Church."

The spread of the practice of inter-communion on college campuses has to be seen as part of the overall philosophy of today's students. As Dr. John E. McCaw, of the Divinity School of Drake University, has expressed it, "The students have said that there should be on the modern campus one believing presence, and that it should find its common expression in action and study."

This reflects the awareness of students that they form a single community with common goals. And because they see these goals as separate from and in large part in conflict with those of the society around them, they make their own decisions as to how they will implement them, with a minimum of concern for the regulations presented to them from areas outside their own ranks. For many of them it is not important whether the institutions survive as we know them, or in any recognizable form. They would agree with the formulation of the problem made by the Catholic scholar Michael Novak.

"The issue is not whether the Christian Churches should find some way of ending the scandal of their separation," he has observed. "The issue is whether the Christian

Churches will survive. The question is even more painful than that. It is whether we should *help* the Christian Churches to survive. Are the Churches worth reforming?"

This trend of thinking and action among students is creating an entirely new situation for the Newman Centers for Catholics, as well as for the Student Christian Association and similar groupings of Protestant students. A progressive integration of the facilities and activities of these organizations is taking place, not only in social and cultural, but in strictly religious areas. The Catholic and Protestant students in these unified activities quickly come to know each other not by denominational contrast but by common Christian concern.

When it is remembered that this young segment of society is already in revolt against the legalism and hypocrisy of the community from which it has sprung, it is easier to understand its scant concern for the niceties of the rules laid down by the various Churches for the conduct of worship, or for the prohibition to express common beliefs and anxieties in the supreme action of Christian worship—the eucharistic commemoration.

What is significant, however, is that we have here in the making a powerful impetus toward secular ecumenism that is completely different in its assumptions and directions from spiritual ecumenism. The Catholic strategists and policy-makers, as late arrivals on the ecumenical scene, had simply assumed that the path to unity was that already traced by the Protestant Churches.

Here is how one Catholic ecumenist, James Gallagher, described their approach: "In most instances official Catholic participation in the United States brand of ecumenism is following the orderly, logical, and mostly theoretical approach of veteran Protestant Church unionists. Catholic commissions are joining in discussion at many Church levels. But they bear out the criticism of the World Council of Churches' Albert van den Huevel that 'the ecumenical movement today is a churchly affair. It is first of all a movement of and for the denominations.' " It is this approach, the logic of which could only lead to one great super-Church embracing all Christians, that many of the more advanced thinkers in the student community find emotionally repugnant and intellectually irrelevant.

Nor is the attitude of these students confined to North America. I was particularly impressed by a workshop on ecumenical dialogue and collaboration that I attended in Rome during the Lay Congress. Summing up the views of this group, the chairman said that they felt that the ecumenical movement had to go beyond structures and human forces to place itself under the influence of the Holy Spirit. They were impatient, for example, with the restrictions on mixed marriages still imposed by the Catholic Church, regarding the automatic excommunication of a Catholic married in a Protestant Church (without special permission) as "a serious offense against charity."

All—especially the younger generation—regarded intercommunion as one of the most important aspects of the ecumenical movement, the chairman concluded. The workshop called on the laity to undertake extensive experimentation in order to discover more natural forms of community, so that "the Christian life can be brought to all and not confined to a small group." It urged the creation of joint lay-clerical commissions at all levels "to promote Christian commitment in the world." It would seem clear, therefore, that the main ecumenical progress in the immediate future is likely to be in this area—secular ecumenism.

On the Protestant side, there is growing approval of this approach. "The secular mission becomes important," says Dr. George A. Lindbeck of the Yale Divinity School, "because God is seen as guiding all that happens toward the final transformation. All that is pure, honorable and of good report, whether it develops within the explicitly Christian sphere or not, whether it is overtly religious or apparently secular in character, will enter into the consummation. Human advances of all sorts, from the technological and scientific to the social, political, cultural and moral, are part of God's preparation for the coming kingdom.

"These advances, of course, are radically ambiguous and can be used for evil purposes as well as good; but God wills that man actualize his potentialities to the uttermost, and whatever is good about these actualizations is relevant. Thus the 'building of the earthly city,' as Vatican II calls it, and the worldly tasks which necessarily occupy the attention of most men most of the time are not simply a meaningless background to spiritual reality, to the new age, but contribute to its very constitution. In promoting so-called secular advances, therefore, the Church and the Christian are directly engaged in God's business, and this is true not only when they struggle for peace and justice, but also when they are concerned with the inseparably related technological, intellectual and cultural domains."

At the very highest levels, this kind of "ecumenical pragmatism" is being fostered by the World Council of Churches and the Vatican's Justice and Peace Commission. They see it as the specifically Christian contribution to the solution of the social and economic crises confronting the contemporary world. Particularly significant is a report prepared in 1967 by a working group composed of World Council and Catholic representatives, and approved by Pope Paul and by the central committee of the World Council of Churches. While noting that "for the moment the common cause of Christian unity would not be furthered if the Catholic Church were to join the Council," it outlined a series of recommendations for joint action. They included proposals for joint emergency relief and development aid, with particular stress on cooperation in medical assistance and the creation of a working party to explore the possibilities of common witness in missionary situations.

Major gatherings to discuss and promote international peace, development, and justice, with active participation of Catholic, Protestant, and Orthodox delegates, have become so common they no longer merit headlines. What is interesting is the fact that stress on development is bringing Marxists into the picture.

Commenting on a Christian/Marxist dialogue held in an ecumenical setting in Western Europe in early 1968, Rev. Paul Abrecht of the World Council of Churches said, "Both Marxists and Christians have one point in common: a real concern for concrete man in his social environment. Both, moreover, are faced with complacency in society about man's condition. In a sense, both have failed in meeting the challenge of the modern age, and this makes them more open to real talk with each other without seeking the other's conversion."

The visit of Roger Garaudy, a French Marxist intellectual, to the United States, while predictably raising the hackles of John Birch followers, was notable for the general receptivity he encountered. The willingness of advanced Christian thinkers to hold dialogues with Communists is reflected also in the Vatican's establishing a Secretariat for Non-Believers, charged with the study of atheism for the purpose of exploring its background philosophy, and to develop a dialogue with non-believers.

The first tentative feelers for a dialogue between Russian Communism and Catholicism have already been put out. Following up the visit of former Premier Khrushchev's son-in-law, Alexei Adzhubei, to Pope John, N. V. Podgorny became the first Russian head of state to enter the Vatican since the time of the czars. He was received by Pope Paul, who has dispatched emissaries to talk over problems with Russian Orthodox leaders known to be beneficiaries of the Kremlin's blessing. Rome never forgets that one of Communism's avowed purposes is to persecute religion, but in the policy of nonalignment that now grips the Vatican, the Church realizes she must coexist with all ideologies.

While a rapprochement with a milder Moscow fits in with the Vatican's drive for peace in the world, it is not unthinkable that a form of socialism might some day receive the Church's tacit blessing. The Church's desire to be an influence among the millions in the developing Third World may hasten this. Critics of all the pettiness in the Church's operations often overlook the really giant strides in progress that have been made. When Pius XII in 1949 imposed excommunication on those voting Communist, it would have been regarded as preposterous that in less than two decades one of his top aides would be opening the Church to the left.

Peace among Christians must obviously have top priority, and indeed most Christians are still blind to the staggering job waiting to be tackled after Christian reunion is achieved, but the most profound realities of pluralism are at last being faced with implications for the benefit of mankind that tower over the new friendships of today's Christian pulpit exchanges. For religious thinkers are finally understanding that no religious, philosophical, or ideological creed is going to dominate the world and we must, therefore, learn how to coexist spiritually.

As a brilliant ecumenist, Willem A. Visser't Hooft, former general secretary of the World Council of Churches, notes: "No Church can claim any more that it alone represents the convictions and aspirations of a whole people. And even to claim that the Christian Churches together are an adequate reflection of the deeper reflections of the community as a whole has become untenable in most so-called Christian countries."

The fact is, Dr. Visser't Hooft observes, the non-Christian religious and ideological forces are making more rapid advances today than Christianity. The statistics bear him out. The percentage of Christians in the world today is steadily declining. An enormous part of the world is now under the influence of Marxism, and in many other countries, notably in Asia, the Christian missions are practically unable to operate.

The Vatican Council's Decree on Ecumenism dealt directly only with other Christians. The logic of this document and of the Council's total reevaluation of the relationship of Catholicism to other religions within the divine plan for mankind required some guidance for Catholics in their dealings with non-Christians, and this was given in the Declaration on Non-Christian Religions.

The most important and most debated part of this document dealt with the Jews, and that for two reasons. One was that Catholics, like other Christians, bore a long heritage of guilt for their anti-Semitism. The World Council of Churches had issued a statement on the subject on behalf of its members at New Delhi in 1961. It was proper that the Catholic Church should also confess its guilt and urge a change of attitude on those members who still continued the tradition of prejudice. The other concerned the fact that Christians are linked, in the words used by the Council, by "a spiritual bond" to the Jews from whom they descend. The Church, the Council accordingly declared, "cannot forget that she received the revelation of the Old Testament through the people with whom God in his inexpressible mercy deigned to establish the Ancient Covenant. . . . According to the Apostle, the Jews still remain most dear to God because of their fathers. . . . Since the spiritual patrimony common to Christians and Jews is thus so great, this sacred Synod wishes to foster and recommend that mutual understanding and respect which is the fruit above all of biblical and theological studies, and of brotherly dialogue."

Although some Jews were at the time saddened by the Council's delays in approving this statement, and by its failure to spell out an anti-Semitic stand as unambiguous as they had requested, the years following the Council have seen a rapid expansion of contacts at all levels, especially in the United States. Such visits as that of Bishop Fulton J. Sheen to a synagogue in Rochester are no longer uncommon, and one frequently finds a rabbi speaking in the company of Christian clergymen in Catholic churches in ecumenical services. Frequently a Jewish theologian will be found on the staff of Catholic seminaries and theology schools.

Early in 1967, the Catholic bishops of the United States issued Guidelines for Catholic-Jewish Relations in order to promote and coordinate existing activities. The Guidelines encourage dialogue, mutual respect and understanding, warn against proselytizing, call for the elimination of offensive material from school texts and prayerbooks, and urge common social action. In addition to such grass-roots activities, they call for "slower and deeper explorations of pertinent issues by Catholic and Jewish scholars."

An innovation in these Guidelines is an emphasis on common prayer for Catholics and Jews, a proposal that follows logically from the Vatican Council stress on "the spiritual patrimony common to Christians and Jews." Such a concept poses the challenge of a return by Christians to worship in the synagogue. It was in the synagogue that Jesus taught and worshipped. The apostles decided at the first Council of Jerusalem that gentile converts were not bound by the prescriptions of the law of Moses, but they never suggested that it was improper to follow them.

As recently as a few years ago, nevertheless, any such suggestion would have been greeted with derision on both sides. It is a measure of the extent of the Catholic revolution that a group as conservative as the American bishops is encouraging Christians to join with Jews in prayer.

CHAPTER 6

Laity: Freedom vs. Control

I was having lunch with a teacher during an education conference when a bishop whom he knew passed by. "Hi, Bishop," my friend called out cheerily, receiving a cordial greeting in reply. He quickly returned his attention to the plate of steak and onions in front of him.

A moment later, he looked up and said to me, "You know, even two years ago, I'd have jumped up, said 'How do you do, Your Excellency,' genuflected, and grabbed his ring to kiss it. I guess things *are* changing in the Church." A little episode.

The ocher cover of the brochure says simply, "The National Association of Laymen Speaks..." Inside one finds such statements as these: "We propose inter-communion by all Christians who accept the presence of Christ in the celebration of the Eucharist... [and] sermons and scripture reading by Protestant ministers during the celebration of Mass, and like participation by priests at Protestant services." "The parish must be free to evolve its own style of life, both in the development of its purposes and in liturgical celebration." "The elective process should be generalized in the Church. It should be established in such a way that all members of the Church may play an essential role in the selection of their pastors, bishops and other major ecclesiastical officials." A very large episode.

In little mannerisms and big policy statements, the mood, style, and character of the laity in the Catholic Church are changing in the biggest transformation of relationships since the Reformation. They are no longer happy sheep, willing to be blindly led by their shepherd pastors and bishops. Not all the laity know enough about the Vatican Council to react to its intellectual challenge, but sufficient numbers are reasonably well informed to provoke a storm of criticism and creativity. Docility has given way to assertiveness.

Very few laymen have mastered the sweeping outlines of a new Church in the 700 pages of Vatican II's sixteen documents, but a sentence in paragraph 37 of Chapter 4 of the Constitution on the Church has constituted a beacon light to nearly everyone: "An individual layman, by reason of the knowledge, competence, or outstanding ability which he may enjoy, is permitted and even sometimes obliged to express his opinion on things which concern the good of the Church."

From the Lay Congress in Rome to the parish precincts of Missouri, the laity have taken the bishops at their word. As a result, educated, informed, articulate men and women are challenging traditions in a way that would have been considered outrageously presumptuous before the Council began.

Where does the money go and why isn't there full public accounting? Why are we building more big churches when underdeveloped countries need all the help we can give them? Why weren't the liturgical changes better explained? Why can't we practice birth control if our consciences tell us it's all right? Why can't the Church operate along democratic lines? These are only a few of the urgent questions being propounded today by thinking and concerned Catholics in all walks of life.

The sudden rush to open season for the tongue after generations of free speech being off limits is a large factor in the present turmoil of the Catholic Church. The clergy and hierarchy interpret such questioning as challenging (which it is), and too often they respond defensively. The criticisms do not admit of easy answers, and the questioners themselves are frequently divided in their premises and the kinds of answers they want.

Despite repeated attempts by the Pope and the bishops to assert their teaching authority, the tones of authority echo from another age. A few conservatives among the laity are still manning the ramparts in behalf of ecclesiastical judgment, but the great majority are confused about what the Church is, should be, and will be.

After being drilled since childhood in the "timeless qualities of a changeless Church," men and women by the millions were swept up in the conciliar hurricane. Although much more change is needed to speed the updating of a Church falling farther behind the needs of modern man, the simple fact is that change has struck too quickly for immediate adaptation, not to mention digestion.

Catholic experts have stopped counting their crises (of faith, of culture, of authority), but at the very least there is a crisis of confidence in the leadership of the Church, and one needs considerable courage to hope that the hierarchy and the laity will get off their collision course.

For thoughtful laymen, the entire Vatican Council can be boiled down to one word: *freedom*. Freedom from an artificial conformity, freedom from an overbearing clericalism, freedom from the fear of asking pointed questions about the Church. But there is one word that has stayed uppermost in the minds of the bishops: *control*.

The bishops control the Church's vast holdings, including church and school properties and a myriad of welfare institutions: This administrative function is in addition to their principal role as teachers of the faith with a divine commission. The bishops made an important legislative advance at the Council by informing the layman that he is a first-class member of the Church and that his advice is needed in the governing of the Church. But both in the academic atmosphere of the Council and especially in the personal encounters of their home dioceses, they have shied away from anything that looks like a surrender of their considerable power to the laity.

The bishops have put themselves in the position of legislating open-ended change ("continual reformation," the Council said) and yet retaining power over even the minutiae of change. It is an impossible position. When the laity, in their new spirit of freedom, move too close to the cutting edge of an issue, the bishops claim their authority is being watered down. Where, in fact, does lay freedom impinge on hierarchical control? That is the great question that embraces every facet of the Catholic revolution. The question becomes more strident as the tensions between laity and bishops bubble to the surface.

"When the bishops unleashed the desire of contemporary Catholics to really get with the world, they unleashed a force which they could not control," says Dr. Eugene Fontinell, a philosopher at Queens College, New York. "When people get more freedom, they get more impatient with even the more advanced structures that replace the old ones." Thus, even though the Church advanced more in the conciliar years than in the previous fifty, "the gap between the attitudes of the younger and more reflective people in the Church and the bishops is so great that it is hard to see how it can be bridged."

In fact, adds history professor Thomas P. Neill of St. Louis

University, the bishop/people gap is the most serious problem in the American Church. And instead of being resolved, it is festering as the bishops continue to safeguard episcopal authority at the expense of developing a dynamic, charismatic laity.

The Catholic Church is squeezed in a revolution of rising expectations. The bishops, who enjoyed a world spotlight on their progressive legislation, feel cheated when they are now accused of resisting reform. The resentful attitude of the laity, however, is too clear to mistake, and it is attested to by qualified observers.

"The Catholic people of the United States are restless, dissatisfied and angry," declares the *Critic,* an influential Catholic monthly.

Priest-sociologist Andrew Greeley sees American Catholicism approaching the 1970s "with a restless liberal elite, a vaguely dissatisfied liberal mass that wants more rapid change but does not understand either the theories or dynamics of change, a youthful population that is bored and apathetic about many religious questions, and a clergy and religious caught in a crisis of ambiguity for which it was not trained."

All these elements are clearly visible, but the total mood of the laity—at least, as I found it on my journey through the United States—is positive as well as negative. It is concerned with growth and progress, as well as with criticisms. It seeks revolutionary change, but has by no means given up hope that it can achieve it by peaceful means.

The new self-awareness of the Catholic laity should not be seen as an isolated phenomenon, but rather as part of the worldwide awakening of the common man to a sense of his power and destiny, an awakening in which modern communications have played a decisive part. What the Vatican Council did was to serve as a catalyst. But the rapidity of the reaction to its initiatives shows that all the elements were already in position, that there would surely have been an explosion if the Council had not provided safety valves.

In the United States, the impact was felt with particular force. Catholics previously had a tradition of following the orders of the priest unquestioningly. They sent their children to the school he recommended. They brought up their families the way he told them. They went to Sunday Mass because he warned them that they'd go to hell if they missed it. In all of this, however, they were running counter to the general mood of the society in which they lived, a fluid and mobile society in which the external pressures to conform are minimal.

Once the Council told them that as laymen they were full members of the Church, called to an active role in performing its mission, obliged to make their own judgments on the basis of general moral principles presented to them by the Church, the social attitudes around them came into play to enable them to apply immediately in practice the newly offered principles.

The communications media quickly responded to the newly awakened interest in religious matters. The general press, radio, and television provided the basic information to permit the formation of a new public opinion on the Catholic Church. Independent Catholic publications were established in response to the need, including the aggressive and astute *National Catholic Reporter,* which serves a broad middle-class readership from coast to coast. Old liberal standard bearers, such as *Commonweal,* were joined by a renewal-committed coterie of a dozen diocesan newspapers in building a climate of reform. The conservative Catholic publications, highlighted by a new entry, *Twin Circle,* have never been a match for the professionalism of the liberal Catholic editors. Though under the control of the bishops, the progressive diocesan weeklies responded to pressure from their readers to give all the religious news and views, knowing that to the extent that they failed, the general news media in their area would supply the deficiency.

Tension between the bishops and the Catholic press, however, is marked. Bishops who dwell on the crisis of obedience have been extremely bitter in their criticisms of Catholic publications. Bishop Bernard Topel of Spokane, Washington, for example, charged that some Catholic publications should not be found in Catholic homes. Cardinal Shehan of Baltimore added that almost wholesale negative criticism has been the stock in trade of some Catholic journalists. For Cardinal Krol of Philadelphia, they are undermining the authority of the hierarchy.

One of the most professional and progressive-minded Catholic editors, John O'Connor, was squeezed out of the Wilmington, Delaware, diocesan newspaper in 1967 because his views were too advanced (though not an inch beyond Vatican II) for the policy-making group in the diocese. His colleague at the *St. Louis Review,* Donald Quinn, put in words the widespread lay reaction to the O'Connor incident, which became a celebrated test case of the new freedom within the Catholic press: "Here was a case that should have worked: good planning, professional skill, creative purposes, lots of energy and zeal went into the project—and it failed. The questions raised by the failure are immense."

Although there are failures, delays, and incidents along the way, the laity are, in fact, gradually moving closer to the power centers of the Church. It is not power for its own sake they want, but an honorable share in the decision-making process. A resolution presented to the Lay Congress in Rome by the United States delegation synthesizes very well the views of thinking American Catholics on their place in the Church. The resolution called for a basic change in the structure of the Council of the laity set up earlier by the Vatican. This body, it said, should be "truly representative of the laity," with its officers and members freely elected by the laity. Truly representative councils of the laity, it added, should be formed at all national, diocesan, and parish levels, with officers and members freely elected by the laity. In addition, national and diocesan pastoral councils, consisting of clergy, religious orders, and laity, should be set up in such a way that the "lay members will be truly representative of the laity and freely elected by the laity."

In a moment we shall see the start that is being made toward implementing this ambitious goal. First, however, we should note an extremely important parallel development. It is the laity's concrete insistence on and practical exercise of their rights as human beings and as members of the People of God. In this sense, the Catholic is showing himself to be a man of the 20th century. This new trend expresses itself graphically in the attitude toward marriage and the decision-making roles of the married couple. As we saw in Chapter 2, the thrust of the Lay Congress turned on this issue.

Allied to the marriage question and very much a part of the Council's insistence on the equality of the People of God is the question of women in the Church. Discrimination against women has been built into the Church for so long that many well-educated women still take for granted their exclusion from the ministerial and governmental areas.

When Cardinal Suenens of Belgium made a plea during the second session of the Vatican Council for the admission of women auditors, he noted drily, "Unless I am mistaken, women make up one half of the world's population." The sheer news value of this statement reverberated around Rome. The Council did admit a few women auditors (not before a guard prevented a woman journalist from receiving Communion at a Council Mass), but refused to let Barbara Ward, an outstanding British economist, speak on the Council floor. The low status of women became highlighted, and opposition against the male mystique began to mount.

"Women now are definitely an issue in the Church," Margaret Mealey told me as we talked in her sleek Washington office where she directs the National Council of Catholic Women. A veteran Catholic actionist with a winning smile, Miss Mealey points to the increasing contribution women are making to their communities and to society in general. In dozens of fields—education, health, the arts, interracial and inter-faith relations, immigration—women stand out. But in the Church they are downgraded because of their sex, despite the quality of their minds.

Although Pope John's great encyclical, *Mater et Magistra*, acknowledged the social and cultural emergence of woman as one of the most significant developments in the modern world, the Church's repression of the female is rooted in a Canon Law which treats them as minors. The law goes back to scriptural interpretations connected to cultures long dead, such as St. Paul's admonition that women should be quiet in Church. St. Paul's other injunction against inequality in the Church "on the basis of race or nationality, social condition or sex" is generally passed over, even though the Council quoted it.

The exclusion of women from the ministry has been accompanied by a prejudice against them as unequal to men that has been handed on from one generation of seminary professors to the next. Even the post-conciliar commission on the liturgy specified that women could not be commentators at Mass or read the Epistle. The function of serving Mass is the preserve of boys. Progressive parishes allow women to walk in the Offertory procession. All this leads Margaret Mealey to note that women are now being dropped back from second- to third-class status as the participation of laymen in the liturgy advances.

The legal barrier to women in the liturgy spills over in the thought processes of bishops and pastors. Miss Mealey tells of a bishop who named a lay committee composed entirely of men. When a woman called and asked why he had not appointed any women, he admitted he had simply not thought of it. It is seldom that women number more than a quarter or a third of the composition of a parish council. Sometimes a bishop or pastor says he wants "a true housewife" on the board or panel. "He is paying a noble tribute to womankind," Miss Mealey notes, "and is putting us all in the exalted company of his beloved mother. But we maintain that imprisonment on a pedestal is as effective as any other."

The Church authorities have simply refused to recognize that the modern woman not only has great capabilities, but is already achieving recognition in many areas of human endeavor—in industry, the arts, communications, and the realm of ideas. Admittedly, contemporary women have not triumphed over the scorn and rejection the secular world has traditionally offered them, the trading on femininity that many women still fall back on, or the erotic philosophy of the eternal *Playboy* that views women as sexual tools, but the 20th-century advance of women out of social enslavement is beyond question. The old-fashioned notion that the brain of a girl-baby just doesn't have to be developed as much as a boy's is dead.

The declining docility of women shows up in the Church, which is as yet unprepared to make the adjustments that secular society is making. As the leading women thinkers press their case, male resistance hardens. Some priests recognize the basic injustice involved here and try to make amends, such as permitting women to participate in forbidden liturgical functions. "This defiance of authority is an unhealthy phenomenon in the Church," Margaret Mealey says, "and will have an especially devastating effect on Catholic women and the children they are raising to be the future people of God."

The St. Joan's International Alliance, a militant women's group, continues to fight discrimination. It has zeroed in on the revision of Canon Law (by competent women as well as men) to end the inferiority status in the Church "which does not correspond to their civic and social status." When this is accomplished, it will bring to the forefront the contentious question of ordaining women to the priesthood. Already, there is a strong male element that rejects discussion of women's rights in the Church on the grounds that "women just want to be priests." Yet, there is probably not one woman in a hundred thousand who has given any thought to being a priest. This emotional male rejection misses the key point entirely.

"It is not that few women have the desire to become priests, which cannot be fulfilled," says Dr. Mary Daly, a leading woman theologian. "It is rather that Catholic women, by the fact of exclusion of all women from such a role, are conditioned to believe that they have an irremediably inferior nature."

Dr. Daly, who holds Doctor of Sacred Theology and Doctor of Philosophy degrees from the University of Fribourg, was the first woman appointed to the theology faculty of the Jesuits' Boston College. In an appraisal of Christian documents, she has cited a record of contradictions between the Christian teaching on the worth of every human person and the "oppressive, misogynistic ideas about women arising from culture conditioning." The exorcism of sexual prejudice is one of the great challenges facing the Church, in her view. The abruptness with which so many males dismiss the idea of women priests is "a deep-seated prejudice which totally identifies women, but not men, with their

157

sexual function." As long as there is ministerial exclusion, there cannot be sexual equality in the Church. Here the battle is joined.

The rising insistence on lay rights within the Church—for both men and women—combined with the new trend among the laity to make their own decisions without waiting for the approval of the Church authorities would seem to spell the dissolution of the character of the Church as it has existed historically. Some Catholics are, in fact, considering such an eventuality, but they are more numerous and more vocal in Europe than in North America. They have even been given a name—the "third man"—meaning one who is personally committed to moral values and to faith in Christ, but who is detached from or unconcerned with institutional structures that cannot keep pace with new modes of thought. He is called "third" to distinguish him from the conservative who wants to defend traditional Church structures, and from the progressive who wants to update them.

In North America, it is the progressive who is most vocal. His ultimate aim is the creation of integrated institutions that will give all the members of the People of God a voice in making policy and supervising its execution. Most progressives would justify the present trends to unapproved liturgical experimentation and to the use of artificial methods of contraception as the result of an abnormal situation in which the institution has become frozen and must be prodded into activity. And many of these would feel that, since they are starting from a historical situation in which all the power structures are under the effective control of the bishops, the first step has to be the creation of parallel but independent organizations of priests, of members of religious orders of men and women, and of the laity. As a matter of practical politics, it is only when such power bases have been formed that it will be possible to take the final step of forming integrated institutions in which all the members will have the voice to which the Vatican Council said they were entitled.

This is definitely the approach of the National Association of Laymen that came into existence at a meeting at St. Paul-Minneapolis, in June, 1967. It grew out of a number of local organizations, of which the most important were in Cleveland, St. Paul-Minneapolis, and Chicago. They had come together in April in Chicago during the meeting of the United States bishops, requesting but failing to obtain an interview with representatives of the bishops. Having made that unsuccessful effort, they decided to go ahead on their own and picked Dennis Landis, head of the St. Paul-Minneapolis group, as their first national president.

Landis is a scientist employed by Honeywell in Minneapolis. Aged 32, he is married and the father of five children. He is short, dark-haired, well-mannered—in fact, rather deferential, but extremely determined. He cares deeply about the Church. "It is much too important to leave to the clergy," is how he summed up his views to me. He has long been active in the Christian Family Movement, the Confraternity of Christian Doctrine, and Church youth work. He and his wife have counseled 500 couples on the use of the rhythm method of family planning.

The 225 people who joined with Landis in forming the National Association of Laymen had backgrounds similar to his own. Most of them were in their thirties, were married, suburbanites, working at the professional or managerial level, active in Church work, experienced in organizational operation, and respectful of the democratic process. They had little difficulty in formulating a program to which all could subscribe.

159

"We are not power hungry," as Landis put it, "but the layman wants a free, open, and responsible voice in the Church's decision-making processes."

Pledging the Association to the promotion and encouragement of continual renewal in the Church, he said that if the present apathy of the adult world and rejection by youth continues, "religion will be gone in fifteen or twenty years." The question is not whether renewal is going too fast, but whether "we have time to slow down."

Other aims of the Association are to stimulate an authentic, free, and responsible lay voice in the Church, to help renewal efforts of individuals and local organizations, to encourage the exchange of ideas at every level, both within and outside the Christian community, and to provide liaison with the bishops and with national organizations.

"The response from all parts of the country was tremendous," Landis told me. "Our membership mushroomed in six months to ten thousand. In addition to individual memberships, we get requests for affiliation from local groups, the Long Island Association of Laymen, the Philadelphia Association of Laymen, the Northern Illinois Conference of Laymen, the Parish Advisory Council of Richardson, Texas."

Landis is not opposed in principle to official organizations of the laity, but he feels that in the present circumstances they don't have enough freedom to say what the people think.

"We feel that we can make a bigger impact on the bishops. I think we have restored hope to a lot of people who had given up. Many of our members see this organization as a final effort. If it doesn't work, I think they will say goodbye. There are also many others who refuse to be kicked out, who say that this is their Church and that they are going to stay in it. What we are working for is a sense of community, a sense of Christian responsibility. We want Christianity to mean more than just going to Mass on Sunday. It must be concerned with the real issues, with peace, with race, with all of today's social problems."

Proving its flexibility and commitment, the NAL moved immediately when the United States Riot Commission made its report condemning white racism as responsible for urban riots and unrest. The NAL took up the challenge by giving top priority to a program of social education at the grass-roots level. The association called on the whole Church "to launch an immediate revolution in attitudes and in financial priorities."

Landis' group was one of the driving forces behind a coalition of laity, clergy, and sisters, calling itself the National Committee on Catholic Concerns, formed at St. Louis in April, 1968. A scorching consensus paper, indicting the institution for a lack of creative and dynamic leadership, deplored the Church's failure "to recognize and seek solutions to problems deeply affecting persons' daily lives—celibacy, laicization of clergy and religious, birth control, divorce and remarriage, the right to selective conscientious objection to war, the morality of the Vietnam war, love and justice to the black people, poverty, and peace."

The Concern Committee deliberately chose the same week and city of the American bishops' meeting in an effort to open up channels of dialogue. The bishops all but rebuffed the committee which, undaunted, determined to hold its next meeting simultaneously with the next episcopal assembly. The specter of the Synod and the World Congress of the Laity meeting separately in Rome was repeated on a smaller scale in St. Louis.

It is this arbitrary division of the business of the bishops and the concerns of the rest of the Church that frustrates growing numbers of mature, educated, responsible Catholics, both clerical and lay. Yet, it is their criticism of the gap between Church teaching and practice, becoming more high-keyed all the time, that makes bishops resist confrontation and commingling with the reform elements.

If there is to be one people in one Church, the blocs must be joined. So far, it is the bishops who resist open discussions with open groups to arrive at open decisions. With post-conciliar issues exploding around them, the bishops feel they are being persecuted by the avant-garde for not being progressive enough and rejected by the traditionalists for allowing changes to threaten faith. The Concern Committee insisted, as a partial answer to the developing splits in the Church, on a new spirit of communications "on all levels of the Church and among all groups—hierarchy and clergy and laity, young and old, conservative and liberal, in a climate of mutual trust, mutual openness, and Christian love."

It is incredible that it should be considered news when a group of bishops and a group of laity sit down to talk over issues. Yet the Catholic press regarded it as very newsworthy when, in November, 1967, Dennis Landis and his associates in the National Association of Laymen were invited to dinner by Archbishop Joseph T. McGucken, episcopal chairman of the Department of Lay Organizations of the U.S. Bishops' Conference, and six other bishops. The Landis group presented NAL views on human dignity, Christian unity, parish life, communications, education, diocesan and parish administration, liturgy, and marriage and the family. The laymen asked that their views be considered by the bishops in the drafting of policy statements in these areas.

The bishops agreed that Catholics were entirely within their rights in supporting an independent structure like the National Association of Laymen. They urged, however, the desirability of exploring ways to relate such independent organizations with existing and projected official bodies, such as the National Councils of Catholic Men and Women, and diocesan pastoral councils. They also agreed with the laymen on the need for more and better communication, while differing with them in their estimate of current defections from the Church. The laymen feel that the rate is higher, especially among young people, than the bishops do.

Although the Association is still involved mainly in organization and the formulation of its views, some indication of the direction it is taking was given at a meeting of the executive board held shortly before the discussion with the bishops just described. A statement on diocesan and parish administration called for "a legislative apparatus" to democratize Church procedures and permit "general participation by Catholics in decisions of Church policy." Denying that democratization would eliminate authority in the Church or adversely affect its efficient exercise, the statement concluded that "there is every reason to believe that the increased involvement of all Catholics in the life of their Church, which will follow upon this democratization, will intensify the community among the people of God and raise the level of their capacity to extend the presence of the Church in the world."

Additional indications of how such groups see their place and function in the Church have been given by the Chicago Conference of Laymen, which is one of the founding bodies of the National Association of Laymen. Its president, Dr. John Bannan, a professor at Loyola College, told 1,500 members that its legitimacy did not rest on episcopal approval, but "on the right of a group of members of the Church to organize freely to act in the interest of the Church as they see that interest. We shall not pretend to speak for the Church. We shall speak for ourselves. But we claim the right to speak to the Church, and to speak from within the Church."

The meeting was extremely critical of the autocratic structures of the archdiocese of Chicago. It complained that a drive for funds, variously estimated as from $80 million to $250 million, had been imposed without adequate information, that on financial matters the archdiocesan officials showed "a lack of trust, candor, and information," and that when the layman attempts to respond to the call to assume responsibility for the Church's mission, he finds that "there is very little room for his effort and not much interest in his experience." A general conclusion was that all members of parish, vicariate, and diocesan councils—made up of both laity and clergy—should be representative of the people, should be elected by the people, should have the power to act, and should be informed by a modern concept of Christian stewardship.

The formation of these independent organizations of Catholics has had a positive effect on the previously existing official organizations in two ways. On the one hand, they have spurred the bishops to give these bodies more important tasks, and to go ahead more rapidly with the creation of parish and diocesan councils, as recommended by Vatican II. On the other, they have encouraged the leaders of the official organizations to express the viewpoints of the laity more strongly than had previously been their practice.

I had the opportunity to discuss these developments at length with the man who probably knows more about them than any other—Martin Work, Executive Director of the National Council of Catholic Men. A Californian, with a previous successful career in radio and advertising, Work at 53 is tall, spare, and driving. He sees the development of the National Association of the Laity as something that was inevitable, and his only surprise was that it took so long in its creation. For him it is complementary to the official NCCM and not in opposition to it. It should stimulate the NCCM and broaden its outlook, just as the independent *National Catholic Reporter* did for the diocesan press. An overlooked by-product of the NCCM is the formation, through extensive training programs, of educated, committed laity who have integrated their apostolic motivation in community concerns. Very often, it is these laymen who now form a solid base in independent organizations such as NAL.

Martin Work insists that the reluctance of the bishops to give more authority to the laity is frequently based on contradictory reasons. Many bishops have grown up with a distrust of the laity. They fear that if the door is opened an inch to them, they will want to take over the whole Church. Some of their experiences confirm their doubts about the ability of the laity to contribute significantly. Bishop Francis Green of Tucson, Arizona, invited the help of laymen, only to find they had little to offer on specifically Catholic matters. They could give sound judgments on real estate, on banking, on legal matters, but they were completely adrift when it came to the implications of the new theology.

Even on financial matters, the ghost of the bitter fight between the bishops and lay trustees a hundred years ago still walks at night. The late Cardinal Ritter established the practice of publishing the diocesan financial report in the *St. Louis Review*, but most bishops are still afraid that the laity would not understand the financial picture of a diocese.

On the parish level, a breakthrough has been made in regard to financial disclosure, although many pastors still insist on keeping the laity completely out of the picture. As Martin Work sees it, approximately one third of the nation's pastors are anxious to move forward, with another third open to involvement, and the final third shaken by the changes they are experiencing. Only a minority of pastors display an interest in learning about Vatican II, while many ignore it because they fear the implications for their own lives that might result from a greater knowledge.

The National Council of Catholic Men experienced what Martin Work describes as the greatest crisis in his long experience early in 1967. Its elected president, John F.

Donnelly, of Holland, Michigan, believed that it should have more autonomy in regard to its policies and operations. When a meeting was arranged with the five bishops who were members of the committee for the laity of the U.S. Bishops' Conference, only one attended. His old-fashioned homily on the thesis that all should man the ramparts unquestioningly in the Church's struggle against creeping materialism did nothing to smooth tempers.

Meanwhile, a new cause of dissension developed. John Donnelly and two employees of NCCM agreed to serve as directors of the newly formed Institute for Freedom in the Church. Archbishop Leo Binz of St. Paul-Minneapolis, chairman of the NCCM, interpreted the move as an act of disloyalty. The Institute had indicated its intention of conducting independent investigations of cases in which individuals claimed that their rights had been violated by the institutional Church, and Archbishop Binz said this would create a conflict of interest. The crisis subsided when Donnelly and one of the two employees resigned.

Since the Institute showed no indication of being more than a paper tiger, the case of the other employee was left in abeyance. Meanwhile, the bishops continue to ignore the Institute, which may be good tactics from their point of view, but is deepening the sense of despair of a highly intelligent group of Catholics who will soon pass beyond the point of even caring what the bishops think or do.

The major continuing effort in which the NCCM is involved is the development of diocesan pastoral councils and parish councils. The creation of such councils is going ahead at a rapid rate. Pastoral councils comprise the representatives of priests, men and women religious, and the laity, to advise the bishop on diocesan affairs. The danger that Martin Work sees here is that they will be dominated by the bishop to the extent that the lay voice will not be effective, and that at the parish level they will be similarly dominated by the pastor. He agrees in principle that the whole People of God should work together, but he fears that an absorption of the laity into unified structures before they have created for themselves a broader power base may simply mean a perpetuation of the old clerical-dominated system.

It may take a long time before the issue is finally resolved, and then it will come through dynamic development rather than as a result of a formal solution of the theoretical issues. This is the conclusion I reached from a study in depth of one parish council, that of St. Roch's Parish in St. Louis. This council has grown out of a concrete situation which the pastor felt unable to handle, forcing a group of laymen to take the initiative.

The activity began seven or eight years ago when Negroes began to move into the parish in considerable numbers. When the pastor just let things slide, some professional men went to the cardinal and asked for a new one. They were given Father Robert M. Peet, a kindly man with 34 years of pastoral experience behind him. He enlarged and modernized the grade school, so that it can accommodate all who wish to attend. There are 560 pupils taught by 6 nuns and 11 lay teachers. Although the parish is still losing some of its white members and few of the Negro newcomers are Catholics, there is no longer any danger of a panic situation.

"I preach openly on integration," Father Peet told me. "I reprimand people who use scare tactics to get whites to run, and I also challenge those who try to stop whites from selling to Negroes."

St. Roch's has joined with the Baptists, the Methodists, Washington University, and businessmen's associations to form a Neighborhood Association. St. Roch's parish pays an assessment of $3,000 a year toward the cost of an office and full-time help. The Association helps to keep the area stabilized both by means of social action and by getting Federal loans to rehabilitate rundown properties.

Father Peet sees the parish council as playing a major part in maintaining the parish. "They want a strong parish," he says, "and they are interested in keeping this parish stable. They recognize that more Negroes will come, but they want to keep a proper balance—what is called a pepper-and-salt balance—in the community. They have taken over some responsibility for running the school and lifted a big load off my shoulders. The school board consists of three men and three women, all elected, plus the assistant priest and the superior of the convent. The council feels the parish can contribute financially more than it does. We have a thousand families, and while some are poor, others earn $25,000 to $100,000 a year. Our total revenue is $185,000, of which $120,000 goes to the school and another $11,000 as our assessment for diocesan high schools."

On one vital point, Father Peet is in disagreement with his parish council, but with typical American pragmatism they continue to get along well in spite of a conflict that would in principle appear to eliminate all hope of progress. Here is how James McCarthy, a lawyer and president of the council, explained the situation to me:

"The pastor said the council had to be advisory. I felt the lay members must have authority in order to participate meaningfully. I checked with a Chancery official to find if there was anything in Church law to prevent the granting of deliberative powers to the council. He eventually called me back and said the law was silent on the point, but that it was more prudent to make it only advisory."

Recognizing that he had reached an impasse, McCarthy simply decided to leave the issue of powers unresolved and get on with the work. "We have spent a disproportionate time on structures," he reported to a meeting. "As far as I am concerned, I propose to go ahead on the assumption that the council has authority. If anyone disagrees, the burden of proof will be on him." And it seems to work fine. "There has not been much tension between the pastor and the council," he told me. "There is much more at times inside the council itself. Although the procedures are vague, we share in the running of the parish. We are consulted on financing, on building, and on liturgy."

Other parish councils in the archdiocese of St. Louis, whose constitutions I have studied, either leave the issue of powers similarly vague or include a phrase enabling the pastor to review the decisions. Elsewhere, as in the experimental Community of John XXIII in Oklahoma City, described in Chapter 4, the parish council can even dismiss the pastor.

In his book on *Parish Councils,* to which Bishop John J. Wright has contributed an introduction, Bernard Lyons gives a specimen constitution based on that of Holy Rosary Parish, Toronto, Canada. It provides that if the pastor judges any action of the council "as being contrary to faith or morals or diocesan policy," he can ask the president to reconsider it. If the conflict continues after reconsideration, the pastor can appeal "to the inter-parish council, diocesan council, or the bishop, depending upon the policies and structures available within the diocese."

The parish council is still very much an experimental structure in North America. In fact, few of them have more than one or two years of existence, and the relationships between the council and the pastor are still to be worked out. But they are mushrooming at an extremely rapid rate, thanks to the fact that many bishops are openly promoting them.

The National Association of Laymen insists "that parochial administration be the responsibility of the total community."

Martin Work, of the National Council of Catholic Men,

pushes parish councils as "the really phenomenal development," the point at which "the most dynamic action is taking place."

Acting upon the initiative of Archbishop Karl Alter, nearly every parish in the archdiocese of Cincinnati has formed one. If this becomes the pattern, the parish council may well become the symbol and focus of untapped reserves of Catholic laity who for generations were content to "pay, pray, and obey," but who now have a heightened sense of Christian reality.

CHAPTER 7

Priests: What the Mirror Shows

Thomas G. Furber is a big man, well over two hundred pounds, with an air of decisiveness about him. He has a quick step and he wastes little time in small talk. His briefcase contains his schedule for the next few days, notes for a speech he will make in a few hours' time, and a tiny tape recorder, ready for instant use. Attached to his belt he wears a small machine that buzzes when his office is trying to locate him. Thoughts and words come quickly to him, and as he sits in an easy chair, his girth amply filling it, he unfolds his life story with a blend of chronological precision and philosophical dimension.

It is an important story, for Thomas G. Furber * is an expressive symbol of the malaise in the Catholic priesthood that has produced the least expected of the post-conciliar developments: the phenomenal rise in priests leaving their ministry. From the obscurity of the priest who now drives a cab in New York City to the national prominence accorded James Kavanaugh, author of *A Modern Priest Looks at His Outdated Church,* priestly departures are the most commented on and least understood new fact of life.

---

* At his request, I have changed the name for professional reasons. The story is true.

Why? What pattern can be seen in the departure of more than 1,000 American priests since Vatican II?

"It used to be whispered around in the Church," Furber said with a smile, "that a priest left for one of two reasons—Punch or Judy. People never thought that a priest could leave for better reasons, namely, to save his soul."

I met Furber through Bearings for Re-establishment, a national office founded in New York in 1966 by William P. Restivo who, as a former priest himself, became deeply concerned at the predicament many priests find themselves in when they return to civilian existence and try to find a job.

Bearings helps priests through a difficult, often agonizing, transition and uses former priests such as Furber, who have made the adaptation successfully, to bolster the confidence of men shorn of the security of their rectories and monasteries. Tom Furber is a jail warden; he earns $13,321 a year; he is 36, married, and, most of all, he is a happy, confident man.

He bustled into my hotel room. "It's a busy day, but let's take a couple of hours for this," he said as he opened his collar and lit a cigar. "Let's start off this way. I am a priest. Notice that I use the word *am* rather than *was* or ex-priest. I am a priest because I was ordained. But I left the active ministry because I wanted to be a good Catholic layman. I don't regard my step as a negative but a positive one."

Furber then told me about his early years that took him into the priesthood.

He was the only son of a "rather strong Irish family" in Cleveland. After two years of college, he entered a religious community that sent him on for an A.B. After his ordination in 1957, his superiors instructed him to do graduate work in math.

"Why math?" I asked.

Furber chuckled. "Because I had received straight As in

math in high school and college even, though the only reason I took math was to escape science. I told my superior I wasn't ordained to teach math in some high school. Anyway, I enrolled at the Catholic University of America and went to the first class, but I didn't know what in heaven's name the professor was talking about. I told the superior this was ridiculous, so he switched me to the speech and drama department, and I began working toward a Master's degree."

Meanwhile, he was assigned to be an assistant chaplain at a prison. "This was considered to be a terrible job, but I liked it and dug in, organized a choir, taught music, things like that." Then a big break came. The local bishop suggested Furber study criminal law; by the mid-Sixties he had a law degree.

He became a full-time prison chaplain, turning over his $13,000 government salary to his religious community. He started branching out, giving instruction classes to prospective Catholics, working closely with lawyers and nurses, writing a radio show.

"After I was ordained, I began working with various families, and some of them I considered almost my own. I blessed their marriages—some had been married outside the Church for ten years—I baptized all their children. I would baby-sit for them so that the husband and wife could go to Mass together. It would get so that the children would sometimes come to me instead of going to someone else. I could change them and feed them just as fast as a real father could.

"After I had been ordained about four years, I gradually began to think of leaving the priesthood. A scene from my seminary days frequently flashed into my mind: I had gone to the rector and told him I didn't think I should be ordained because I didn't believe I had a vocation to the priesthood. Well, he didn't think this was sufficient reason.

"Now, with a little more maturity behind me, I realized that if I was going to make the break I would have to do it before I hit forty. What precipitated it was the attitude of the pastor in the parish where I lived. Two other prison chaplains lived there, and although we brought in more than $30,000, we were treated as second-class citizens because we gave priority to our jobs rather than to his wishes about rectory duties. There were power politics all around me in the rectory, and I just couldn't get interested in all the in-fighting. Naturally, I fell into political disfavor.

"There's an old saying, 'Politics is rotten, but ecclesiastical politics is perpetual suicide.' When you fall into disfavor with your religious superiors, you just get phased out. You don't have any wife who understands, you have no incentive to fight back. And so you find the easiest way to survive is to sit back and do nothing. If you do nothing, you're not rocking the boat and you're not upsetting people.

"Most of all, never become popular, because once you do, people start coming to you instead of to the pastor or somebody else in the house who looks upon himself as God's gift to the people, and this is potential suicide. So you have the priest who is filled with the zeal of perpetuating Christ, who has a burning desire for the creativity of spreading the Gospel. Then on the other side, you have the restrictions—not the restrictions of prudence as St. Thomas tells us—but restrictions that the superior is the superior and the people come second. I think you'll find this in the history of the Church. Many of the saints were not accepted in the religious communities of their time. They burned the books of St. Thomas Aquinas up to fifty years after he was dead.

"You can see now why the Vatican Council has rocked many of our pastors. They have suddenly realized their own insecurity. All of a sudden, people are asking questions that priests don't have answers for. We still have missionaries living in the grand old days, still getting up in the pulpit and threatening hell, fire, and brimstone. But people are better educated now, and they aren't going to listen to some priest use the pulpit to further some idiosyncrasy he may have."

I asked Furber whether the Vatican Council had a direct influence on his decision to leave the ministry.

"I don't think so," he said. "The one thing that had been in the back of my mind, even before the Council started, was that I wanted to remain a Catholic in good standing. I wasn't angry with the Church as such. I just became convinced that I could best save my soul and serve Almighty God as a Catholic layman. The Council was influential in changing public thinking about priests leaving, however. It used to be that a stigma was placed on anyone leaving the priesthood. You were told beforehand that you would be an outcast if you left. What gradually started to happen with Pope John was a more merciful and humane treatment of priests who wanted to leave. It became easier to get dispensed from the ministry.

"I still had a certain naiveté about the procedure and believed that if I applied for a dispensation I could get it. I felt that I should get it because I had spent many years as a good priest and I had not brought any scandal upon the Church or my religious community. The fact remained that it was a free choice of mine to go into the priesthood, and I couldn't see why it wouldn't be a free choice of mine to leave the active ministry.

"In the hazy years before I actually took the step, I began to do something that was strictly forbidden: I established checking and savings accounts and personal financial credit so that I would be protected against that cold, rainy day."

In September, 1966, Furber took the long-contemplated step. He filled out two sets of forms, one applying for dispensation from his vows as a priest, the other for dispensation from the vow of celibacy. The applications went off to the Sacred Congregation for Religious in Rome. Furber made a couple of phone calls to friends in Rome, and by the middle of November the approved dispensation from the priesthood was back on his desk, a dispensation that contained the words "without hope of being restored to the active priesthood."

Through his administrative connections in the prison field, he had been offered a warden's job, and the day following his release from the priesthood he went back on the government payroll, this time without the "Reverend" in front of his name.

"The day the dispensation arrived in the mail, I returned to the parish for dinner. I still hadn't opened my mail. The superior came up to me and said, 'Hi, Tom. Your dispensation came today, so you are no longer a religious. So first of all, give me the keys to the car; secondly, you owe us a check which is due tomorrow; thirdly, since you are a lay person you can no longer stay in the house, so you can't stay here tonight. I'll stretch it for you. I'll let you stay here tonight, but you can't eat here.' I wasn't really upset by all this. I just said to myself, small mind, small acts.

"Then the phone rang, and it was the bishop wanting to see me. He was now involved because my dispensation from celibacy had not accompanied the dispensation from the priesthood. Rather, I was told that if it was granted it would come from Rome through the local bishop. I went to see him, and he told me that he didn't want me living in his diocese. I said that was fine, except for a little problem of money. I told him about my salary, my health policy, retirement fund, sick leave, and so on. Then I said, 'Now, you match this with something comparable in some other place and I'll be glad to talk about it, but I'm not going out to California and get a teacher's job paying $6,000 or $7,000 a year.'

"Next, I told the bishop that I had met a widow with two

children. I told him frankly that there had been no liaison between us but that we wanted to be married, and therefore I wanted the dispensation from celibacy. Her children were in school, and I wasn't going to transfer them just because my presence would embarrass the bishop.

"Then the waiting period began. Rome sent back a questionnaire asking if I was attacking the validity of my vows. All this had been made clear in my original petition. It was pure stalling tactics. One of the things about Rome is that you send everything to them by air mail, but they reply by surface mail. There were more queries, more trips to the Chancery office. Finally in February, six months after I had made the original application, still with no official release from celibacy, I said to the bishop, 'All right, that's the end of it, we are getting married.' So a chaplain friend of mine conducted a private ceremony, with no witnesses. We began married life together and continued to attend Mass and receive the sacraments.

"I phoned an official in the Congregation for Religious in Rome and told him I was married. I told him, 'I did everything I possibly could. Now it's your problem, not mine. When the dispensation is granted, you let me know.'

"Two months later, the local Chancery said the dispensation was in, but they still wanted me to move, because you're not supposed to live as a married man in the area where you were known as a priest. I said, 'Look, I'm working here, I've been married a couple of months, and as far as everyone is concerned I was married in the Church. There's no problem. People have forgotten it. Why prolong this?'

"My wife and I went down to see the bishop. Untrustful people that we are"—Furber gave a little laugh—"we tape-recorded our conversation with the bishop. He finally said, 'All right, when do you want to have your marriage blessed?' We said right now, so we went over to the cathedral rectory and the chancellor blessed our marriage."

I asked Furber what the general reaction was to him in the community among those who had know him as a priest.

"Among the more educated people, there's no problem. My best friends as a priest were lawyers and nurses, because I worked with both groups. I find them completely accepting me. I've been amazed at the number of teenagers, whom I had helped as a priest, still coming to me with their problems. Of course, the secret to acceptance is not to slink around trying to hide the fact that I was a priest. The best way is to grab the bull by the horns.

"For example, I went into a store one day and the owner, whom I had long known, called me 'Father.' I put on a big beam and asked him hadn't he heard the good news. Now I was 'Mr.' He immediately picked up my approach and said, 'Wonderful, so happy to hear it.' No problem, complete acceptance.

"The exception, of course, was among the priests in the rectory where I lived. A woman started to write poison-pen letters, declaring that 'the savior of men's souls has now become the jailer of men's bodies.' Naturally, I found out about this and learned that she had called the rectory and was told that I had been kicked out of my order, that I was not married in the Church, and that I was a public sinner.

"I went over to the rectory, saw the superior, and asked him what was going on. I said that he himself knew I had been dispensed and that I was married in the Church. He said, 'We don't know that officially.' I said, 'Fine. I will now talk to my lawyer. You are affecting my life, my wife's life, my children's lives, my present position, and my future. I think we are talking a couple of million dollars and I intend to file suit against you.' I went to my lawyer and he sent the superior a letter to cease and desist; if they did not, there would be a suit for punitive damages. Since then there hasn't been a whisper.

"Grabbing the bull by the horns again, I took my wife

and my children to Mass there on a feast day. We all approached the altar together for Communion. Afterwards there was a buffet reception downstairs, and all the people we had known gave us a fantastic welcome. But some of the priests, when they saw us in the reception, turned around and walked out. They wouldn't even step inside the door. Some ushers were giving out a form asking for volunteers to teach special classes in theology of the laity that were about to begin. I filled out the form and listed my degrees. Funny, I've never been called."

There is no one answer to why priests are leaving their ministry, and I do not present the story of Tom Furber as a "typical case." Yet in candid conversations with many priests and former priests, I realized that the Furber history contained many of the elements basic to the anxiety that is so notable a characteristic of the priesthood today—dissatisfaction with "the system," a personal need to break away from the restrictiveness of the clerical outlook and demeanor, a need for human companionship of both sexes.

There have always been priests who came to a point in their lives when they looked straight into a mirror and said to themselves, "What am I doing wearing this Roman collar?" But what has startlingly occurred since Vatican II is a collective reappraisal. Thinking priests are either working desperately to reform the priesthood, or they're getting out. And whichever route they take, they are increasingly winning public support. For the communications media have successfully transmitted this unique story: the collective identity crisis in the priesthood.

It is strange that the identity crisis was not foreseen during the Vatican Council. The Council was concerned about bishops, who had previously been downgraded to the level of servants of the Roman Curia. Its teaching on collegiality was intended to restore their status as successors of the apostles and co-rulers of the Church with the Pope. It was concerned about the laity, long treated as marginal members of the Church. Its teaching on the People of God reasserted their rights to full citizenship and active participation. It was concerned about the religious life and called on the orders of men and women to revise their rules and practices to make them relevant to the contemporary world and its needs.

Regarding priests, on the contrary, the Council did not feel that it had anything important to say, and for a time it appeared as if it would not bother to discuss their problems formally. It finally changed its mind, under pressures which seemed to stem more from a priestly demand for attention than from any definable problems. In the end, nevertheless, the short Council statement on priests, taken in the context of its statements on the other members of the Church, served to sharpen and spotlight the previously hidden problems.

Formerly, as far as the sacrament of orders is concerned, the tendency was to see the priesthood as the point of departure from the people, with the bishop receiving an addition of jurisdiction and extra sacramental powers. The Council presented the episcopate as the starting point containing a full complement of orders, with the bishop communicating a subordinate participation to his priests. When to this was coupled the participation of the laity in the universal priesthood of Christ through baptism, the priest was forced to ask himself what specifically was allocated to him in the middle.

In addition, the stress on service pulled the prop of status from under him. "He is bidden to serve eagerly those in want, to identify—even radically—with the poor in spirit," as Dr. John Oliver Nelson, a distinguished Protestant commentator, summed it up. "Here is no authoritarian cleric prompting sentimental veneration or advertising novenas with guaranteed benefits, moving among mere communicants in haughty eminence; he is the gracious, unassuming, joyful, completely honest and dependable servant of God and of common folk."

This theoretical reformulation of his position came at the very moment when the priest was experiencing in his daily life a parallel narrowing of his functions and downgrading of his authority as a result of the contemporary explosion of knowledge and expansion of education. In a primitive society, the cleric's monopoly of knowledge, and consequently of authority, had developed a priestly caste and surrounded it with protective devices: distinctive dress, titles, manners, language (Latin), the monopolization of worship and moral teaching, compulsory celibacy.

In today's community, the leadership functions have passed to professionals, many of them more highly educated than the priest. Protective devices no longer suffice, and to an increasing extent they discredit the person who relies on them. What counts is a man's intrinsic worth and the distinctive contribution he makes. This is why we no longer have simply the personal crisis of the priest who asks himself who he is and why he is wearing this collar. It is a collective anxiety, a group crisis of men who ask: What is the priesthood; what is the role of the priest; what can a priest do; are we doing anything laymen cannot do; what justification remains for celibacy and our other protective devices?

Before the Council, the priest lived within a system that helped him to stifle any doubts he might experience. Authority had been glorified in his training to such a point that he could usually dismiss his doubt as a temptation, regard as an unhappy exception the injustice he experienced or the harm to souls he witnessed, and resign himself to patience and silence for the sake of some greater good which he could not see but had to take on faith.

The rigid control of expression, the silencing of dissidents, and the climate of condemnation of any protester prevented the formation of a public opinion. The unhappy priest suffered in silence or slunk away in secret, often accepting as the true verdict the universally held belief that personal weakness had caused him to be derelict in his duty.

The Council told the Christian to use his own judgment, and many priests have taken this advice seriously. The open discussion of all issues in both the Catholic and the general press have made priests aware that their particular problems usually form part of a total pattern, that they are not freaks, oddballs, or derelicts because they see things the way they do. But it is not easy for them to react in a logical, coherent way, and so we have the formation of three major groups differentiated principally by age, though with much crossing of age lines in response to personal temperament and local situations.

Older priests tend to be the least involved emotionally. They feel they have passed the age when the changes affect them personally. Each has made his niche, big or small, and he can cling to it.

The middle group is experiencing a deep insecurity. All they have to support them is their scholastic training in the seminary many years ago, and they know that it has little meaning for the contemporary world. They have studied little during their active lives. As they look at what they are doing and compare it with the contributions of their peers in the professional and business world, they realize the claim that celibacy has left them a freedom for work denied to the married man can seldom stand up. While some of them work hard, much of what they do is peripheral to what could be a dynamic ministry. They think of themselves as chosen to lead, yet recognize that they lack the know-how to lead in this community.

The young priest, on the contrary, is not afflicted with this kind of insecurity. He knows he should be where the action is, and that is where he wants to be. He feels no need for a collar or other status symbols. He is ready to protest, to picket, to march. But that does not mean that life for him is going to be simple. Within the system in which he is being asked to work, he can easily reach a point of total frustration.

Father James Hennessy, O.M.I., a British Columbia missionary with many years of pastoral experience, describes what can happen to the forward-looking priest in a parish situation. He meets divorced Catholics, invalidly remarried, who must lead their Christian lives at the door of the Church without benefit of its sacraments. He buoys them up with a promise of possible validation and absolution, only to see the petition papers molder unanswered in chancery and curial offices. He listens to married persons bewildered by conflicting advice from confessors on the lawfulness of contraceptive practices which they honestly believe are needed to save their marriages. His efforts to provide more meaningful forms of worship for teenagers turned off by impersonal Masses are stepped on by his superiors. Attempts to update the sacrament of penance for those who have abandoned the assembly-line approach are tagged as heretical. He has no explanation to satisfy either himself or the enquirer of the Church's assertion that a Catholic can properly marry a Protestant in a Protestant church with the signature of a curial official, while without that signature there is no marriage and these two Christians will "live in sin."

Father Peter J. Riga of St. Mary's College, California, a nationally known exponent of the Church's social teaching, puts the dilemma of the sensitive priest this way. "When you get home from a chancery office after being told that you may not speak on Vietnam when your conscience tells you to speak, or that your sermons 'disturb' people because you tell them of their sins of racism and heartlessness with regard to the poor—then you go to your lonely room and you cry because there is no one to say to you: 'I disagree with you completely, but I love you and will stand with you.' Then your thoughts naturally turn to the woman who would have understood, in other circumstances and in another vocation."

Compulsory celibacy is frequently identified as the key issue in the current crisis. "It's tearing the priesthood apart," according to Robert Francoeur, a nationally known and respected priest who himself left the active ministry in order to marry, "and forcing the best men to lead unreal lives." It seems clear, nevertheless, that celibacy is a symptom of a deeper malaise, or at best one of a complex of factors.

Father John L. McKenzie, S.J., says the crisis is over authority. "Our system degrades both the governors and the governed, so we wind up with despotism tempered by rebellion."

"Total institutionalism" is the villain, according to Dutch psychologist Father Henri J. M. Nouwen. He says the priest is caught in a system that submerges his private life, leaving him with little idea of when he is off duty, or even who he is.

French Jesuit Emile Pin, director of the Institute of Sociology of the Gregorian University in Rome, attributes the priest's present confusion to the loss of his former role without having yet found a new one. He does not think that marriage would resolve the psychological crisis in its full depth.

"While the ordination of a man who is already married may to him mean the intensification of his work, the apotheosis of a process of human and spiritual maturation, the marriage of an already ordained priest most probably would not resolve his affective crisis. When a man becomes a priest, he responds to a universal vocation which can only be truly satisfied by self-fulfillment on a communal scale. Unless the priest can reinsert himself in society as a whole, or at least in a community that is sufficiently large and exacting, he will remain alone even if he has a family. He would, in effect, run the risk of communicating to his wife and chidren the feeling of estranged isolation from which he himself suffers. His real problem is that of reinsertion, whether he be married or not. His real choice is between renouncing his priesthood in order to reinsert himself, or trying to reinsert the priesthood."

Father Gilbert Graham, a Dominican who heads the National Conference of Major Superiors, expressed this same analysis to me in the American idiom. "It's true that many priests are attracted by a family life and the love of a woman, and to that extent celibacy is a factor in the crisis. But many priests are no more suited for marriage than they are for the religious life."

An observation of *New York Times* reporter John Leo, an astringent Catholic commentator, backed up this viewpoint. "According to commonly accepted statistics," he notes, "one out of every twelve American priests is an alcoholic. Though the pressures of celibacy are usually blamed, two other factors are receiving increased attention: the effects on the personality of 'total institutionalization,' and the problem of suppressed hostility in an institutional system that is still— by normal American standards, at least—too authoritarian."

These various factors are now discernibly affecting the priesthood through priests abandoning the ministry in increasing numbers, and a dwindling number of candidates for the priesthood. It is estimated that there was a 5 to 10 percent decline in vocations to the priesthood in 1967 and that, as Father Graham says, "the crisis is only beginning." In 1958, 37 percent of seminary students dropped out in their first year, a percentage that had risen to 44 in 1963 and 50 in 1968.

Nobody knows exactly how many priests leave the active ministry, because many chancery offices cover up resignations by listing priests as being "on leave." A group of priests known as the National Association for Pastoral Renewal compiled a list of 711 priests who had left in two years, and incomplete research made it an obvious undercount. Of the

711 priests, 108 had been ordained 15 years or more. The list included 39 seminary professors, nine chancery officials, and 34 pastors.

"In my diocese," a bishop told me, "we hardly ever lost anyone, but in 1967 we lost eleven men, two percent of our total."

In one year, twelve priests left the 400-member Dominican province of St. Albert the Great; in the previous 25 years, five priests left. In another religious community, five priests were ordained in 1966 and within a year all five had petitioned for laicization. Communities that put a stress on men with advanced degrees, such as the Jesuits and Dominicans, have been particularly hard hit; the more education he has beyond seminary years, the easier it is for a priest to get a job.

William Restivo, who heads Bearings for Re-establishment, estimates that there are 15,000 former priests in the U.S. and that the rate of departures in 1968 will double that of 1967. The renowned Dutch theologian, Edward Schillebeeckx, shook up the Catholic establishment by predicting, after a two-month tour of the U.S., that ten thousand priests would leave their ministry in the next three years (the official 1968 total, 59,803, was 89 fewer than the previous year and represented the first decline in the national total of priests since records were started). Discontent is indescribable, he said, adding, "Celibacy is a much bigger problem than in the Netherlands."

I think that Father Schillebeeckx's dire prediction does not take sufficiently into account the significant positive steps now being taken by priest leaders in reforming the priesthood—steps we will examine in a moment. Nonetheless, there is no gainsaying priestly disillusionment.

A California Paulist put into a few words for me the mood I sensed everywhere on my journey. "I care less and less," he said, "about priestly ministrations which seem to offer only flights from the reality of human freedom to the safety of an imagined refuge in the sacred. This goes for all manner of instrumentalism: the incomprehensible jabberings and gesticulations whereby we once tried to convince ourselves and the docile faithful that they were being saved. I want to be a priest to the real world that has no more use for the medicine man I was trained to be."

The American bishops have started a detailed, in-depth study of the ministry and life of priests, but their announcement of this research tended to downplay, at least in public eyes, the magnitude of the crisis. A bishop told me frankly, "The bishops don't know how to cope with this problem." The headlines have fixed on celibacy, and this has compounded the confusion.

The pressures for a change in the law to make celibacy optional first came into the open at the Council in October, 1965. Brazilian Bishop Pedro Koop, with the backing of some other bishops, decided to suggest that special arrangements be made for countries like Brazil in which there was a great shortage of priests. "Latin America represents 33 percent of the universal Church. Yet it has only 6 percent of all priests. In the year 2000, Latin America will have 600 million souls, 50 percent of the universal Church. . . . The choice is urgent; either we multiply the number of priests, or we can expect the fall of the Church in Latin America."

Bishop Koop did not suggest a change in the law for those already priests. "I propose that the Council make it possible to confer the priesthood on worthy laymen who have been married for at least five years. After suitable formation they would exercise the priestly ministry as substitutes and assistants. They could administer to small communities in their free time."

The proposal never reached the Council floor. Under the rules of procedure, the text was submitted in advance to the secretariat, causing a behind-the-scenes furor. The upshot was a letter from Pope Paul read in the Council chamber. "We know that some Fathers intend to discuss in the Council the law of ecclesiastical celibacy as it is established in the Latin Church. Thus, while respecting the assembly's freedom of expression, we would like to offer our personal opinion: this is not the time to debate publicly a subject which requires the greatest prudence and is of such importance. It is our purpose not only to do everything we can to conserve this ancient, holy, and providential law, but to enforce its greater observance. . . . If any Father wants to talk about this question, let him do so in writing, and let him remit his exposition to the Council presidency, which will in turn transmit it to us."

Although the Council agreed to the Pope's request, the text of the proposed Koop intervention was leaked to the press, and from that time onward all the efforts of Roman officialdom have been unable to still the discussion and agitation. The challenge is not to the value of a celibate life voluntarily embraced for positive motives. Scripture and Christian tradition clearly assert its excellence. But they also stress its difficulty and call it a gift not granted to all. What is being questioned is the modern practice of the Latin Church making celibacy a condition for exercising the priesthood. The obligation, universal in the West for only 400 or 500 years, has never existed in the East, either Catholic or Orthodox. And even in the West, as Pope Paul indicated when he said that he intended "to enforce its greater observance," a gap between commitment and practice continues to exist. The diocesan priest does not take a vow, as members of religious orders do. He is bound by a prescription of canon law, Canon 132.

It has long been a criticism that the Roman authorities dispense much more easily from a vow, which is technically a promise made directly to God and witnessed by the Church, than from the priest's commitment to celibacy, which is simply a Church law. Dispensations have become more frequent since the time of Pope John, though always with a condition that priestly functions are no longer exercised. In practice, also, a priest who asks for a dispensation can expect a delay of several years, unless he has influence in high places. The only way he can hope to speed the process (as the case of Tom Furber indicates) is by going through a form of marriage before a judge or a Protestant clergyman in violation of Canon 1072, thereby incurring (and involving the other party in) excommunication and other penalties prescribed in Canon 2388.

In a June, 1967, encyclical, in which he rejected in the most absolute terms the requests for a relaxation of the law to permit married priests to continue in the ministry, Pope Paul promised that those who wished to leave and showed "serious and good dispositions for leading the Christian life of a layman" could expect dispensation. No immediate change in practice, however, followed this encyclical. The only quick approach to "the Christian life of a layman" continued to be through the gate of "attempted marriage" and excommunication.

While compulsory celibacy may not be the basic reason for the group anxiety of priests today, it is the specific factor that induces many to leave.

"I can find no common denominator among those who made this decision, but celibacy is a big factor," Auxiliary Bishop James Shannon of St. Paul-Minneapolis told me. "This view is shared by bishops, diocesan priests, and members of religious orders with whom I have discussed it. Since the Council, the atmosphere has changed significantly. Tradition and authority no longer dominate Catholic life to the same extent as formerly. Evidence coming from the behavioral sciences is shedding light on celibacy. There is, for example, the evidence of the Christian witness of married Protestant ministers. Their fidelity to Christ and to the

Christian witness is not necessarily compromised but may in some instances be enhanced by their marriage.

"Then there is the psychological impact on the priest who remains celibate when this might not have been the best way for him to live. Is it not possible that as a priest he may have changed, may have become selfish and less generous? I personally think there is validity to this argument. I think there is no profession in which a man can be selfish for so long as the priesthood. The priest's favorite cuisine is respected. His privacy is respected. A wife and children would not let him get away with this. He would give much more of himself to other people, because his marriage would compel him to. I am not making a general criticism. I simply note that the behavioral sciences are raising such questions, and so is our new evaluation of the Protestant ministry under the impact of ecumenism.

"I give two or three priests' retreats each year, and I find that the priests bring this question up every time. They are more free with me than they would be with their own bishop. My experience, however unscientific, confirms Father Joseph Fichter's research. American priests widely hold the view that celibacy should be optional, that the Church should distinguish between the priesthood and celibacy."

Father Fichter, Stillman professor of Roman Catholic studies at Harvard University, surveyed American priests who were not pastors and not monsignors and found that 62 percent of the respondents favor the diocesan priest's freedom of choice to marry.

"This means," explained Father Fichter in the *National Catholic Reporter*, "not only that they accept the statement of the Council that celibacy is not demanded by the very nature of the priesthood, but also that they want to remove celibacy as a condition of ordination to the priesthood. This position is perfectly orthodox and unassailable on doctrinal grounds."

Of course, the celibacy problem cannot be treated in isolation from the total institutional structure. If optional celibacy were suddenly approved, it is doubtful that the Catholic laity, accustomed to financially supporting their clergy, schools, and other good causes, would accept the extra cost of priests' wives. The whole rectory system, in which three and four priests live under one roof, would have to be abandoned. And the end of celibacy would almost certainly be accompanied by the rapid development of the worker priest. Thus, the entire manner of diocesan clergy service would be transformed. The institution is not psychologically ready to take on a headache of this magnitude. Yet the celibacy law will very likely be unable to stand up against mounting pressure, especially from the generation now coming to maturity, a generation growing up with an enriched concept of the nobility of married love which Vatican II underscored.

As long as sexual love was presented as necessary "for the alleviation of concupiscence" or the procreation of children, then celibacy could be put under the mantle of ordination without too much objection. But an enlightened, and official, teaching on the inherent spiritual value of married love now means that celibacy will have to be presented as a positive alternative. Hence, it must be willingly embraced for its own sake, not forced upon those who want to be priests.

A significant development was the formation in 1966 of the National Association for Pastoral Renewal. Membership is secret, on the ground that some bishops might make life unpleasant for any of their priests who join, but there was nothing secret about a symposium it held at Notre Dame University in 1967.

A group consisting of nearly 200 priests, a few former priests, several nuns, and some laymen heard celibacy discussed in great detail by such distinguished speakers as Father Alfred McBride, O. Praem., of the Catholic University of America, Father Fichter, Father John A. O'Brien, of Notre Dame, and Father Ignatius Hunt, O.S.B., visiting professor at the Chicago Theological Seminary. The symposium called for optional celibacy for diocesan priests, urged that married priests currently outside the ministry be readmitted to the sacraments and be given the opportunity to return to the active ministry, and asked that priests who leave the active ministry be permitted to do so "with dignity and honor."

In a series of surveys conducted among 46 percent of the diocesan priests of the United States during 1967, the Association reached the conclusion that more than 7,000 of the country's 36,000 diocesan priests (as distinguished from priests in religious orders) want optional celibacy. Even more important is the fact that most of those in favor are young priests. "In practically all dioceses, whether large or small and in all parts of the country, assistant pastors in significant majorities favor the right to marry."

Also noteworthy is the refusal of the priests to regard the issue as closed by Pope Paul's encyclical. A comparison of surveys conducted during May and June—shortly before and after the encyclical was published—with those run in September shows a marked increase both in the proportion of questionnaires returned and in the proportion of those favoring optional celibacy.

The conclusion reached in the Association's final report on the surveys is that "celibacy is an urgent problem of significant dimensions in the American Church. As such it deserves the urgent and serious attention of the National Conference of Bishops, lest those who now look to their bishops for leadership be disappointed and turn elsewhere. However one interprets the percentages yielded by these surveys, the fact remains that a large body of American priests are on record as favoring optional celibacy. Unless this problem is resolved in the very near future, an alarming number of these priests may swell the ranks of those who have withdrawn from pastoral work in order to marry."

To that, the American bishops responded "with a single voice" that priestly celibacy "has been and will be a source of great advantage to the Church particularly in the United States." The hierarchy emphasized that it would be "irresponsible on our part to hold out any hope that this discipline will be changed." The line of demarcation is clearly being drawn more sharply right down the celibacy issue.

Public discussion of celibacy has quickly brought a change in the social status of the priest who has left the ministry, as we have seen. Formerly shunned as a weakling unable to live up to his public commitment, he is now given credit for having the courage to recognize that he may perhaps be able to serve God better in a different calling. The new concern in the Church for the rights of its members as human beings is also helping him. It is now being publicly argued that the priest is the beneficiary of the affirmation by Pope John and Pope Paul that the right to marry is inalienable. As canon lawyer Father David F. Born, of Youngstown, Ohio, expresses it, an inalienable right is one which neither the lawmaker nor the possessor can alienate. "It follows from this that a priest or religious who would marry, with or without a dispensation, would commit no sin."

The Church authorities, however, are not by any means willing to accept these conclusions. As far as they are concerned, any priest who goes through a form of marriage without the proper dispensations is excommunicated, whereas for an increasing number of both priests and lay people he is doing no wrong when he has applied for a dispensation and waited a reasonable time without receiving a reply.

I know a specific instance in which a nationally known priest in his mid-forties, with an excellent record as administrator and pastor, submitted his application to be dispensed from the ministry and celibacy, then went to another city and got a job. After several months, he reapplied, then waited many more months before marrying in a private civil ceremony. Some days later, before beginning married life together, the couple had a religious service in their apartment. Three priests dressed in vestments concelebrated the nuptial Mass, assisted by several friends of the couple. Afterwards, all stayed on for a champagne supper. The reasoning of those involved was that the couple were being wrongly deprived by canon law of their right to a Church wedding, and that a wrongful law does not bind. Regardless of the rights and wrongs of the situation, it is obvious that such developments threaten the social cohesion of the institution.

Dan Herr, the leading critic-humorist of the Catholic Church in America, issued this directive: "Will all malcontent priests who intend to leave the priesthood and/or the Church please do so by March 12, 1968, so that their colleagues and the rest of us can get on with the very serious business of reform and renewal."

Herr's scalpel was sharp, as usual. For the spotlight has inevitably fallen on those walking under the exit sign. Less attention is given the far greater number who are actively engaged in developing new ways in which to make their ministry more effective for the people and more meaningful for themselves. Here one can observe three phenomena which are interacting dynamically on one another—the initiatives of individuals, the formation of unofficial associations of priests, and the creation of official senates of priests to help the bishop in the governing of his diocese.

Up to Vatican II, the activities of priests were strictly determined by their bishops or religious superiors within traditionally set patterns. The first priests who tried to take literally the Council declarations that every Christian had to make his own judgments and act accordingly were quickly undermined by their superiors.

The brothers Philip and Daniel Berrigan, one a member of the Society of St. Joseph and the other a Jesuit, were transferred when they openly opposed United States policies in Vietnam. Public opinion, however, quickly formed in their favor, and gradually their superiors decided to let them proclaim their beliefs. National public opinion, quite apart from white segregationists in Milwaukee, helped to sustain Father James Groppi.

Others have fared less well. Father William DuBay of Los Angeles was suspended by Cardinal McIntyre for attempting to form a labor union for priests and otherwise challenging the Cardinal's authority. Father James Drane, a professor at St. John's Seminary in Little Rock, Arkansas, was similarly suspended by his bishop for offenses that included the assertion that the Church needs a new set of rules on birth control and that they should not be written by celibates, because "love cannot be understood from the outside but must be experienced."

One Sunday I went to Baltimore to see Father Philip Berrigan, and the two hours I spent talking to him were among the most inspiring of my journey. Berrigan at that time was very much in the headlines. He had just been released from jail following an inter-faith anti-Vietnam war protest in which he and others had poured blood over Selective Service files. He had been on a liquid fast for eight days in jail, refused an out-of-court settlement, and demanded trial on four Federal charges in order to focus the public spotlight on Christian witness against the inhumanity of the Vietnam war. He was later convicted and sentenced to six years, but not before he, his brother Dan, and a group of fellow protesters struck another Selective Service office, burning 600 individual draft files.

As well as being a vociferous opponent of U.S. policies in Vietnam, Berrigan has been a stern critic of institutional complacency in the Church in both the peace and civil rights movements. Yet, as he welcomed me into the spartan parlor of St. Peter Claver rectory in a Negro ghetto of Baltimore, I did not find him the prototype of the agitator or angry cleric. In fact, he does not have a clerical demeanor, but talks simply, openly, and unreservedly about what he feels as a Christian.

Philip Berrigan, in his late forties, is tall and spare. The handsomeness of deep blue eyes and short-cropped, steel-gray hair is counterbalanced by deep lines in his face and, on the day I was with him, a penetrating fatigue. In slow and measured language, he talked about the need for priests to work militantly against the laborious institutional machinery of the Church.

"We're hung up in categorical fixations in the priesthood and the laity," he said. "Second-class citizenship of the laity is so enmeshed in the system that dramatic action is needed by the priest to illustrate the life-and-death measures needed to involve the Church in America's moral and social issues. We have to realize that the ministerial function is second to baptism and that all of us have a primary obligation to work for the betterment of social conditions. It's nonsense for a priest to be tied down to the parlor and the parish. I like to think that I can't be a decent citizen unless I am a decent Christian."

He scorned narrow Catholic thinking. If birth control and celibacy were solved tomorrow, they would not seriously affect the course mankind is taking. For the world is in the throes of revolution involving the black man's rights, the hungry people of Latin America, the hopeless millions of Asia, plus war and the threat of nuclear annihilation.

"There's a new type of religious community forming," he said, "and it takes its theology from issues rather than from a pre-formed set of propositions. You learn the issues from involvement."

Humanists are involved. Atheists are involved. They're

not learning about God through Christians; rather, they're experiencing God through a deep commitment to their fellow man.

The silence of the American hierarchy on war and peace, Berrigan holds, "is a depressing scandal." So is the absence of an all-out commitment in behalf of justice for Negroes. Most priests, however, have a false sense of loyalty to the institution and are not prepared to do anything out of line. Even a routine protest march would be a traumatic experience for most, much less asserting that the institution must start living up to the demands of Christ. Philip and Dan are regarded as zealots because they believe so ardently in civil disobedience, but they may also be forerunners of a new breed of prophet-priests. The road for prophets who go against the grain of the institution that gave them birth is a lonely one.

By their prophetic courage, priests who have stood out individually have served a breakthrough function in the reformation of the priesthood. They have broken out of clerical rigidity and frozen patterns of action. They have shown that ordination and personal initiative are not incompatible. But a more profound effect on the shaping of the new priesthood is being accomplished by collective action. Just as collectivity is a dominant feature of the identity crisis, so joint action is building a momentum of reform. Here the Council laid the groundwork by calling for senates of priests.

In a context in which it is dealing with the unity of consecration and mission of the bishop and his priests, the Council says that "the bishop should regard priests as his brothers and friends. As far as in him lies, he should have at heart the material and especially spiritual welfare of his priests. For, above all, upon the bishop rests the heavy responsibility for the sanctity of his priests. Hence, he should exercise the greatest care on behalf of the continual formation of his priests. He should gladly listen to them, indeed, consult them, and have discussions with them about those matters which concern the necessities of pastoral work and the welfare of the diocese. In order to put these ideals into effect, a group or senate of priests representing the presbytery should be established. It is to operate in a manner adapted to modern circumstances and needs and have a form and norms to be determined by law. By its counsel, this body will be able to give effective assistance to the bishop in his government of the diocese."

Whether the Council intended the new associations of priests to be of such an official character that they would operate only under the direction of the bishop is not clear. Certainly most diocesan senates of priests that developed in the years immediately following the Council clearly deferred to the authority of the local bishop. Progressive-minded bishops, extending the principle of collegiality that they had obtained for themselves at Vatican II, began to involve senates (for the most part elected by their fellow priests) in meaningful consultation. Yet many priests saw senates as too much under the wing of the hierarchy.

Priests' unions were not the answer. Father DuBay of Los Angeles has never been able to win much support for this idea because priests regard unions as putting bishops and priests into an employer/employee relationship that is theologically unsound and pragmatically frustrating. A new type of priests' organization was called for that would be at once united with the bishops, yet separated from their control. In both the United States and Canada, this idea gave birth to independent national federations of priests that show signs of enriching the Church far beyond the expectations of the malcontents.

The American federation of priests came out of Chicago. The archdiocese of Chicago, largest in the United States, has long enjoyed a reputation of fostering and supporting new ideas. As the sociologist Andrew Greeley notes, a series of experiments began in Chicago in the 1930s "that would anticipate in many respects the spirit and teachings of the Vatican Council."

Under the permissive leadership of three successive open-minded bishops, Cardinals George Mundelein, Samuel Stritch, and Albert Meyer, experiments in lay action, social action, catechetics, liturgy, and marriage education were started and later imitated all over the United States. The men who launched them became national heroes to the growing band of progressives in every part of the country. The greatest of these liberal heroes was Monsignor Reynold Hillenbrand, a liturgist, social reconstructionist and dynamic visionary, who stimulated young priests and laity to new goals in the Church's role in the modern world. Hillenbrand's charismatic influence was a foundation for the new-style Church that slowly began to take shape.

Among the coterie of young priests who surrounded Hillenbrand was John Hill, who had been Hillenbrand's assistant as national chaplain of the Christian Family Movement, Young Christian Workers, and Young Christian Students. To Hill fell the leadership of a new age: organizing the Chicago priests into an association.

As Vatican II came to a close, the morale of the almost 3,000 priests in Chicago was low. It took thirty years to become a pastor. And by the time priests moved into the pastor's chair, they had developed strong authoritarian streaks. There was a lot of bad blood among the clergy. When Archbishop (later Cardinal) John Cody came on the scene in 1965, following the death of Cardinal Meyer, who departed this earth with a lion's reputation because of his spectacular fight for religious liberty at the Council, one of the first actions of the new administration was the compulsory retirement of aging pastors and the election of two young assistant priests as canonical consultors.

However, this wasn't enough for forward-minded priests who began to see, in the light of Vatican II, that the clerical system had kept them like children. One day sixteen assistant priests had lunch together and spontaneously decided to develop a leadership of intelligent priests who were not at the same time identified as radicals. They set up three regional exploratory meetings without asking the permission of Archbishop Cody, because they did not want to imply that those in authority had the right to deny this kind of assembly.

The meetings were organized secretly, and Cody was informed by special delivery letter, timed to arrive at his office a few hours before the first meeting. The letter actually was handed to Cody a day later as he was getting on a plane for Rome at Kennedy Airport in New York. At the last minute, a pastor called Father Hill, one of the central organizers, urging him in fearful tones to cease organizing.

"It's your kind of fear that keeps me going," Hill replied.

Four hundred priests came to the first three meetings, which were deliberately kept low-key to avoid giving the impression that a new power bloc was developing within the Church. The priest leaders then approached Cody for recognition, gambling that the archbishop's political realism would lead him not to stamp out the new association and thus hurt his national reputation as a liberal. "Survival was our main question at that point," says Hill.

After a period of sparring, the archbishop agreed to the creation of a body representative of all priests in the archdiocese. The result was a nationally acclaimed organization democratically structured and geared to achieve effective liaison among the priests themselves and between them and the archbishop. Its first concerns were with internal institutional problems, personnel, promotion and retirement policies, relationships of pastors and their assistants, pay scales, time off.

It quickly moved forward to offer proposals on general policy, voting to investigate the role of the laity, nuns, brothers, and clergy in electing bishops and other Church officials. It also voted to provide the resources, in ideas, plans, staff and money, to implement two pilot projects designed to "work out a complete and responsible participation by the total Catholic community in the decision-making and functioning of already existing parish structures."

On a still wider scale, the Association decided to include among its interests the social problems of the general community, committing itself to the apostolates of poverty, race relations and peace. By the end of 1967, 85 percent of diocesan priests and 22 percent of priests belonging to religious orders had joined the association.

I interviewed Father Hill and his successor as president, Father Raymond Goedert, in the small office the Chicago association operates out of its own funds. They seemed convinced that the openness of the association meetings and the monthly convocation of the steering committee with Cardinal Cody were already paying dividends. A greater freedom of action in solving the problems of priests had already been established through this kind of association than through an official senate tightly connected to the bishop, they felt.

"Our most important accomplishment," Father Goedert said, "has been the development of a professional organization independent of the chancery office and yet without excluding the bishop. This has been a creative act and the priests' morale has improved, especially with the kind of seminars we hold."

I went to one of these seminars—on "Ministry in the Church"—held at the Center for Continuing Education at the University of Chicago and found the professional level of speeches and workshops akin to what one finds at a conference of mature executives reappraising their business in a changing world.

While the old-style priesthood with its automatic status is breaking up, it is not yet clear what form the new priesthood will take. This, too, is a cause of anguish, but the seminar revealed the concern of some 350 priests in charting a new path. Some hold that the cultic function of the priest, which keeps him on the altar ministering to his people, should be preserved. Others opt for the hyphenated priest, one who is trained in an allied field, such as psychology, sociology, economics, community planning, and so on, so that he is able to give a more expert and influential witness to his Christian commitment. The priesthood of the future will clearly be more flexible, with room for an ordained man to follow his own bent, including the ability to dissent from institutional opinion if he wishes.

Such priests are here already, and Philip Berrigan is one. One of the most influential internationally is the German Redemptorist and outstanding moral theologian, Bernard Haring, who spoke to the seminar.

"Priests should reject titles," he admonished his brothers. "They are making fools of themselves with their Right Reverends and Very Reverends. We are searching for a new kind of service, a witness as priests. Christ abolished the privileged class of the priesthood. We are not an established social class. We should not separate ourselves from the visibility of God's brotherliness in the real world."

With the exception of an elderly priest sitting beside me who snorted disapproval, I could sense the audience identifying itself with Haring's comments.

"We are concerned with chasubles," he went on, "and not paying attention to the many lying in the street in their own blood. The priesthood today has power, privilege, and monopoly, but it lacks concern for people as people."

The priest must be a man anointed by the spirit and filled with the joy of the Gospel, Haring added. Christ did not tell priests to memorize the Baltimore Catechism. The whole system of counting mortal sins has to die. Our celibacy is not credible if it does not make us willing to give our hearts more openly to others. Priests who, psychologically and sociologically, through a mistaken choice or later development, cannot maintain their celibacy should be helped by the professionals. We are dealing not with the "sacred law of celibacy but the law of sacred celibacy."

The priest who decides he cannot live a celibate life should be respected. He should be helped to return to the lay state, and his request should not go unanswered, as often now happens. The authorization given by the Vatican Council to ordain married men as deacons should be implemented, and perhaps later some of the deacons can be ordained priests.

Later, the discussants were asked to contribute a concrete idea that might help to free a priest who has a "hang-up" over his role. Start your own community, said one priest. Try experimental ministries on an ecumenical basis, said another. Study history. Promote democratic structures. Wear a suit and tie and live outside the rectory. Suffer through this moment in history. Fight for optional celibacy.

Then Father William Nerin of Oklahoma City, whom we met in Chapter 4, spoke up and cut through the gloom that enshrouded the table. "Why, this is the best time of all to live as a priest," he said. "There is a richness and openness and marvelous opportunity. We have to be able to respond to the challenges." Nerin, we recall, has the freedom to experiment.

Out of Hillenbrand seed, a flower has bloomed. Spurred on by the success of the Association of Chicago Priests, 326 representatives of 114 diocesan priests' senates and associations met in Chicago in February, 1968, and launched a national federation, a move that will change the structure of the Church in the United States. For the priests, while continuing to work in union with the bishops, will for the first time have a voice apart from them. As with the laity and the nuns, it is only by developing an independent basis of action that these elements making up with the bishops the total People of God can have a structured voice in Church policy.

Father Hill gave a ringing speech to the first national assembly, emphasizing that the Schillebeeckx prediction that ten thousand priests would leave must not come to pass. The priesthood must be shaped by priests themselves, he said. "We stand in solidarity with other priests of our age whose lives testified to the capacity of priests to shape events and times—yes, to shape history. I think of Virgil Michel, John Ryan, Joseph Cardijn, and John Courtney Murray. In their spirit . . . we shall not let it be said that in these uncertain times we failed to come together, that we failed to act."

Their new brotherhood enables priests to take actions they would not have previously dared. New York's new archbishop, Terence J. Cooke, was hardly on the job when a group of clergy presented him with a 37-page report calling for sweeping reforms. The priests wanted a limited term of office for the archbishop and senior officials, full financial disclosure, and decentralization in the decision-making process.

While the U.S. movement was from Chicago and other individual dioceses outward to a national federation, the priests in Canada began with a nationwide assembly. The first steps were taken at an International Theology Congress held in Toronto in 1967, when Father Ora McManus, a young priest who had just returned with a doctorate in philosophy from Catholic University, where he numbered among his close friends James Kavanaugh, brought together some 25 priests.

They agreed to take the Association of Chicago Priests as a model for a national Canadian organization. The day after their first meeting, they assembled again, this time inviting into their midst Bishop Alexander Carter of Sault Ste. Marie, president of the Canadian Catholic Conference. He not only gave his personal approval, but undertook to act as a liaison with the upcoming bishops' meeting.

Following that meeting, Bishop Carter told a press conference that the bishops had given "enthusiastic approval" to the project. A series of three regional seminars was then set up, the first one being held in Edmonton, Alberta, where Western Canadian priests came together in congenial surroundings and in the presence of several bishops, including Edmonton's Anthony Jordan, O.M.I., vented clerical problems with a ruthless honesty. The conference established itself not as a band of wild-eyed radicals, but as a group of pastorally concerned priests who feel deeply their responsibility to make the theory of Vatican II a realization at home.

All the ferment among the priests is inevitably reflected in the seminaries, often in a magnified form. One obvious result is the big drop in the number of seminarians. This is one reason for the amalgamation of seminaries that is taking place, but it is not the only reason. The Vatican Council called for a thorough overhaul of seminary training, which had remained unchanged in its major characteristics since the seminaries called for by the Council of Trent in the 16th century came into existence.

That regime provided for a total separation from outside influences, including university life. It produced men highly motivated but progressively isolated from the world they were intended to serve. The current trend is in the opposite direction. One of its elements is the amalgamation of seminaries into bigger units to provide a fully professional staff of professors, a good library, and all the other material elements required by an institute of advanced education. With increasing frequency, such new seminaries are being incorporated into the theology faculties of universities, thereby ensuring for the seminarian the intellectual climate enjoyed by other professionals. The Jesuits announced the relocation of Woodstock College in the Morningside Heights area of Manhattan to take advantage of personal and official associations with Union Theological Seminary and Columbia University.

The proposal for a joint Catholic-Protestant seminary in Rochester, New York, mentioned in Chapter 3, is also an indication of a major change in seminary training. For today's theologians and seminarians, the issues dividing Christians are far less important than the problems they have in common, such as how to confront the dehumanizing aspects of contemporary technology. They are discovering a common core of Christianity that stresses individual freedom, a sense of community based on close personal relationships, and an understanding of Jesus as someone who identified with suffering humanity and urges them to make the same identification and to express it in social action.

The progress of this movement of Christian consolidation can be illustrated by one significant development. Father Bernard Haring was a major attraction as visiting professor at Union Theological Seminary in New York for the first semester of the 1967-68 academic year, and he was followed by Swiss Catholic theologian Hans Kung for the second semester. Meanwhile, the student body of this very Protestant institution has grown to number 95 Catholics, nearly a fifth of the total.

The new seminarian himself tends to be a different type from the traditional one. In the past, much of the recruiting was done by priests who encouraged their altar boys to join the clergy, and by parents whose motivation usually included the attractiveness of the status of the priest.

Today, priests are less inclined to bring Johnny in, because they are unsure of themselves, and parents no longer have the inducement of a status that the priest is rapidly losing. Moreover, the sociologist Joseph Fichter has spotted two trends that are on a collision course as far as vocations go: Catholic parents seem increasingly ready to permit their children to marry at an earlier age, and are less and less inclined to encourage their children to choose the priesthood or religious life at an early age.

The modern seminarian—and the young priest—is a self-starting, highly motivated man, convinced or at least hopeful that he can change the image and reality of the priesthood to restore its relevance and make a contribution to society. He wants to be a part of the community rather than of the institution. He prefers a sports shirt to a cassock, is more involved in slum clearance than parlor calls in the rectory. Like other Americans of his generation, he is turned off by hairsplitting over abstract formulas. He is a member of a scientific culture that cares little what a thing is, as long as it works.

And right here, of course, is the issue that challenges the institutional priesthood in North America today. How can this independent young man coexist with the older priests and bishops brought up in a world that for him is meaningless and absurd? Most observers agree that changes must be much more radical than those we have yet seen.

Monsignor Ivan Illich, a priest of the New York archdiocese who heads an institute of intercultural research in Mexico, welcomes the drop in vocations on the ground that the Church has far more priests than it needs. The ever-expanding ecclesiastical bureaucracy is for him an illustration of Parkinson's Law that work grows with available personnel.

"Ecclesiastical employees," he wrote in the *Critic,* "live in comfortable church-owned housing, are assured preferential treatment in church-owned and operated health services, are mostly trained in ecclesiastical educational institutions and are buried in hallowed ground—after which they are prayed for. The habit or collar, not competent productivity, assures one's status and living."

He points out, for example, that theological training is not needed to exercise the ministry. "We shall not look for professional competence to teach the public, but prophetic humility to moderate a Christian group." Neither does the theologian need to be a priest or even a Catholic. "Nearly all of what is now considered theological science will pass out of the exclusive competence of the Church. Already, most of the subjects of the seminary curriculum are competently taught in secular universities by men of all faiths."

For Monsignor Illich, the typical priest of the future will be an adult layman ordained to the ministry as an exercise of leisure rather than a job. "The periodic meeting of friends will replace the Sunday assembly of strangers. A self-supporting dentist, factory worker, professor, rather than a church-employed scribe or functionary, will preside over the meeting. The minister will be a man mature in Christian wisdom through his lifelong participation in an intimate liturgy, rather than a seminary graduate formed professionally through 'theological' formulae. Marriage and the education of growing children, rather than the acceptance of celibacy as a legal condition for ordination, will confer responsible leadership on him."

Though Illich's views are regarded as extreme, it is clear that the death of paternalism and isolation will eventually enable a new theology, sociology, psychology, and economy of the priesthood to develop.

Tom Furber. Philip Berrigan. John Hill. Bernard Haring. Ivan Illich. William Restivo. The thoughts, words, and actions of these ordained men sketch a new outline of the future priesthood. There will be diversity of service, an understanding of the prophetic role, a welcoming back to the laity for those who wish to terminate a service of ministry. The rigidity of clerical conformity will be gone, and a growing maturity in the Church will enable priests to give an obedience to their bishops that is less subservient and fearful, to match a hierarchical authority that is more permissive and humane. The priests will be closer to both people and bishops, and they can be expected—once the threatening, emotion-filled first years of the new age have passed—to align themselves with all Christians in a more meaningful ministry to humanity at large.

CHAPTER 8

Nuns: Minds of Their Own

The woman sitting on the chesterfield across from me wore a pale green blouse and matching cardigan, with an olive skirt and black pumps. Her red hair was modishly set, and her blue eyes danced behind soft-rimmed glasses. Yellow and greens dominated in the curtains and rugs of the living room. *The New Yorker, Look, Time,* and *Commonweal* were scattered on a coffee table. A record player provided light background music while we talked.

The woman is a theologian and a film buff, and she has been, for the past twenty years, a nun. Her name is Sister Ann Richard White, a member of the 156-year-old Sisters of Loretto, who are a community of 1,100 American nuns in the vanguard of Catholic renewal.

All told, there are 176,341 nuns in the United States—three times the number of priests. Although they have their diehards, the nuns have so far achieved the greatest success in rebuilding their lives in the spirit of Vatican II. I sat, fascinated, as Sister Ann Richard talked about the kind of unfettered life she is now able to lead as a result of the Council.

We had begun by talking about what had motivated the Loretto Sisters to transform Webster College, outside

St. Louis, into a secular institution (a subject I shall return to in Chapter 10).

"We want to get rid of all property we can do without," Sister Ann Richard explained. "Our main concern is not to be free of Church authority, but to unload commitments which tie us down without any commensurate gain."

She gestured to embrace the room and the six-bedroom house across from the Webster campus which she shares with five other nuns. "We have three houses like this on the campus, with four or five sisters in each. We think we can form a deeper community spirit in this way, a spirit that embraces the total community around us. Our home is open. Adults come to visit, and so do the students. There is always somebody to welcome them, day and evening. We have no superior. At our chapter we got rid of a lot of the old conventions. Nobody opens our mail. There are no rules of precedence.

"As for our dress, we have many options. Anyone who wishes can wear the traditional habit. Then we have a suit in four styles and ten colors, allowing an enormous number of combinations. A veil may be worn with the suit, if desired. Those who prefer can wear regular street clothes, and this is becoming very common."

I asked Sister Ann Richard if she thought it important to get out of the habit. Her answer was in the affirmative.

"What you wear is a reflection of what you stand for. Since I changed to ordinary dress, I have discovered a new dimension. People, especially students, find me more human, easier to react to. A habit makes the wearer anonymous, so that people don't distinguish one nun from another. When I went home for Thanksgiving, my mother was very pleased to find me in ordinary clothes. She mentioned a family who told a daughter not to come home unless she was wearing a habit. That was a terrible thing, my mother commented. It showed that these people were only proud of the habit, and not of their daughter."

As I listened to her, I began to understand better the tremendous fuss in the clerical world about the habit. The resistance to change is, if anything, stronger among bishops and priests than among the nuns themselves, and one can only conclude that the men subconsciously view the habit as an element in the subject status of the nuns, just as their own distinctive dress is an element in their superior status. If the nuns get rid of the habit, they are emancipating themselves. They are also indirectly increasing the pressure for eliminating the distinctive dress of bishops and priests.

"Some people say nuns won't get respect without the habit," Sister Ann Richard observed. "The last thing I'd want is that kind of artificial respect. I don't want a seat in a bus because of my dress, but because of myself. If I am given a seat, it should be because a man respects me as a woman. My behavior should identify me, not my clothes. The other day on a plane from Denver to Chicago, the stewardess asked me if I was a nun, and this is all I had to identify me." She held out her left hand to show me a gold ring on the wedding finger, inscribed with a black cross.

What struck me particularly about Sister Ann Richard was that she had gladly changed her whole way of life because she considered this necessary in order to perform her mission in life. She and her companions had decided they had to live like everyone else, if they were to reach their students and influence them.

Each nun gets up on her own schedule, says her own prayers, meditates in private, makes her own breakfast, has her own schedule of classes. Sister Ann Richard usually buys lunch in the faculty quarters because of the opportunity to talk to other professors. They attend Mass in a school at 5:10 in the afternoon. Each takes her turn in preparing dinner, and they try as far as possible to eat dinner together. It is the point of community for them.

Afterwards, they study, correct papers, go out to meetings or events. They have a car, which anyone can use in terms of the ordinary give-and-take that characterizes a family car. The old rule about having a companion when going out has disappeared, as has the silence at night. If one comes home late and feels like talking, all she has to do is find somebody ready to listen to her adventures.

As far as employment goes, Webster treats the nuns like everyone else, paying professional salaries based on competence and experience. The house is run on a budget and has its bank account. Each nun also has a personal budget, and when she cashes her check, she keeps what she needs and turns the balance in to the house. What remains in the house account at the end of the month is transferred to the mother house.

"We no longer have to ask permission for everything we do," Sister Ann Richard said. "Though permission was usually given, it was somewhat degrading. It is more responsible to live on a budget, as most people must. We have our professional obligations, conferences, and seminars to attend. Each of us decides for herself and then she adjusts her budget accordingly. It encourages personal maturity."

Sister Ann Richard is interested in the dance, the theater, and art films. She goes to as many plays and movies as her budget will permit. She believes that in the future theology will be taught not only in the classroom but by means of such vehicles of communication as art and the theater, with far more people reached by these media than in the classroom.

"We are already seeing the beginnings of this trend," she says. "Religion and life are greatly intertwined. You can recognize yourself in a play. In the films of Bergman and

Fellini, as in the novels of Dostoyevsky, you see man's concern with the absurdity of life."

At this point our conversation was momentarily interrupted as two other sisters returned from a long weekend. There were affectionate greetings and lively banter. Gradually the talk swung around to the students and the more significant ways emancipated nuns are able to communicate with them.

These Loretto nuns have discovered that youth no longer constitutes a captive audience. Their students will not accept anything as fact simply because an older person tells them it is so. One must establish communication.

"Students in general are unconcerned for the Church as a Church," Sister Ann Richard observed. "This doesn't mean that they are without faith, because they are concerned with being authentic and humanistic. Many are humanists and wonder how Christ fits into their human concern. Most associate the Church with a series of moral rules, the reasons for which they don't understand. Often, they are talking off the top of their head, but frequently they have a valid point. They ask how the Church can declare that it is a mortal sin not to go to Mass on Sunday, and theologians today ask the very same question.

"I can't imagine students being even remotely interested in the kind of things the bishops do when they get together. To ban the Dutch Catechism or to impose restrictive rules on liturgical experimentation is to turn them off. What impresses them is the kind of discussion we had right here in this room with Robert McAfee Brown. 'Gee,' they said afterwards, 'a middle-aged man and he is going to jail!' I never saw a bishop get across to young people like that."

Sister Ann Richard is extremely aware that what they are doing is experimental. The one thing she seems certain of, however, is that the old way has ceased to be viable. Beyond that, it is only possible to find new ways by trying. The

Loretto Sisters are not getting many vocations, though this is explained in part by the change of regulations that has raised the entry age. Formerly they took girls straight from high school. Now they must work or go to college for two years.

Sister Ann Richard also sees the changes as a concrete part of the effort by women to assert their rights in the Church. "Many men simply turn off any assertion of the rights of women or any suggestion that women are being discriminated against in the Church. They have a blind spot, so they will dismiss the subject with the comment that all the women want is to be priests. But the issues are far more complex. I taught at the seminary last year, and it was quite a shock for the seminarians to have a woman teach them theology. For them a nun was someone who taught first or second grade. It took them about a month to get the picture, and after that we had some worthwhile sessions."

For a long time, the world has regarded the one million nuns in the Catholic Church as demure ladies of service, self-sacrificing and at times heroic, gladly submerging their true personalities to perform better their educational, nursing, and other prayerful tasks. They were present everywhere, it seemed, except in the decision-making areas of the Church. But why should they be involved in the sweaty mills of power? They are above the mundane pursuits of man as they live reflective lives of consecration in their polished convents, never eating with strangers, venturing out only in pairs, and generally behaving like the most genteel of Henry James's ladies.

That is the image nuns must transform to get society, and the rest of the Church, to take them seriously. When some nuns marched in Selma, when they demonstrated in peace marches, when they stood up to the Cardinal of Los Angeles, they signified their move into the post-conciliar

Church. The simple truth is that, as Sister Aloysius of the Sisters of St. Joseph in New Orleans says, nuns no longer see any value in being the "faceless wonders" of the Church.

They are beginning to be aware of their power in an institutional Church that depends heavily on their services. The 6,000 nuns in Detroit, for example, are the largest single personnel force the archdiocese has. When nuns start saying that they don't want to teach arithmetic to Johnny in suburbia, but want to be personal witnesses to Christ among the poor in the Inner City, the institutional leaders listen. The consequences of their not listening are becoming clearer.

There were 4,750 fewer sisters in America in 1967 than in the previous year. A spiraling rate of departures combined with a notable slackening of vocations forces countless communities of nuns to modernize faster than they themselves would have ever thought possible in pre-conciliar days. As with priests, great numbers of departing sisters are not rejecting the religious life so much as chucking the kind of life that constricts a religious spirit. Progressive sisters are struggling to break out of outmoded sociological and cultural forms—and their struggle makes headlines because it has the ingredients of drama, a sports feat, a political convention.

To begin with, nuns are trying to discard the shackles imposed by a male-dominated culture on women simply because they were women, so that they will be able to develop their own personalities and make a contribution to society on the same level as other 20th-century women. When they have done that, they will still have to determine —in more or less the same way as the priest is doing—what is the distinctive quality of being a nun in the Church as self-identified by Vatican II. The forms of spirituality and types of activity developed when the stress was on individual salvation and a direct communication between the believer and God are not viable for those who accept the Council's stress on the social nature of faith, the common destiny of the People of God, the identification of worship of God with service to Christ in the person of his needy members.

"The appropriate renewal of religious life," the Vatican Council said, "involves two simultaneous processes: (1) a continuous return to the sources of all Christian life and to the original inspiration behind a given community; and (2) an adjustment of the community to the changed conditions of the times."

To carry out this renewal, it was subsequently decided that every religious institution would hold a general chapter in two parts, at intervals of about a year. The first would permit a general evaluation of the problem and the introduction of experimental changes. The second would permit more basic decisions in the light of experiences.

For many who had followed an unquestioned routine as "the will of God" for years, such a challenge was terrifying. They were made suddenly conscious of the change in the status of woman in contemporary society, of the opportunities for service denied to them as nuns because of their physical and emotional separation from the world, including the barrier created by a medieval dress. Professional girls were leading equally edifying and dedicated lives, while contributing more to society because of their identification with their contemporaries.

The response to the challenge varied from one institution to another. Much effort was expended on projects to modernize dress without altering its distinctiveness by evolving in the direction of spiritual airline hostesses, an approach serving to confirm the middle-class respectability of convent existence and making the nun even less a witness than before to the poverty of which she professes to be a sign.

Institutions seeking radical updating quickly ran into

roadblocks erected by the very people who had issued the challenge to them. The all-male Congregation for Religious in Rome, ably abetted by many elderly bishops who appreciate little of woman's emancipation, vetoed even quite timid changes. With the addition of four nuns to the Congregation for Religious in October, 1967, some slow change of heart in this body can be anticipated.

Meanwhile, however, many of the most dynamic and forward-looking nuns have simply left their convents. The crisis is by no means confined to the United States. A Brazilian spiritual magazine, *Sponsa Christi,* devoted an entire issue to the problem in Brazil, stressing the urgent need for modernization if convents are to survive. It quotes as typical a 45-year-old woman who left a convent after twenty years.

"In my few years outside, I feel more inside than ever in my consecration to God. I am persuaded that in this short time, I have done more for God than in all my years as a nun."

A letter written to the Vatican by representatives of 29,000 Dutch nuns in late 1967 warned that many convents faced a slow death if they did not change rapidly so as to allow nuns to live a life more like that of other women.

In Canada, a brief on behalf of 60,000 nuns criticized the structures of religious life that have "cramped, not developed, us as persons." The Canadian nuns complained that "the ascetic life and its emphasis has actually fostered the destruction of the person."

In order to be full-fledged citizens, sisters must have freedom to participate on an adult level in the work around them. Professional religious should have the same opportunity to be professional as have laywomen. Consultation and dialogue should replace the series of permissions from religious authorities. Referring to the impulsive do-goodism projected by television's version of religious service, the

Canadian nuns wryly noted, "If superiors are not professional and mature, the sisters under them cannot be."

For nuns to think and speak in these terms is not only to challenge the whole tradition of convent life, but to hit the entire institutional Church at its most sensitive point. For the past century, the men who control the Church have determined the lives of nuns with little regard for their physical, emotional, or spiritual well-being. Canon law treats nuns as "minors" in the Church, and the bishops and priests have followed its lead faithfully.

In 1887 there were approximately 2,700 elementary schools in the United States taught by nuns. The system expanded over the next half-century at a rate of more than a hundred yearly. By 1930, the number exceeded 7,000, and by 1965 it was in the vicinity of 11,000. It was all possible only because superiors kept pouring nuns into the system. The one thing they had learned was the virtue of blind obedience to the bishop who made their decisions for them. Superiors took the young nuns fresh from the novitiate, even if only partly trained, and put them in classrooms in charge of 50, 80, or even 100 pupils. On top of this impossible work load, they had to live in a convent that imposed on them a regime of religious exercises designed for an entirely different kind of existence. There was neither the atmosphere nor the opportunity to continue professional studies in order to acquire the academic formation that had become standard for teachers in the public elementary schools.

Since World War II, much has been done to improve that situation. As far back as 1941, Sister Bertrande Meyer wrote a doctoral dissertation on the education of nuns in which she incorporated the results of hundreds of interviews. She placed the blame squarely on the shoulders of the bishops and priests who could not grasp "the necessity of holding the young sister back until she was fully formed, academically and spiritually, to enter the professions of teaching and nursing."

Little attention was given to Sister Bertrande's warnings and pleas until she was joined eight years later by a nun with a national reputation as a poet and intellectual—Sister Madeleva Wolff, head of St. Mary's College, Notre Dame, Indiana. While Sister Bertrande had concentrated on the professional issue, Sister Madeleva bore down heavily on the personal one also.

In *The Education of Sister Lucy,* she insisted that the nun's sense of dignity had to be respected. It was no longer possible in the middle of the 20th century to treat her as a cog in a machine and get away with it. She at least succeeded in getting the opposition to defend itself. Bishops and priests asked why a fifth-grade teacher needed a college degree. Old nuns, raised in a tradition of pietism and anti-intellectualism, saw their whole way of life under challenge. In addition, they feared that the young nun with a Ph.D. would become restless and leave the convent, a point which was certainly valid on the assumption that the convent was going to stay unchanged.

By the mid-1950s the pressures were building up. A Sister Formation Conference was organized under the auspices of the National Catholic Educational Association. Headed by a dynamic nun with professional training in philosophy, Sister Mary Emil Penet, it developed 150 Sister Formation Centers across the United States, then sponsored six special colleges for nuns based on the premise that "the spiritual and intellectual life reinforce each other."

All this activity laid the foundation for the new phase introduced by the Vatican Council, a phase in which "community" and "witness" are added to the earlier notions of "education" and "formation." That is the kind of thing Sister Ann Richard was talking about when she said that the Loretto Sisters were no longer willing to support an institution simply because it existed, that they wanted instead to go where they were most needed, where they could, in fact, be witnesses to the teaching of Christ.

The present mood of American sisters, said Sister Maryellen Muckenhirn, a Holy Cross theologian and renewal leader shortly before returning to lay life, is like the contemporary greeting card with the cover, "I'm with you" and the inner message, "But where are we?" The sisters themselves have not become accustomed to the new idea that even within a given community there can be multiple styles of life. This plurality causes tensions not only within cloisters, but in the larger ecclesiastical system that does not yet accept the non-monolith approach to religious life. The more education a nun receives, the more she realizes she is not an automaton. She wants flexibility to find a form of life to accommodate her own creative powers that have been stimulated by the experience of 20th-century living.

Her three vows of poverty, chastity, and obedience are valid for any century because in their pristine meaning they bring her closer to the Christ to whom the woman wishes to consecrate herself.

But is it poverty to live in a well-furnished convent where there is never a trace of dust, where the larder is kept full, where there are no worries about the next meal or the crippling illness, where the madness of the world can be shut out to facilitate uninterrupted and tranquil prayer to God?

Does chastity require an artificial decorum, the submergence of friendly relations with the other sex, traveling in pairs, a fear of the night, and the unspoken assertion that virginity is prized above all?

Does obedience consist of sublimating the human personality so that one can hear the call of Christ through a superior, of giving up one's baptismal name and wearing the clothes that reflect a culture long dead, of following the commands of men who do not exhibit any awareness of the psychology of women and control a government that automatically excludes women because they are women?

Self-determination—that is what nuns want. The type of change envisaged by the more advanced institutes of nuns is illustrated by the decisions of the Medical Mission Sisters at their general chapter. This group of 350 nuns, with headquarters in the United States and convents in 18 countries of Asia, Africa, and Latin America, decided to operate like a family, with all members of each convent involved in decision-making under a leader elected by themselves.

Newcomers will, after a novitiate, make a simple promise to live in the community for a period. Vows will be taken much later, after a tour of duty overseas. The old routine of religious exercises at fixed times has been abandoned. Each community will fix its program of prayers according to its work. The nuns can wear ordinary clothes whenever they wish. And a new category of associate membership has been created for women who want to share the life and work without becoming nuns.

Other communities have made lesser, yet significant, changes. The 500-member Sisters of the Holy Child of Jesus have updated their habit, can now go out unaccompanied and engage in civic or Church-sponsored summer projects. The Sisters of the Holy Humility of Mary dropped "Holy" from the title, eliminated the chapter of faults, in which nuns publicly confess their personal failings, and agreed to make petty cash available to sisters who should take turns shopping in order to get a better insight into the cost of living.

While these changes, which are representative of what is happening across the broad sweep of 500 communities in the United States, hardly meet the expectations of those who see the need of wholly new forms, they are nonetheless difficult and even bitter for many older nuns to accept. The young and the creative know that their drive for reality is the community's greatest asset for continuing existence in a swiftly changing world. But it is obviously wrong to pressure elderly sisters into forms of life that do not express their sense of holiness formed in a different age of the Church. Thus, we have tensions, confusions, stalemate, compromise. And departures.

I interviewed the most publicized ex-nun in America, Jacqueline Grennan, an intense, attractive woman who commands attention wherever she goes. *Life* devoted a four-page picture spread to her versatile direction of Webster College and involvement in the great issues of peace and justice, calling her brilliant, burning with ambition and energy, "a woman who could run U.S. Steel as easily as a college." On the speaker's platform, another writer insisted, her ideas come across like an atom exploding in a million directions at the same time.

Miss Grennan wore a gray checked suit with matching blue accessories the day we spoke. She acknowledged the accumulated fatigue of rearranging her life in the full glare of publicity. But the reward was that now she was "a freer person."

"I wanted to be really free to help the Church, because the Church means a great deal to me," she said. "And I came to the point where I felt I couldn't carry this kind of emotional fight as a sister for the next twenty years of my life and continue to be productive, that I would defend myself with cynicism or protection. I don't know whether that is strength or weakness. I think it is honesty, and I think some of my critics are beginning to realize that is my position, and so they don't see my leaving the sisterhood as a rejection of the sisterhood.

"I don't ever say that religious life as now structured is incompatible with full development and creativity for all women," she went on. "I only say that it was incompatible for me. I think there are some nuns who are staying for the same reason I left. They are trying to solve the question of commitment and freedom, of affectivity and personal response. The marriage state hasn't solved it, either. It is on the way, but few marriages make it. If you see the anguish and frustration in this creative movement as having implications for the larger society, as if my life has something to say to your little daughter, whether she marries or not, then my whole creative life will have been worthwhile. In that sense, my nineteen years as a nun provided some things for society which it would lack if I had not led that life. I think that what one learns from an experience is what is created. Much of the result is not what you strip out of it, but what you leave in it."

Miss Grennan left the Loretto Sisters, which, as we have seen, is one of the most advanced communities. There is no assurance that modernizing rules will solve the crisis of religious life. For every individual is encompassed by experiences and viewpoints that force her to make constant reevaluations. As with the priesthood, the social barriers against sisters returning to lay life are coming down.

"I don't regard religious life as *the* way in which you have to live in order to express a certain kind of holiness," says Sister Ann Richard, Jacqueline Grennan's friend and professional associate. "Rather, I am in favor of diversity within the Christian community. We as nuns need the companionship of those who are married, and I think married people need us. We all need each other to experience the fullness of the People of God."

While the departure of individual nuns has always been a fact of life in the Church, what has caused surprise is the breakup of whole communities. There have been several cases of blocs of sisters splitting off from their mother house and starting their own associations, free of canonical control.

The most significant development in this area involved the Glenmary Sisters, founded in Cincinnati in 1941. Their specific work was to help in rural Appalachia, and by 1966 they numbered more than a hundred. They did not open schools or hospitals. Instead, they spread out over Appalachia in a variety of social-service activities, some under Church auspices and others under community auspices.

As the rural people moved north in search of jobs, some of the nuns followed them and set up a base in an apartment in Chicago where 30,000 white Appalachians live in an area of approximately two and a half square miles. They come from the most primitive surroundings and lack the skills needed for success in the city environment. There are many social agencies, but the Appalachians don't know how to use their services, so the Glenmarys try to keep in touch with them as they drift from one address to another. Very few of them are Catholics, and the Glenmarys work with the other Churches as well as the Catholic Church, but they find that none of the Churches is geared to help these people.

"The institution has no meaning for them," was how one Glenmary member explained it to me. "They know that the Church doesn't want them."

The work in Chicago was expanding as the word came from the Vatican Council that nuns should modernize their ways to meet their various situations, and the Glenmarys in various locations embraced the invitation as heaven-sent. They took apartments in slum neighborhoods. They experimented with short, unobtrusive habits. Protests from conservative Catholics reached Archbishop Karl Alter in Cincinnati, and he issued instructions that they were to slow down, take a year to assess their goals, and during that time to refrain from accepting new members, opening new houses or taking on new assignments. During the year, some

35 nuns left the institution one by one, and by the time it had ended, most of the others had reached their decision.

Led by Sister Mary Catherine Rumschlag, the mother superior for 14 years, and her entire governing council, 44 of them left in a body to establish a lay association with the same objectives as the one they were leaving. The new federation was incorporated as a nonprofit group. A board of elected representatives was formed and the federation divided into four regions, each making its own decisions on the extent of common prayer, the pooling of salaries, and training of new members.

I visited some of these girls on the eve of Thanksgiving, 1967, just three months after they had started their new life. They were living in a slum area of north Chicago. The group consisted of four staff members and seven trainees housed in a third-story walk-up flat. Decay was written large across the neighborhood, as I approached, in the hollow eyes of the alcoholics and drug addicts with their shoulders hunched against the icy wind, in the broken glass littering the streets, in the dingy store fronts. This is the urban Appalachia to which the poor whites of Kentucky and Ohio have been driven by the relentless march of progress.

At the very hour of my arrival, *To Tell the Truth* was coming on television, and the girls were anxious to see it because Barbara Kuess, one of the former Glenmary nuns and now also a member of the new group, was on the program. Miss Kuess had previously achieved a fleeting moment of fame when, as Sister Marie Bernadette attending the University of Detroit, she had been forbidden by the Roman Curia to play a dramatic role in a university play. The fact that she had the lead and there were only three days left before opening night did not sway the finality of the Curia's ruling. Now here was Barbara trying to fool a panel about her identity as an "ex-nun." The panel picked her out without much difficulty.

"She has that warm and friendly smile that sisters have," ventured Peggy Cass.

Evelyn Eaton, spokesman for her colleagues, is 27, the eldest of six children. She grew up in New Orleans, but her father was from West Virginia and had given her an understanding of life in Appalachia. "I knew what Southern poverty was like," she said.

After graduation from an exclusive school, she joined the Glenmarys at age 17. She was a bright girl and went on to get a Master's degree in philosophy and is now working toward her Master's in clinical psychology. Blond, articulate, with flashing eyes and a trim figure, she is far from crushed by the squalor around her. Her hobby in Chicago is work with the Theater of the Absurd, which may be what keeps her sane.

"I think that perhaps our move was prophetic," Evelyn told me. "What we are saying is that the Vatican Council has not worked, at least in implementing the decree on religious life, because we started to do what the Council had ordered, and the axe fell on us. I think the whole notion of religious life is changing. We need to be with the people who think like us, who are prepared like us to give themselves full-time to dedicated Christian service, and we have to find our own way to do this.

"Our concept is one of total service. The commitment is not necessarily total in time, but it is total in intensity. We stay for as long as this life is meaningful to us. There is no stigma in leaving. Right now we have 43 members in our group and 12 affiliates, but we have no intention of making an institutional commitment. What we have are interpersonal relations, and many nuns are thinking in the same terms. They are blaming the structures for the emptiness in their lives. They are tired of irrelevant controls and rejecting a commitment to irrelevancy."

Inevitably, the new Glenmarys carry some emotional

scars from their experience. In the conversation, someone described 69-year-old Cardinal Ildebrando Antoniutti, head of the Vatican Congregation for Religious, which has been blocking many of the attempts by nuns to update their institutes, as "bad news."

Kathleen Harkins, one of the group, interrupted. "He *was* bad news," she said. The clear inference was that he no longer counted, that they had passed him by.

Evelyn Eaton made a very similar remark in describing the reaction of the Church authorities to their move. "The very day of our ceremony of inauguration, Cardinal Cody wrote to our local parish to say we were not to be treated as nuns. And a Catholic television program about our work was canceled without explanation. But it doesn't make much difference any more what the bishops think. You could say that we'd be worried about the Dutch Catechism if the bishops had failed to ban it. So you get some stability and go on your own."

The atmosphere was extremely informal and relaxed while we talked. People were coming and going all the time, Girl Scouts bringing food for Thanksgiving dinners for the poor, adults seeking information or just wanting to chat, two or three ministers of different Protestant denominations, a young Catholic priest.

"We are always open," one of them explained to me. "Often we have conferences late at night. Some of our neighbors like to stop by at midnight or one in the morning. We do our best to lead a community life. We have common prayer in the morning, when we can make it. We have a Scripture reading. We try to meet for supper. We have Mass here once or twice a week, usually quite informally. Sometimes the priest vests, sometimes not. We go to our parish church Sundays, but the priests there don't want to have too much to do with us."

The Glenmary girls maintain their existence through a

communal approach; some work full-time as teachers or social workers, using their salaries to subsidize those who spend each day trying to help the Appalachians survive in a terrifying jungle.

In other parts of the country, groups similar to the new Glenmarys are coming into existence. Each has a somewhat different style. Experimentation and flexibility are the operative concepts. Permanence is a word that is not thought about very much. What is common to the groups is a concern for individual development, a belief in community life and service to society—all of this in a setting outside the restrictions of canon law.

Twenty-six of the fewer than 100 members of the Daughters of the Cross withdrew from their convents in Louisiana in 1967 and re-formed in Milwaukee as a lay community, known as the Christian Institute for People, living with minimal structures, no spiritual rules, and shared authority. Most of them are highly qualified teachers, and several hold Master's degrees. In Milwaukee they live in rented apartments, no more than five in each. Most of them teach in public elementary and high schools as employees of the Board of Education. They do not pool their salaries, since they hold to the belief that the experience of personally managing a budget is more beneficial. However, 10 percent of their salaries is placed in a central fund for the education of novices who left with the sisters. They meet regularly for the Eucharist; otherwise, the girls in each apartment plan their own prayer services. They have made no written pledge to one another. Yet they claim to have achieved a feeling of community. "Community is above all a spirit," said one. "We aren't a group coming to live together as much as we are people with common ideas and readiness to become aware of each other."

Oklahoma City has a somewhat different group, the Sisters for Christian Service. They were members of a community of 131 Benedictine nuns in Tulsa involved in a program of renewal that was suddenly disrupted by the appointment by Rome of an outsider to govern them. After a considerable number of the nuns had simply dropped out in frustration, six of them decided to create the new institute.

They live in community, pray and work together. They visit jails, tutor in underprivileged areas, teach school, conduct catechetical classes, perform social work in the slums. They were dispensed from their vows as nuns and now have private vows, so that they are no longer under the bishop, except in the same general sense as are other members of his diocese. But their relations are excellent both with the community they left and with Bishop Victor Reed of Oklahoma City, who celebrated the Mass at which they formalized their new commitment.

In Pueblo, Colorado, eleven former Notre Dame Sisters from Cleveland set up an experimental community with the blessing of Bishop Charles A. Buswell. Some teach, others work in welfare jobs, and they live in three apartments.

"We wish to live a celibate life in community in an atmosphere of such open, responsible freedom that each may be encouraged to give spontaneous, prayerful response to the inspiration and need of the moment," their guidelines state.

No one person has veto or decision-making power. Any change in policy requires a three-fourths majority vote.

"The guidelines are mimeographed," one member noted. "That's an indication of their permanency."

Only a small minority of American sisters have joined these new lay associations, but their number shows every sign of increasing. More and more nuns have passed the normal frustration level in putting up with episcopal and curial interference in doing the modernizing jobs that are required. As long as the nuns are told that a life of religious dedication must be accompanied by certain prescribed forms, then the experiments they are simultaneously enjoined to try become a mockery. The clearest case of this fundamental conflict between the teaching of Vatican II and the implementation of Vatican II was the celebrated dispute between the Sisters of the Immaculate Heart of Mary and Cardinal James McIntyre of Los Angeles.

The IHM controversy began when Cardinal McIntyre opposed a temporary experiment in renewal under which the sisters were permitted to wear secular clothing, keep their own hours, and find ways of serving Church and society other than by teaching in parochial schools. The IHM Sisters said their experiments were a response to the decrees of Vatican II and also to a directive by Pope Paul mandating self-renewal by religious communities.

Cardinal McIntyre said they were being disobedient to him in carrying out reform without his direction. The sisters, moreover, insisted on a written contract guaranteeing freedom from interference by bishop or pastor in the 35 parochial schools under their direction; they wanted teachers whose qualifications were not equal to those demanded in public schools withdrawn for further study and each teaching nun paid the same salary as a lay teacher.

Cardinal McIntyre asked the Vatican Congregation for Religious, headed by the equally intransigent Cardinal Antoniutti, for a ruling. Antoniutti sided with McIntyre. He ordered the sisters back into habits, common community prayer, and a retention of their teaching commitment and told them to work in "collaboration" with the local bishop.

The IHM Sisters' friends, who are legion, exploded. Bishop Remi de Roo, young, progressive Bishop of Victoria, B.C., who had previously told an IHM branch in his diocese to experiment, attacked the Antoniutti order as containing the seeds of disaster for all sisters. Sisters by the thousands petitioned the United States Bishops' Conference to get a reversal. Columnist Gary MacEoin deplored the ruling as "brutal," and said the Antoniutti-McIntyre axis would destroy the hope of enlightened people that the institutional Church really intends to implement the reform it has voted. Father John Reedy, Holy Cross editor of *Ave Maria* magazine, deplored the Curia's "insensitivity" and warned of massive unnecessary departures from the religious life. Thirteen members of the theological faculty at the Jesuits' Alma College in Los Gatos, California, praised the IHM nuns for their "creative maturity" and faithfulness to the norms of Vatican II.

The reformers achieved a reasonable victory. A committee of American bishops, named by the Vatican to mediate the dispute, ruled that the IHM order could split into two groups, one pursuing liberal experimentation and the other following the traditional rules. Individual members were given the option of joining either group.

Sister Helen Kelly, president of Immaculate Heart College, put the IHM case succinctly, and spoke for thousands of sisters beyond her community, when she spoke to a convocation.

"Let me say briefly, and once and for all, that I attach no importance to the fact that I am wearing this cap and gown, or this beautiful pink suit, or that I didn't get up at 5:20 this morning, or that I made what I think was a pretty good meditation under a hair dryer, or that I flew from Washington to Pittsburgh yesterday, alone, and had lunch there with a young man, or that I bought a drink during the flight from Pittsburgh to Los Angeles. None of these is worth burning at the stake or being crucified for.

"The significant thing is that the sisters looked at themselves, at their lives, at their work, at those with whom and for whom they worked, at their times and what their times are doing to people and the way they live, and they said: Not only our lives but the lives of almost everyone are very much in need of fundamental change, change of mode growing out of change of heart. We and the world need to grow up. We need to move in all directions indicated by painful self-examination. We can no longer rely solely on the judgments of others who do not live our lives and who cannot know what our consciences indicate.

"This is what it means to be grownup, and part of it is suffering the consequences of personal decisions. This is what it means to be a grownup religious, a grownup husband or wife, a grownup Christian in relation to his Church: It means not letting anyone else's conscience (individual or corporate) rob me of the responsibility for my life, no matter how tempting an alternative that may continue to be. To be burned at the stake in defense of that responsibility makes sense to me."

What reform-minded sisters are up against is a mind-set in the Vatican as exemplified in Cardinal Antoniutti's philosophy of renewal.

"Up-to-date renewal does not imply the indiscriminate introduction of lay customs and ideas into religious life," he declared, adding that the laity wish religious to distinguish themselves in manner, words, and dress as persons "unmistakably dedicated" to God. The religious habit can be modified, but not eliminated, "because it serves to distinguish religious life as a sign of the Church's sanctity." Certainly change "may not be left to free choice," and the nun who told *Newsweek* that sisters should go to a tailor to change their habit, not to the Congregation for Religious, was branded by Antoniutti as "ultra-progressive."

Whenever there are doubts or problems, not to mention arguments, come to the Congregation for Religious for counsel and direction, he said. In any event, don't deny the spirit of your founder, he admonished sisterhoods, by introducing ideas "contrary to the Gospel and the norms of religious discipline."

This paternalism, revealing a Curia-knows-best mentality that the Council and Synod tried to break, is slowing renewal, but it, too, will inevitably be swept aside along with culture accumulation in the papal court. The question is: How much damage, meanwhile, will be done to the sisterhoods?

The desire to be an authentic Christian person and a committed religious servant has split in two and polarized. The former nun leader, Maryellen Muckenhirn, conceding that genuine new forms of religious life will probably not be immediately acceptable to Rome, maintains there are many educated and experienced nuns willing to implement the decrees and spirit of Vatican II, and who are able to make the necessary changes in themselves. They are the ones, and the only ones, who can modernize the nun's life, in her view. The first step is a more profound study of the Council teaching. Next is a greater effort to formulate creative ideas for experimental community and experimental apostolic works, combined with a determination to fight for what they are convinced is necessary, including "new and much more adult ways of dealing with authorities in the Church—for example, with the Congregation for Religious and with the bishops both singly and collectively." But as for herself, "I feel that Christ wants me to live out my commitment in the reality of today's world."

What Miss Muckenhirn says stems from her concept of the nature of the evolving nun in today's society—a woman with a sense of genuine freedom, personally secure, conscious that it is not disloyal to be articulate, free, intelligent, and personally committed. She believes there are already enough nuns measuring up to this description to lead the revolution in the convents. That is why she is convinced that the Church will continue to have nuns around for the foreseeable future, perhaps fewer in numbers but certainly contributing more to themselves and to the total community.

A widely published photo of Harvey Cox, the Protestant theologian, bestowing a friendly kiss on the cheek of Sister Corita, the famous Immaculate Heart artist who wears secular clothing, carries wonderful symbolism. Rome loves symbolism, and officials in the Curia should have been able to get the message here: American nuns possess minds of their own and will choose their own company.

CHAPTER 9

Youth: The Big Turn-Off

One Friday afternoon, during the course of my research for this book, I flew from Washington, D.C., to Detroit. I had spent a week observing the American bishops at their semiannual meeting. "Observing" is a little strong, since the meetings are conducted in total secrecy. In fact, when I walked into the America Hotel during the first day of the meeting and inquired at the desk outside the episcopal assembly room what time the meeting was expected to adjourn, a priest assistant rushed up to me, grabbed my arm, and hustled me out to a main corridor.

"Nobody's allowed near the bishops' meeting room," he admonished me.

A uniformed guard, heading toward me, was obviously prepared to back up the priest's warning.

Of course, among the innovations in Catholic life are the press conferences that accompany bishops' meetings. Thus, the Church (and the public generally) is given a reasonably good idea of the actions of the bishops, if not the ideas and speeches that put these actions in a proper context. At this particular meeting, the bishops reinforced their commitment to Catholic education, upheld compulsory celibacy for the priesthood, voted a $9,618,000 budget, urged the U.S. government on to greater efforts at negotiating a peace in Vietnam, and banned the new and widely acclaimed Dutch Catechism as an unsuitable text for the teaching of religion.

On Friday evening of the same week, I found myself in Wayne State University in Detroit, attending a Newman Club lecture on the new theology by Father Eugene Burke. A Paulist who teaches at the Catholic University of America, Father Burke is a notable example of the intellectual transformation that has taken place in the Church because, whereas he was once a traditionalist theologian without any doubts, he has undergone a "conversion" and is now a leading progressive. He has, in fact, been banned in the archdiocese of Los Angeles for his leadership in the strike at Catholic University in support of Father Charles Curran, as well as for his open advocacy of optional celibacy for priests.

For approximately one hour Burke gave a masterful exposition of how the Church is moving from a static to a dynamic theology to recognize the continuing intervention of God in humanity. Modern theology cannot simply be a defender of the denominational Church looking in on itself; rather, it must go on interpreting the good news of salvation, making God relevant for each new age. The students seemed to grasp Burke's vivid insights and warmly applauded him.

Then a student stood to ask a question. Why, if the Church now professes a new openness, was the Dutch Catechism, which had been praised by catechetical experts, banned by the American bishops? Doesn't this action reveal that, despite the Council, the authoritarian tradition of the bishops will prevail? Father Burke acknowledged the point of the question. The bishops, he said, should have cited specific objections so that the validity of the ban could have been tested. Heavy-handed exercise of authority makes authority less and less credible, "and when you really need it, it's lost its punch."

In this little exchange, I could feel the forward thrust of Burke's lecture on the new theology blunted by the bishops' hasty ban of a new theological work (a work that was commissioned by the Dutch hierarchy). The students very likely had not even read the Dutch Catechism and would have been only marginally aware that it is an adult book containing fresh and exhilarating insights into the Gospel. Yet the cloud cast upon the work by the bishops made the students react—not against the book, but against the American bishops. Here, in this room, was a microcosm of the grave dilemma in the post-conciliar Church: the cynicism of the young toward antiquated institutional authority, with a modern-minded theologian standing in the middle.

I had selected Wayne State as a principal viewing point of young Catholics largely because I had read a book, *The Restless Believers,* by a leading Paulist, Father John J. Kirvan, who is the Newman Chaplain at Wayne State.

On Sunday morning, I attended Mass at the Newman Centre where some 200 students had gathered. We sat in the lounge for the first part of the Mass, which comprised hymns sung to guitar accompaniment, the Epistle and Gospel, and a sermon by Father Kirvan, who talked animatedly about the need for a free response to Christ's love. Then we all filed into the chapel to stand around the altar for the Eucharist. After the Mass we returned to the lounge for coffee, and I spent a long time listening to the free-flowing student conversation.

An attractive brunette, an education major, was speaking. "I had canceled out a lot of older people, but I now see they have something to offer in the renewal of the Church. However, I don't think the Church is important as a structure. We want a structure that is responsive to our needs."

A boy in an open-necked white shirt cut in. "Structures

238

divide, and especially the Church structures. The Church has abdicated its social responsibility."

"That is why the Church is thought to be irrelevant," the girl continued. "The Church should say what needs to be done to solve more problems. Instead, we get a few little whispers of leadership. I have no idea what the bishops are doing. I just don't hear them. Maybe that is why the institution means so little to me. The greatest crime of the Church is not giving inspiration on political and moral questions. They should be giving us leadership in regard to selective conscientious objection, which is very real to us."

Another boy took over. "In the parishes you don't hear these new ideas, although the leadership at the top of the Church is pretty good. I am praying for the roof to open up and see the pastor floated off on a cloud."

Another boy: "Too many of those in leadership have not expressed views on real issues. The priests should be talking about these things."

All of them are desperately earnest. "Where do I get my inspiration?" a graduate student repeated my question. "I get it from people like Malcolm X, from a book like *Honest to God,* from Mahatma Gandhi."

"I get it from people," stated another young man, this one bearded and wearing sneakers, "from books, from the study of logic, from the interactions of persons."

There was general agreement that many of the Catholic students on the campus don't go to Mass at all, that they rush around to check where the local parishes are when their parents are coming to visit them. On the issue of sex, they agreed that there is little promiscuity.

"The great disillusionment," one observed to the laughter of his friends, "is to find out there is no free sex and LSD. There is, however, lots of 'grass' around, if you are looking for it, lots of kids making their first experiment with dope."

As conversations go, this one was not particularly enlightening, but it served to focus a lot of questions in my mind about the casual disdain the college generation exhibits toward the institutional Church. There are many observers of the current scene who think the Church in America is already facing a massive "intellectual turn-off."

Half the population of the United States is under 25. From the viewpoint of the nation's institutions, including the religious institutions, the attitudes, values, and commitments of this half are decisive. And as of now, what these attitudes, values, and commitments really are is largely a mystery to the other half, and even to the young people themselves.

It is, of course, a truism that parents never understand their children. Those who have reached an age at which sensuous pleasures pall have always found an astringent satisfaction in bemoaning the moral decline since their youth. All of this remains true, but additional factors now seem to escalate the generation gap to the point where it becomes different not only in degree but in nature.

Today we have the first generation of the nuclear era. There may yet be no biological alteration from fission fall-out, but there is an emotional alteration. Nuclear man is conscious both of his totally new control of his environment as expressed in technological progress and the snowballing of utilizable knowledge stored in and manipulated by electronic brains, and of the tenuousness of his hold on survival because those older people who achieved the technological and nuclear breakthrough failed to include a safety valve in the design.

Today's young people, in addition, are understandably unimpressed by an education system that is only marginally adjusted to the forms of electronic communication with which they have lived from infancy. They are acutely conscious not only of this failing, but of all the inconsistencies in contemporary society. In particular, they are painfully cognizant of the gaps between the ethical and moral professions of the older generation and its actual behavior patterns.

Furthermore, youth has for the first time become aware of itself as a moving social force, a breakthrough as momentous as that of the common man into political life in the 19th century and the rise of woman to equal status in the early 20th century. Young people cannot be pushed around any more. They speak their own language, make their own moral judgments, and are conscious of their power.

All of this change is itself progressively escalated by the accelerated rhythm of human existence. From the dawn of history the evolution of the human mind proceeded at a rate that produced a new intellectual generation in three or four biological generations, remembering that the human life span averaged 30 to 35 years. Now with the life span doubled in advanced countries, the intellectual generation has shortened to as little as five years and continues to shrink. The effect is dizzying for the young people themselves, who find they can communicate with a constantly narrowing band of their own contemporaries, and even more for those who are professionally involved with the high school and college strata.

What is true for youth in general is true for young Catholics. They had no part in starting the Catholic revolution, which in its essence was proclaimed by the staid, elderly gentlemen of Vatican II. The preceding chapters, however, give some inkling of the impact of youth on the progress of that revolution.

In particular, they are challenging the traditional structures and forms. They won't accept something simply because somebody says that's the way it should be. The scientific method is the characteristic of their approach to life. It is a method that concerns itself not with objective truth, but with practical results.

This is not a denial of truths, whether in the realm of religion or of other areas of life, but a challenge of the practical conclusions drawn by human beings from a series of premises or assumptions. How does the Church come to the conclusion that God will condemn me to hell for all eternity if I miss Mass once on Sunday? Who says you have to put the book in one place for the Epistle and in another for the Gospel? What do celibates know about two people being in love?

In the Constitution on the Church in the Modern World, the Vatican Council gave a very fair analysis of the viewpoint of the young. "A change in attitudes and in human structures frequently calls accepted values into question. This is especially true of young people, who have grown impatient on more than one occasion, and indeed become rebels in their distress. Aware of their own influence in the life of society, they want a role in it sooner. As a result, parents and educators frequently experience greater difficulties day by day in discharging their tasks.

"The institutions, laws, and modes of thinking and feeling as handed down from previous generations do not always seem to be well adapted to the contemporary state of affairs. Hence arises an upheaval in the manner and even the norms of behavior. Finally, these new conditions have their impact on religion. On the one hand, a more critical ability to distinguish religion from a magical view of the world and from the superstitions which still circulate purifies it and exacts day by day a more personal and explicit adherence to faith. As a result, many persons are achieving a more vivid sense of God.

"On the other hand, growing numbers of people are abandoning religion in practice. Unlike former days, the denial of God or of religion, or the abandonment of them, are no longer unusual and individual occurrences. For today it is not rare for such decisions to be presented as requirements of scientific progress or of a certain new humanism. In numerous places these views are voiced not only in the teachings of philosophers, but on every side they influence literature, the arts, the interpretation of the humanities and of history, and civil laws themselves. As a consequence, many people are shaken."

I have quoted this section because it illustrates one of the basic issues in the relationship between the institutional Catholic Church and today's youth. Anyone who has the courage and perseverance to wade through it and digest it will, I think, agree that it hits a lot of the major issues. But the problem is one of language. It is on a different wave-length. How does the college student react who is subjected to it? "Dig that crazy jazz, man," he says, as he turns it off.

All these questions formed a backdrop for a lengthy talk I had with Father Kirvan after the last of the Newman students had drifted away. A wiry, balding man in his late thirties, Kirvan holds degrees from St. Paul's College in Washington, D.C., and the Catholic University of America.

"One thing is certain," he said as he slumped down in a chair in his cluttered office and lit a cigarette, "a new generation of believers will not and cannot accept faith as a heritage. They won't accept it as part of some family tradition. They cannot accept it as some manifest destiny. Either it is something in which they can find needed dimensions of their own desperate search for self-identity, or they will abandon it as irrelevant.

"The kids today tend to be more indifferent about the Church as an institution than was true as recently as three years ago," he said. "We had a meeting with a distinguished ecumenist from New York. It was well attended and we were telling the kids about the big progress being made toward unity of the Churches. I could see they were being turned off rapidly, so I put a pointblank question to one of them, and he said, 'That's a very interesting institutional question you are discussing, and I'm sure you institutional types can work it out. But for us it has no meaning whatsoever. To be interested in ecumenism would be for us to regress. We no longer accept identification with denominations, and consequently we couldn't care less whether they get together or not.'

"I did some more investigating later, and it confirmed what this young man said. The fact is that the people seem to be far more unified than the Churches. It is a heartening phenomenon, but also a disturbing one, because it demonstrates the gap between the people and the bishops. If the bishops don't understand what the people are thinking and saying, it means that they have lost their potential for leadership."

I referred to some of the points covered in his book, then about two years old. It dealt with the thought and behavior of the Catholic college students with whom he had long worked, pointing out their slight interest in institutions, their different scale of moral values, the stress on the individual conscience, the refusal to accept things on the say-so of authority figures, and some of the other characteristics of youth that have already been described. His overall conclusion was quite optimistic. Youth is always restless, he said in effect. It is impatient and simplistic. But these young people are still believers, and from their doubt and struggle will emerge a stronger and more purified faith.

I asked him whether he still saw things in the same terms. Not entirely, he told me. "The crisis now seems to me to be deeper. I hate to use a cliché, but the only expression that fits is a crisis of identity. Everything is moving so fast that young people cannot grasp the meaning of their lives. There is nothing solid with which they can identify themselves. We older people are still working on the assumption that our traditional churchly tools—the liturgical celebration, the sacraments and preaching—can be formulated in a way

244

meaningful for youth. I suspect we have overestimated the message they have for this new group that is placing all its hopes in one basket called human relationships. This is a very emotional thing, a close, tender relationship with another human being, a real nakedness in front of other individuals, self-disclosure, a total self-revelation. It can include a sexual relationship, but not a promiscuous one—there is absolutely no evidence of more promiscuity today than at other times."

Do you mean, I asked him, that all students think like that?

No, of course not, he explained. "You never had any great involvement with issues among students, and you don't today. The vast majority, eighty percent or more, just don't give a damn about anything except making their grades. That is the mass, and you hardly notice them; you take them for granted. What one sees is what comes out at the two ends—at one end a bunch of neurotics, maybe ten percent; and at the other end, the articulate, concerned people, maybe ten percent also. They are the ones we are talking about, not many, but important, because they create the atmosphere in which the others float.

"They are Christians, believers in Christ, but they are unchurched and fundamentally de-institutionalized. They consider themselves Catholic Christians, but the standards we have developed to determine if someone is a practicing Catholic don't apply. They seldom go to confession, for example. I did a quick survey of daily communicants and found not a single one of them had been to confession in eighteen months. Their concept of sin is quite different from ours. They scoff at numbers or quantities. They laugh at the idea of a laundry list of sins. It means more to them to come into my office and discuss in broad terms what they interpret as signs of alienation or revolt in themselves."

Extremely religious, but totally uninterested in speculative theology—that is how Father Kirvan sums up today's committed young people, boys and girls alike, products of Catholic education and products of public education.

"They are isolated from religious questions as such. The nearest they get to them is the war situation, or the race situation. Other than that, they don't ask religious questions, and consequently they don't want religious answers. I don't think they accept the previous definitions of God or care about them; but they have a kind of instinctive or basic conviction about God, and that is what troubles them. They are disengaged from the past, and you can speak only to their experience. A speculative theology doesn't come through to them, not even the theology of the new wave, like Rahner, Haring, or Schillebeeckx.

"The theology I work with today is 180 degrees from the theology I brought with me here. Part of it is that I have begun to listen to questions. From an *a priori*, absolute, syllogistic way of thinking religiously about life, I have substituted an almost totally personal existential thought pattern. The way I theologize is by reporting. I observe. I hardly ever say anything. Some of my Paulist colleagues blew their stacks about a year ago when a Detroit newsman quoted me as saying I considered myself a reporter. But that's what I am, a reporter in the most profound sense. I see what is happening, I try to observe very closely, and I try to penetrate the significance.

"Formerly, I thought I knew in advance how to judge something that had not yet happened. Now I realize I can't tell in 1967 what will be the human, moral and religious significance of an action I am going to perform in 1972, because I am not now the person I then will be. It's more like playing in a jazz combo. You know the theme and you begin to beat it out. But you never know what the next note is going to be until you have created the situation in which the next note has to be played."

One of the most interesting aspects of the situation Father Kirvan was explaining was the impact the students had on his own view of reality, and I told him so.

"Oh, yes," he agreed, "I know I have lost some things, but I'm not panicky about having lost them. I'll gain them back sometime. I don't know where or when, but I will. A lot of priests are being affected like this, and it's making many of them try to get out of pastoral situations. They don't think they can speak effectively any more in the institutional setting, because much of what they believe doesn't square with the institutional position—on birth control, for example. So they are retreating into academic positions where they can speculate with more freedom and are not forced to make concrete decisions. But some of them feel guilt. They see themselves as scavengers on the institution, living off it but not accepting it. The tragedy is that we lack a good theology of the priesthood, having lived on a sociology and a history of the priesthood which have today been dissipated and left us defenseless."

More evidence of the credibility gap between the skepticism of the young and the faith of their fathers was offered by Father Bruce M. Ritter, a Franciscan who teaches theology at Manhattan College in New York City. Some 3,000 of the college's 3,500 students at this all-male school run by the Christian Brothers answered a 152-question survey.

Of these Catholic students, 41 percent don't go to Sunday Mass regularly; 45 percent don't believe in the real presence of Christ in the Eucharist; 88 percent don't believe the pope is personally infallible; only 21 percent believe that premarital sex is always wrong; only 33 percent think a bishop has, in practice, much influence on Catholic life in his diocese; only 7 percent think that the use of contraceptive devices is always wrong.

One of the many contradictions exposed by the survey

is that, while only 6 percent of the respondents said they were influenced by the Church's teaching in making moral decisions, and only 3 percent said they were influenced by their parents' teaching, a high proportion observe a moral code stricter than they actually profess. Though only 21 percent believe that premarital sexual intercourse is always morally wrong, 80 percent of freshmen came to Manhattan without the experience, and 50 percent of seniors had not had the experience. Though only 22 percent accept a distinction in theory between mortal and venial sin, 72 percent will not receive the Eucharist without confessing their mortal sins—and this in spite of the fact that only 17 percent believe confession is necessary for forgiveness.

As Father Ritter sees it, all this adds up to a love-hate relationship with the institutional Church, producing an almost schizoid attitude to religion. A factor in the situation, he says, is the lack of impact of clergy on the students. Large majorities of those surveyed felt that their bishops and parish priests had no influence on their lives.

In a broader context, the Catholic commentator John Cogley has offered an explanation of the lack of impact of parents, teachers, and clergy on the young.

"They lost any real confidence in what their elders told them," he said. "The leaders of society talked one way and lived quite another."

A young friend of his, Cogley said, had wrapped it all up in a few neat sentences. "We heard about loving our neighbor in lily-white suburbs. We were lectured on the evils of violence in a nation armed to the teeth. We learned about the dangers of materialism from clergymen who spent most of their time heading building funds. We were warned against pornography by people who approved napalming babies. We were given lessons on responsible citizenship by politicians who collapsed in the face of McCarthyism and had nothing to offer but sterile cold-war slogans in confronting the nuclear dilemma. The simple fact is, we don't believe you. You have never given us any reason to. That's the real hang-up."

The cynicism that runs through young Catholics stood out in a symposium organized by *Commonweal* magazine. It brought together six students with Catholic college backgrounds, opinion-makers among their peers, most of them associated with student community and activist organizations, notably in the areas of peace and civil rights.

One question they were asked was whether they agreed with statements made shortly before by two women theologians, Rosemary Ruether and Mary Daly. Rosemary had said that among students she knew there definitely was no interest in any doctrine about the supernatural, that their interest was in human values. Mary had said that many students wouldn't even read Catholic theologians any more, that they felt they only got the party line with some liberal ideas thrown in.

"There is not so much rejection of the supernatural as there is rejection of the idea that there's a great difference between supernatural and human values," was the comment of Frank Carling, a Fordham graduate now studying international law at Yale. "Students today are trying to find some way of fusing the two."

"The type of thing Rosemary Ruether is describing has been occurring in Catholic schools for a long time," said John J. Burke, Jr., a Jesuit seminarian, "but I think it a bit inaccurate to say people are uninterested in reading Catholic theologians. Look at how Teilhard de Chardin is read. I do admit, though, that in many respects Catholic theology is sterile, and I'm not particularly convinced by anybody on the contemporary scene that it is balanced."

William T. Wilson, an undergraduate at La Salle College,

Philadelphia, said the reason he didn't read Catholic theologians was that he found it hard to read with his eyes closed. "I fall asleep when I read Catholic theologians. Young people I know are interested in living, about how tomorrow's going to get on, about whether you're going to be here tomorrow. We're interested in having fun. And we're not such bad people, either; we're not killing people. But we're not obeying sex laws, either."

Kathleen A. McHale, a graduate of Newton College of the Sacred Heart, Massachusetts, who then went on to Stanford for a Master's degree, said she did read Catholic theologians. "But I have great difficulty doing so. They are dull. Besides that, there's a language problem. I was asked recently to read some ecumenical documents and I started with one by Pope John. I was so offended that I had to put it down. The language of the Church is really offensive. It's not very direct. There's a restraint even in the most modern theologians, because they are trying to talk to the older Church. This is a restraint which is not easy for me to adjust to. Rage operates much more freely in my mind than a desire to communicate."

Discussion of language quickly led to honesty of expression, and here the comments were still more devastating. "Many theologians have a valid point to make," said Mary Frances Campion, an alumna of Rosary College, River Forest, Illinois, and a graduate student at Temple University, "but they ensconce it in verbal compromise so that it won't be too offensive to the powers that be. Students are very aware of this tactic; they can spot this kind of phoniness a mile away."

Frank Carling added an important distinction. "We [young people] wish that President Johnson would lie less, but at the same time we know a political figure must present his case in the best light possible, and that often borders on duplicity of some kind or another. But in the religious sphere, we expect no equivocating. So when you have Pope Paul saying that the Church is not significantly divided on birth control, or not divided to the point where the issue is in doubt, we get turned off. His is an obvious lie. You see, we expect religious issues not to be treated the same as political issues; we expect the supernatural not to be pleaded the same way a dubious political cause might be. If the man who is the official pronouncer, guardian, and proclaimer of the supernatural truths finds it necessary to lie or to tamper with supernatural truths, it is understandable that students should regard the values they are intended to reflect as irrelevant."

Perhaps the most important part of the symposium was the attempt the participants made to define their relationship to the Catholic Church as an institution. Only one, William Wilson, would write it off totally. "I really don't give a damn what the Church has to say. . . . As far as I'm concerned, it's lost. . . . Leave us alone and we'll leave Church people alone to follow their foolish practices, their superstitions, their Masses. We have a world that has relevance to the way we live."

The others didn't find it necessary to reject the institution, but for most of them acceptance was on their own terms.

"Even on liturgical matters, I don't think anybody any longer cares what the Pope says," was Carling's summing-up.

Kathleen McHale offered a comparison between the hippies, the New Leftists with their parallel institutions, and "radical Catholics my age who are attempting to develop community, either in houses or unions—you find a great deal in common among all. In a way all have dropped out. All have stopped worrying about how you get the archbishop or the President, or the mayor, or anybody, to see your point of view. You just act; as the hippies say, you do your thing."

251

Mary Ann Brazier, an undergraduate at Boston College, interpreted what was happening as a return to the early Church, "the twelve apostles, and Antioch, and small communities." She thought there would always be a universal Church, but not with the present hierarchical structure. Instead, she envisages a situation in which each community will make its own decisions. The source of unity will be not the institution, but faith. Her suggestion produced a very positive response from the others.

"When you read the Gospel concept of Jesus Christ," said Wilson, "he seems to be—pardon the expression—hip, cool, with it. Right? But the Church today is so different from what Christ had in mind; it just doesn't jive. Someone said youth groups resemble the early Church. That's a good observation. We're starting all over again. Christ would have fit right in at a pot party."

The self-righteous attitude of the young, as typified in this symposium, is to doubt everything except themselves. The adult generation is despised. Communication is shut off. What institution—especially one as tradition-bound as the Catholic Church—can possibly adjust fast enough to satisfy their minimum demands? Although, as we have seen, the Catholic Church is wrenching loose from its medieval past and advancing toward a genuine encounter with man in the secular city, it is moving too slowly to interest (much less impress) today's youth. Very little is written or spoken about this in the Church, but it is becoming clearer that a great segment of the current generation is already lost to the Church.

Actually, the disenchantment of the young is one of the ironies of the Catholic revolution. The generation behind the articulate, impassioned young adults of today is another story, but the Church of the immediate future faces not only chaos, which is present in abundance, but collapse as a strong institution. The combination of departure of many of the best priests and sisters and a dearth of vocations to the priesthood and sisterhood will force many religious communities to shut down. A continuance of the ban on contraception, episcopal talking down to people, and stultifying parish life will combine to drive more and more people away from any meaningful connection with the institution. All of these circumstances will eventually hasten the full measure of the reforms that appear tantalizingly elusive today. But the present generation is trapped in the institutional no-man's-land between what was and what will be.

A pastor with a big youth program told me, "We're knocking ourselves out, trying experiments, bringing in speakers, movies, music, and they simply patronize us, smile, and say, 'Don't stay out in the sun too long, Father.' I am very disturbed because I don't exactly understand what is happening. To be emancipated is one thing. To be unbuttoned is another, and I think they are becoming unbuttoned. I think we have the prospect of real chaos with our youth."

At least one expert on the problems of youth and faith isn't baffled at all by the perplexities. He is a slim, mild-mannered theologian, Brother Gabriel Moran, of Manhattan College, who enjoys a growing reputation in the United States. His cool appraisal goes this way: Caught in the crossfire of religion and personality, youth's response to faith must largely be that of either apathy or attack. The one thing about Christianity many young people are sure of is that the Christian faith has nothing to offer, that it shot its bolt long ago in their lives, that it has been tried and found wanting. And the more desperately religious salesmen try to answer all adolescent problems with Christian faith, the more the young people are convinced that faith is hopelessly irrelevant. When religious faith does appear to have something to say, it is not to be trusted, for it has too often lied, mistaking fairy tales for facts and confusing loyalty to ideals with blindness to faults.

Brother Moran suggests that "the breakthrough must come from adult human beings and most preferably from a dedicated Christian community. What those growing up so desperately need is a human being who will take them from where they are, who will believe in them to such an extent that they also will come to believe, who hold on with an adult love that will never overwhelm but will never let go."

The new or "now" generation is frequently accused of rejecting authority and all moral restraints. But the rebellion of the young is more properly against the abuse of authority, and insofar as it is directed against the Church, it is only against that Church which is seen as part of the total hypocritical establishment, as identified with the selfish rich. The young would have no difficulty in identifying with a Church that would take the Sermon on the Mount seriously—such a Church would be identifiable as the servant of Christ. If they are not interested in becoming priests or nuns, it is because they see other ways of service which for them are more meaningful and less encumbered with idle pomp and circumstance.

As for the new morality, the image of large numbers of college students "sleeping around," indiscriminately indulging in sex for kicks and pleasure without any concern for consequences or permanence appears to reflect more the frustrated yearnings of writers and readers than it does actual campus life. A series of studies of sex habits does not reveal a widespread trend to sexual promiscuity among college students. The young person is, of course, subjected to a continual barrage of sexual images in the mass media which reflect this erotic phase of America's history. If a moral collapse is not imminent, Father Joseph L. Walsh, a Paulist chaplain at Brandeis University, notes, "important changes are definitely in progress.

"A person enters college and soon forms closer and more personal relationships with the other sex than before. The urge to express this new intensity; to show, particularly in the girl's case, that she feels more deeply than she did for the high-school friend with whom she tolerated necking; the continued fascination with sex that the culture creates and the freedom that the automobile and urban anonymity provide—all these factors make much more frequent among college students a bodily intimacy and pleasure that in previous times was reserved only for the engaged and married. A line, however, is drawn usually at intercourse. . . . All the studies indicate that among college students intercourse is considered definitely wrong (which doesn't mean indulgence doesn't occur) if love is not involved, possibly right if it is, and definitely allowable if the couples are engaged."

Putting all this together, the doubts, rejections, and anxieties of young Catholics reflect a generation of men and women determined to find their own way to faith. It is a risky route, and certainly they will stumble into a religionless society, a development which the pluralistic character of American society makes not only possible, but attractive. In spite of the ubiquitous and aggressive presence of the institutional Church, the students have learned how to turn off.

I spent some time talking to a Peace Corps volunteer from Oklahoma, a Catholic College graduate who had just returned from a two-year stint in South America. An agrarian expert and economist, he had worked in small villages, teaching people how to make their land productive. With the eagerness of a young professional, he talked about how people's lives were being visibly strengthened by Peace Corps endeavors. He expressed a deep Christian concern for the Latins he had come to know personally.

"What about the Church in this work?" I asked. "How does the Church fit into all these great social issues?"

The question made him pause a minute before answering. "I just haven't thought about the Church lately," he said. "Does the Church really matter in the modern world?"

CHAPTER 10

Education: A Broken Assembly Line

The men and women gathered around the green felt table owned some of the most high-powered names in the American Church. There was Philip Scharper, erudite editor of the prestigious Catholic book-publishing firm, Sheed and Ward; Jacqueline Grennan, the former nun who stays in the headlines as president of the de-institutionalized Webster College; Mary Perkins Ryan, who earned the wrath of Catholic educators for writing a book that said Catholic education was a lot bigger thing than parochial schools; Father Andrew Greeley, sociologist and co-author of the Greeley-Rossi report on Catholic schools, which was the first significant analysis ever made of a system that educates one out of every seven Americans in elementary and high schools and costs two billion dollars a year.

They were part of a team of 120 invited experts who came to a motel on the outskirts of Washington, D.C., to draw up a blueprint for the future of Catholic education. The extent of the reappraisal of everything Catholic today is remarkably apparent in the field of education, which is in a deep ideological and financial crisis.

"What *is* the role of the Catholic school today?" one of

the symposium participants asked. "To form the intellect, or to form the whole individual?"

"We are vague on the rationale for our schools," a priest said. "Should our schools be a witness—and a witness to what?"

Jacqueline Grennan spoke up: "You can best prepare Christians for involvement in the modern world by educating them in a Christian environment, but you can't let the Catholic school remain a ghetto box."

Another priest challenged the implication that Catholic school children are ghettoized.

Then the committed yet detached Scharper spoke. "We should be asking ourselves, will our schools fulfill the needs ten years from now? What will future sisters be like? What about the laity? Will they send their children to the kind of schools we now have?"

For five days the debate raged as conflicting opinions were voiced. The Church is spending more and more money to educate an elite group, relegating millions of Catholic children to "second-class" status. The strength of the Church in America is directly attributable to parochial schools. What about giving a Christian education to Negroes in the Inner City? Where will the sisters come from? We need fiscal accountability by the bishops. Get out of the total education business. Stay in.

In the end, the experts could say little except to recommend an increase in research. Their debate served, however, to focus on the corner into which Catholic education has painted itself. Throughout America, thinking Catholics are asking, ever more insistently: What good is it all doing? What difference would it make if the Church got out of education entirely? What greater benefits might be reaped by putting the same people, money, and effort into alternative activities?

John Carroll, first Catholic bishop of the United States,

admonished his scattered little flock in 1792 to make provision for "the pious and Catholic education of the young." A series of provincial and plenary councils of the American bishops in the 19th century proclaimed the ideal that every Catholic child should be in a Catholic school. That ideal was, of course, never realized.

In round figures, six million students are attending Catholic schools and colleges: 4.4 million in 11,000 grade schools, 1.1 million in 2,400 high schools, 430,000 in 325 universities and colleges, and 45,000 seminarians in 450 seminaries. It is an operation without precedent or parallel either in the Catholic Church or in any other Church. Except for the most minimal marginal aid from public funds in the form of school lunches, busing of students, and similar fringe benefits in some parts of the country, the operation is financed entirely by the Catholic community. The cost averages out to $375 per student annually, or about $200 for every Catholic family in the country, including those who have no children in the Catholic schools.

Other countries which have substantial numbers of Catholic schools depend on the state to absorb all or most of the cost. In eight of the ten Canadian provinces, for example, the provincial governments allocate to Church-related schools a representative proportion of school taxes. In Britain, the Church pays most of the cost of school construction, but the state pays the operating cost, which is very much bigger. Today in the United States, for example, a 12-room grammar school will cost about $1 million to build, but $250,000 a year to run.

Just over half (52 percent) of Catholic children of grade-school age are in Catholic schools, while only 35 percent of Catholic children attending high school are in Catholic high schools. At the college level, the proportion is much lower and falling rapidly. In the past ten years it dropped from 29 to 24 percent. There is no likelihood of the proportion of Catholic students in Catholic grade and high schools increasing; rather, it is reasonably safe to predict that it will decline steadily. This will result primarily from the impact of the financial costs. While the intellectuals have begun to ask whether Catholic schools are effective instruments of education, their answers are unlikely to influence trends for at least 10 or 15 years. One force already at work is the demand from parents for an education in Catholic schools at least as good as that provided in the parallel public schools, at a time when public-school costs are mounting rapidly and the Catholic system has reached the effective limits of its budgets.

One insistent demand is for more parochial-school teachers in order to reduce the size of classes to the usual norm followed in public schools. Another is the upgrading of teacher qualifications to match that of the public-school teachers. Simultaneously, the number of nuns available as teachers is expected to decrease, both because of the need to improve their professional preparation and because of the declining intake of new nuns.

The proportion of lay teachers in Catholic schools has grown substantially over the past decade, with an increase in costs not nearly as great as had been calculated. The reason was that the nun had cost considerably more than her nominal salary, the balance of her living costs being absorbed by the parish at large, while the lay teacher was paid a salary considerably lower than that of the public-school teacher. A natural consequence of this arrangement, of course, was that the Catholic school tended to get teachers with inferior qualifications, and this is something that the Catholic parent is less and less willing to accept.

Cost must always be related to performance. In order to determine how much American Catholics will or should invest in Catholic education, they must first decide what benefits it provides. The traditionally formulated answer has been that separate schools are necessary in order to protect and develop the Catholic faith of the young. The Vatican Council reaffirmed a long series of official statements to this effect.

The Declaration on Christian Education said, "The Church's involvement in the field of education is demonstrated especially by the Catholic school. No less than other schools does the Catholic school pursue cultural goals and the natural development of youth. But it has several distinctive purposes. It aims to create for the school community an atmosphere enlivened by the gospel spirit of freedom and charity. It aims to help the adolescent in such a way that the development of his own personality will be matched by the growth of that new creation which he became by baptism. It strives to relate all human culture eventually to the news of salvation, so that the light of faith will illumine the knowledge which the students gradually gain of the world, of life, and of mankind. . . .

"The Catholic school retains its immense importance in the circumstances of our times. . . . As for Catholic parents, the Council calls to mind their duty to entrust their children to Catholic schools, when and where this is possible, to support such schools to the extent of their ability, and to work along with them for the welfare of their children."

Catholics probably needed their own Church-related schools in order to attain these objectives in the United States in the 19th century, when Catholics were 10 percent of a population overwhelmingly hostile to their faith and anxious to maintain them in the lower social strata to which most of them belonged. But it is doubtful if the religious motive alone would have stirred Catholics to the enormous sacrifices they made to build their school system, were it not for the social benefits it simultaneously provided. These were significant from the outset, particularly for the Irish and the Germans who reached the country in great numbers in the second half of the century, and who utilized the Catholic schools to protect their Catholic-ethnic identity. A similar function was performed in the first quarter of the 20th century for Italians, Poles, and other Europeans.

In each case, the school played a vital part in the first settlement of the group and its gradual absorption into the mainstream of society, leaving behind its language and other distinctive characteristics, intermarrying, extending its range of occupations and moving up the socio-economic ladder into the professions and the business community.

This gradual process was largely completed by the middle of the 20th century, with an expansion of Catholic colleges and universities to the point where Catholics now share in the sophistication, the intellectual orientation and the educational concerns that characterize the American upper-middle class. The result is that today the typical Catholic has most of the features of the typical middle-class American. His sense of ethnic isolation is slight. He is not distinguished by occupation, income, or status.

Somewhat ironically, the objections that used to be raised by other Americans against the Catholic schools are being progressively muted as it becomes apparent that Catholics will have to divert a bigger proportion of their students to the public schools, thereby augmenting the tax bill for education. The biggest protest used to be that Catholic schools were divisive, that they inevitably taught prejudice against other religious bodies and against ethnic and socio-economic groups who were underrepresented in their ranks.

The criticism, if founded, is an obviously serious one in a pluralist society. But lack of a serious objective foundation has been conclusively established by sociologists Andrew M. Greeley and Peter H. Rossi in a report prepared in 1963-64 under the auspices of the National Opinion Research Center of the University of Chicago. They compared Catholics with an all-Catholic education, Catholics educated in public schools, and Protestants of a comparable level of education. There was no major difference in the three groups on attitudes regarding civil liberties, anti-Semitism, or racial justice. Insofar as differences do exist, Catholics with an all-Catholic education tend to be more liberal and less anti-Semitic.

Catholic education has performed its social function so well, in fact, that it has become superfluous. The United States still has depressed ethnic groups, but the Catholic school is not deeply involved with any of them. Although Negroes make up 12 percent of the United States population, they are only 1.1 percent of the Catholic population. At one time Negro parents in city slums preferred the Catholic school because they believed it provided a better education than the public school. That day is gone, however, and the Negro now finds himself more at home in the public school than in the Catholic one. Strangely, the same is true of the Puerto Ricans, Cubans, and Mexicans, all traditionally Catholic, which is an ironic reflection on the success of the Catholic schools in instilling American middle-class standards in their students and alumni—that is to say, inoculating them with the white racism that the United States Riot Commission said is "essentially responsible" for present-day racial conflict.

In fact, says Monsignor James C. Donohue, education director of the United States Catholic Conference, many Catholic schools are segregated both North and South along racial and economic-class lines. "Schools in the big cities are more segregated today than they were in 1954 when the Supreme Court outlawed segregation. We are increasingly serving a middle-class and upper-middle-class school population."

Catholics long ago joined the rush to the suburbs, leaving behind inner-city schools (452 were closed in 1966) with fewer pupils and a higher proportion of economically depressed families. Thousands of sisters have come to the sudden realization that they are wasting their time teaching secular subjects in lily-white suburbia when they could and should be bringing the love and lessons of Christ to disadvantaged children in the Inner City. Nuns are thus becoming increasingly uncomfortable in the security of suburbia, especially as the concept of the Church as a perpetual missionary to the poor becomes more deeply imbedded in Catholic life.

The Catholic school system is in danger of being preserved as an institution rather than for its Christian message. Yet through programs of sharing in some dioceses, the parishes of suburbia are contributing to the support of the inner-city Catholic schools. And to complete the riddle of Catholic education, Catholic parents in suburbia are paying for their own schools, and sending excess money to the inner-city parochial schools that educate many non-Catholic children entitled to free education in public schools.

I visited one such inner-city parish, St. Agnes in Detroit, which contained 2,500 families in its heyday but now cannot even muster 400. The whites have fled the area, which was caught up in the 1967 summer riots. Although not more than 2 or 3 percent of the Negroes in the area are Catholics, according to the pastor, Father John Markham, the aging parochial school appeals to the more stable element of Negroes.

"If we closed the school," Father Markham says, "it would be the complete abandonment of the Catholic presence." Tuition is $50 per family for the year. Combined tuition payments for all students are only enough to meet the annual salaries of two of the teachers in the school. The subsidy from the inter-parish sharing fund keeps the school going.

With white/black attitudes hardening all the time, no

one talks of integration any more. The traditional Saturday night confessions have been abandoned because people are afraid to go out at night. Prostitution is flourishing. Fathers simply disappear. And the number of emotionally disturbed children is rapidly rising.

"The future of the Church in the Inner City is one of leaven, certainly not triumphalism," says the pastor. "We just make the Church present, not necessarily to have the Negroes become Catholic, but to help them reach for dignity and rights. As long as the nuns and the money come, we can keep it up. Maybe nuns who are now leaving their orders because they want to work in the social apostolate will come here in greater numbers. But even with that, the major handicap remains—the nuns are white. There is only one Negro priest in the archdiocese."

In the Inner City then, the Church is the school. What is needed most of all to keep going, Father Markham added with a grin, is the quality of "failability." "We are going to fail plenty of times, but we have to keep on trying."

Forward-minded educators in the Catholic school system are trying to divert a greater share of resources to the Inner City.

"It would be cowardly to shrink from trying, to consign another generation to the frozen attitudes that have imprisoned our own," warns Monsignor Donohue.

In the view of Robert J. Havighurst, professor of urban education at Fordham, "unconventional procedures" are needed, such as stepping up federally supported programs (like Head Start) for socially disadvantaged pre-schoolers. He sees the possibility of grants of public funds to non-public schools that have proved their ability to specialize in programs for the socially disadvantaged. "The courts would probably find it in the public interest to use government funds through private and even church agencies so as to better serve disadvantaged children and youth."

The issue of public funds for non-public schools is the thorniest question facing the Catholic system, because if Catholic schools cannot share in the Federal aid to elementary and secondary education that seems sure to come, then the Catholic struggle to match public-school quality will become hopeless.

However, if Catholic schools hope to obtain Federal aid, says Philip Des Marais, a top government official, they will have to show Washington that they are more than religious indoctrination centers.

Who would really control the public money used by Catholic schools? The bishops and their priest superintendents are not likely to be able to retain sole control of administration and policy. And without public accountability, there will certainly be no public money. From a tradition of Catholic schools being the preserve of bishops, pastors, and sisters, it is now easy to see that the laity will soon have a major responsibility in running the schools. Through the expediency of hard cash, the goal of Vatican II's lay responsibility is being reached.

"A truly radical restructuring process" has been proposed by two officials of the National Catholic Education Association, Father C. A. Koob, executive secretary, and Russell Shaw, director of editorial services. Pointing out that other social services are now planned and administered largely at the diocesan level, they propose a financial and administrative pooling for grade schools leading to a rationalization and specialization of their services.

They offer the example of how a specific geographical area could be better served. Suppose, for example, that in one area there are four neighboring parishes, each with its own school. Koob and Russell would unite the educational interests of the four parishes and save money in the following way:

School "A" could become a non-graded school for kindergarten and the first four grades; school "B" could convert to a middle school offering departmental instruction of a kind few isolated parish schools can now provide. School "C" could be closed down entirely, and school "D" would be transformed into a resource center providing special services, especially Confraternity of Christian Doctrine (CCD) programs for children attending public schools.

A reform of such modest dimensions would run into considerable opposition from pastors and nuns accustomed to running their own shows, and from many old-style parishioners for whom the school, even more than the Church itself, is the symbol of their achievement. Most of those who have studied the issues, however, view it as a bare minimum program for immediate implementation, and the number of those who seek to move gradually to a more radical solution is growing. I stress the word *gradually* because everyone involved agrees that the Catholic education system in the United States is a phenomenon of such dimensions that its quick elimination would upset the equilibrium not only of the Catholic Church but of the entire public-education system.

The question being asked with increasing insistence is whether the kind of goal set by Koob and Shaw is adequate. Now that the social function formerly performed by Catholic schools has ceased to be important, a closer look is being taken at their contribution to what was always proclaimed to be their primary function—the imparting of a Catholic education to all Catholic children. One part of the answer is clear. They reach only a small and diminishing proportion of Catholic children. And a further element is becoming clearer. The concentration of personnel, money, and effort in this sector leaves a minimum of resources for the major and growing segment of the student population.

At issue is the definition of Catholic education. At one time, it was fashionable to argue that only one method existed for ensuring an education that could properly be called Catholic. This was to teach the child everything he learned, from mathematics to languages, in a Catholic framework. Ideally, the arithmetic problems should be calculations of the number of days of indulgences to be gained by certain types of devotions, and the French conversation should involve pilgrimages to Lisieux and Lourdes. The central part of this process was religious instruction, which meant the memorizing of formulas and logical categories from the Baltimore Catechism.

Such a definition automatically assumed the impossibility of giving a Catholic education to children not attending Catholic schools. This, of course, ran counter to experience, an experience scientifically confirmed by a series of sociological studies, of which the most often quoted is the Greeley-Rossi survey. The studies have not negated the value of Catholic schools; but they place them in a relative perspective. Greeley and Rossi found, for example, that Catholic education has its greatest impact on students from devoutly religious families who go exclusively to Catholic schools and colleges. Classroom religion, however, is no substitute for home example, and non-school influences can compensate in a large measure for an education conducted completely outside a Catholic school environment.

Two other factors have also changed. One is the assumption that the child acquired his general education in science, mathematics, languages, and similar subjects either in a pro-Catholic or in an anti-Catholic environment. This assumption undoubtedly had some validity in the 19th century, but is totally at variance with the contemporary scene in the United States. Textbooks, techniques, and emotional attitudes of teachers toward such subjects today are virtually indistinguishable in the average public school and average Catholic school.

The second changed factor concerns the teaching of religion. Since Vatican II, the emphasis has changed from memorization and logical argument to an awareness that faith precedes intellectual assent and comes through contact with Christ in the Christian community. Spiritual growth, in this understanding, depends more on experience than on learning. It begins before school and continues through one's entire life.

Assuming the presence of the proper environment in the pre-school years and in adulthood, a Catholic school environment would undoubtedly be a benefit. But if it is the only religious factor in a person's life, it is largely wasted, and this is precisely the conclusion of the Greeley-Rossi studies. Furthermore, a more inquiring approach to dogma and ethics is encouraged, and the student is no longer expected to accept and learn by rote.

Whatever resources the Catholic Church has available for educating its members should be distributed more equitably for the benefit of all, rather than just those who can gain entrance to parochial schools. Such a step would involve a transfer of much of the present effort from Catholic schools providing general education for some, to a wide-scale program of religious education of Catholic students in public grade and high schools. The resources of Newman Centers in universities would have to be augmented. Also, there would have to be a renewed effort to educate adults in order to develop their own spiritual lives and ensure a Christian home atmosphere for their children.

"The Catholic educational system has become a huge obstacle preventing the Church from fulfilling its true educational responsibility," John Cogley has commented. Even admitting that Catholic schools are better than public schools, he says, this is beside the point. "The point is that they are a massive diversion from the apostolic and pastoral mission of the Church. The critics of the system are not asking the Church to get out of education but to reconsider its basic educational task and broaden its concern to include all Catholics."

One parish that has made its decision in these terms is Westhampton Beach, Long Island, New York. Having first polled the 600 parish families, the pastor named a 15-man committee that included real estate experts, contractors, and lawyers. They rejected a school and convent that would have cost $1 million (and would have created a big debt without guaranteeing a desk for every Catholic child) in favor of a $400,000 parish center in which only religion will be taught. Among the advantages cited by Monsignor James J. Griffin, the pastor, is that his "all-CCD" parish, by relying mainly on lay people as teachers of religion, will create obligations for parents far weightier than ironing a school uniform or signing a report card. It will also eliminate "the first- and second-class citizenship of many parishes" which offer parochial education to some Catholic children and CCD teaching to the others who must go to public school, often creating social disunity, particularly among teenagers. This and similar solutions are being applied to an increasing extent across the country.

The St. Louis suburb of Webster Groves is a placid, grassy, antiseptic community embracing, as far as the visitor's eye can see, all the comforts of modern America. The pride of the town is Webster College which, on the surface, appears to be a high-class finishing school for Catholic young ladies. Actually, it is an aggressive idea factory run by Jacqueline Grennan, whom we met in Chapter 8. Webster's 1,000 girls are as likely to find their "classes" in slums, mental hospitals, and county political activities as in the traditional theology seminars. In an atmosphere of ferment and freedom, discussions between faculty and students bubble from morning till night with a constant drive to adapt ghetto Catholic thinking to "the real world."

The wide latitude of Webster's operation was not enough, however, for Jacqueline Grennan, who led the college out of the control of the Sisters of Loretto, and even out of the institutional control of the Catholic Church. The manner in which she won the approval of the late Cardinal Ritter of St. Louis and the Vatican for the move, which shocked the whole Church, is a testimony to her political skill.

Because she believes there is an inherent contradiction between academic freedom and hierarchical control, Miss Grennan made Webster a legally secular institution with a Christian presence. She herself left the convent and reverted to lay status, underscoring the new secularity of Webster. Is this the wave of the future? Catholics everywhere asked.

Shortly after this spectacular transformation, some of the biggest names in the U.S. Catholic university world—St. Louis, Notre Dame, and Fordham—announced plans to change their manner of operation. No longer would the religious communities that run these institutions retain exclusive ownership and control over policy. Instead, boards of trustees responsible to civil authorities would exercise control. Unlike Webster, however, these universities intend to retain their denominational character.

These changes add up to the most sweeping innovations in the history of Catholic higher education. And it is now clear that Catholic institutions have finally embarked on the process undergone much earlier by universities and colleges established by or affiliated with Protestant Churches. This process has, by now, integrated most Protestant-related institutes of higher learning into the general university structure of the United States.

Almost all Catholic colleges were established by religious orders and staffed mainly by priests, brothers, and nuns. They started out in the last century with a regime little different from that found in a seminary, and there was strict control over all activities of students—academic and non-academic alike. The societal pressures of the United States gradually imposed some relaxation of the semi-monastic regime, but the big breakthrough came only in the wake of World War II.

The G.I. Bill of Rights increased enormously the number of applicants, and the colleges packed their classrooms, rushed through crash expansion programs, and hired great numbers of lay teachers to meet the demand for larger faculty staffs. Veterans, many of them married, were not ready to be treated like children. Lay professors had a sense of American conventions different from that of the priests and nuns. And deans of discipline were responsible for so many students that the latter became numbers in a register. The combined effect of these factors was to transform the climate of the Catholic college, reducing significantly the educational and sociological differences between it and the typical American college.

Vatican II arrived in the 1960s just in time to catalyze all the new elements. The lay people who had previously been thought of as emergency junior aides on the teaching staff, to be replaced by a priest or a nun when one became available, gradually achieved equal academic status and acquired a voice in the decision-making process in their area of competence. It was a hard struggle, but by the mid-1960s the figures were decisive. Lay people constituted more than 80 percent of the entire teaching staff of Catholic universities and colleges for men and just under half of the teaching staff of universities and colleges for women.

The next step has been the sharing of administrative control with lay trustees representing the general community which the particular institute served. The presence of some laymen on boards of Catholic colleges is not new. The practice goes back to the last century in the case of such well-known institutes as Fordham University, Villanova University, Manhattan College, the College of St. Thomas in St. Paul (Minnesota), and St. Francis College in Brooklyn. But what is new is the trend toward transferring control and even (in the case of Webster) ownership to a body other than the religious order that founded a given institution.

What is behind these new changes? Money, of course. When the Maryland Court of Appeals ruled that three state grants to church-affiliated colleges were invalid (and the U.S. Supreme Court allowed the decision to stand), it was widely predicted that the eligibility of any sectarian institution for Federal grants would be challenged. Without Federal and state assistance, the financial problems of Catholic institutions would reach staggering proportions. So finances have provided the impetus for speedy change.

But the roots of the change are much deeper and are entangled in the conflict of interest between the educational institution and the religious community that owns it. Different rules apply to each and, as a matter of fact, they belong in different leagues. Catholic colleges that depend on the cloister for their administrative talent are drifting further away from the mainstream of American education.

"A blank check on the state treasury or Federal reserve," notes Father Neil G. McCluskey, a Jesuit education expert, "would not solve problems like the dominance of religious orders, reliance on old-world tradition, amateurish administration, short-sighted financial policies, confusion between the pastoral and academic areas, insulation from the main stream of contemporary thought, lack of definition of purpose."

In short, religious paternalism is out of place in the university community. And the intellectual thrust of the Vatican Council, with its explosive aftermath, spotlighted the anachronism of a religious community running an educational institution as a law unto itself. In their post-conciliar reevaluation, it became clear to many that the norms, values, and administrative styles of the typical religious community are far from appropriate to an American university. The training of the priest or nun is not conducive to producing an aggressive and efficient administrator. The reference group of one is his religious community, while that of the other should be his professional associates.

The specific point at which the conflict between the administrator as member of a religious order and the administrator as member of the academic community came into open and violent conflict was academic freedom.

Following an age-long formulation, all the other disciplines were subject to philosophy as the queen of the sciences; philosophy, in turn, was subject to theology interpreted as a direct line to the formulator of truths in language fixed once and for all and covering all things actual and possible.

Vatican II swept away the foundation for this simplistic stance. It proclaimed that the Church's pastors didn't always have the answer to everything, that the Church was involved with the rest of mankind in the unending search for truth, that truth was to be revered above institutional advantages, and that man had to be free in his search for truth.

The Catholic university was thus compelled to confront a basic issue. Is it possible for a university to be free and Catholic at the same time? Can it be open to all points of view, all modes of enquiry, without jeopardizing its Catholicism? If there is an "official" Catholic position in possession, can other views claim equal time?

From being speculative, the issue became dramatically concrete on April 17, 1967, when Bishop William J. McDonald, the Irish-born rector of the Catholic University of America in Washington, D.C., fired Father Charles E. Curran, 33-year-old associate professor of theology. In an unprecedented action, faculty and students immediately joined in a strike that shut down the university until the board of trustees rescinded the rector's action—an action originally taken with their approval.

The previous October, Father Curran had been questioned by university officials about some of his theological views (particularly his open approach to birth control) but no charge had been laid. The board of trustees had, however, named three conservative prelates, Archbishop (now Cardinal) John Krol of Philadelphia, Archbishop Philip Hannan of New Orleans, and Bishop McDonald as a committee to investigate Father Curran's orthodoxy.

Without presenting specific charges or giving him an opportunity to defend himself, the committee recommended that he be dropped from the staff just after the School of Theology faculty and the full Academic Senate of the university had recommended him for promotion. The board of trustees reportedly approved the recommendation 28 to 1, with only the late Archbishop Paul J. Hallinan of Atlanta dissenting. All the trustees are bishops, chosen by and responsible to the conference of bishops of the United States.

When Father Curran was notified, he protested that the action was a violation of both the letter and the spirit of the *motu proprio* of Pope Paul VI, *Integrae servandae,* which grants controversial authors a hearing and a full opportunity of defending themselves. He also insisted that if there were to be a hearing, he should be judged by his theological peers and have counsel present. University regulations provide that a professor can be dismissed only if found guilty of teaching heresy, or of immorality.

When the news became public, the 600 full-time faculty members were summoned to a faculty assembly, and nearly 500 attended. With only 18 objecting, a resolution to boycott classes until Father Curran was reinstated was adopted. It said that the action of the trustees had put Catholic University "outside the academic community" and "raised grave questions for the continuation of Catholic higher education in America, in the minds and hearts of Catholic teachers and students over the entire country." The academic competence and integrity of the faculty and the Senate had been called in question, it said, and "the academic freedom of the man, of the faculty of the School (of Sacred Theology), and of the whole university is thereby jeopardized to the peril of its reputation, accreditation and academic standing."

Meanwhile, led by the 360 seminarians and student priests of the School of Theology, the students began mass demonstrations on campus. The university remained closed from April 20 until Bishop McDonald announced on April 24 that the board of trustees had rescinded its decision. This followed public statements from Cardinals Shehan of Baltimore and Cushing of Boston, and of Archbishop Hallinan and Bishop Thomas Connolly of Seattle taking exception to the board's earlier action.

The Curran affair did not, of course, settle once and for all the issue of academic freedom on Catholic campuses. It did not even define the term. No theological question was raised or settled, but only a question of procedure. There was no explicit law preventing the trustees from refusing to renew Father Curran's contract, and what the incident showed was that there is a spirit of the law which can and will be enforced even when the letter is not explicit.

As David M. Knight, a Jesuit student at the university, put it, "The demonstrators—and the bishops—recognized that conscience is broader than law. Here is the breakthrough of our age."

The unanimity of opinion in the Catholic academic community—both clerical and lay—in favor of Father Curran will make any religious superior or bishop extremely cautious from now on in handling issues involving academic freedom. Enlightened paternalism, of course, is only a stopgap. The real advance has been charted by John J. McGrath, a priest holding degrees in civil and canon law, who has done a penetrating study of the legality of Catholic institutions.

American Catholic institutions of higher learning receive their charters not from the Holy See or the Roman Congregation of Seminaries and Universities, but by the acts of the particular states in which they are located.

"The legal title to the real and personal property is vested in the corporation," says Father McGrath. "If anyone owns the assets of the charitable or educational institutions, it is the general public. Failure to appreciate this fact has led to the mistaken idea that the property of the institution is the property of the sponsoring body." Thus, their boards of trustees should represent the general public. Staff personnel, including religious, should be subject to the same hiring and firing procedures used in civil institutions. "The indiscriminate placement or removal of religious personnel violates sound management principles and reflects upon their professional integrity."

The transfer of control at St. Louis, Notre Dame, and Fordham implements the McGrath thesis. I spoke to Father Paul J. Reinert, Jesuit president of St. Louis, shortly after his congregation empowered an autonomous board of eighteen laymen and ten Jesuits.

"It's important to realize that the religious communities are not giving up the universities but are sharing their control with the public," he said. "Modern higher education is too important, too complicated and too costly for a religious community to bear the sole responsibility."

"But isn't this development just a step along the way to the complete break that Webster has made?" I asked Father Reinert.

He said he did not think many colleges would follow

Webster in a complete religious disaffiliation. "It's harder to justify being in education if the religious link is lost. I think we can make a unique contribution by being a private Church-related college."

He stresses the absolute separation at St. Louis between the Jesuit community and the university administration. This will satisfy the demands of accrediting associations and the dispensers of public funds and thus enable updated institutions to be Catholic and public at the same time.

Despite the rapidity and extent of the changes, nagging suspicions still abound that there is an irreconcilable conflict between Church and academic freedom. A Catholic university, George Bernard Shaw said, is a contradiction in terms. Harvey Cox, leading exponent of a theology of the secular city, says, "The idea of developing Christian universities in America was bankrupt before it began." And Jacqueline Grennan summarizes her philosophy, "The very nature of higher education is opposed to juridical control by the Church."

But Father Theodore Hesburgh, president of Notre Dame, widely regarded as the foremost Catholic university in the land, says the word "universal" provides a key to the answer. Catholic means universal, he says. This universality is emphasized by engaging theology on the highest level of intellectual inquiry so that it may be in living dialogue with all other disciplines in the university.

"The presence of philosophy and theology," he says, "simply completes the total field of inquiry, raises additional and ultimate questions, moves every scholar to look beyond his immediate field of vision to the total landscape of God and man and the universe."

As to the practicalities of the Grennan objection, Hesburgh emphasizes that Notre Dame's new form of administration makes it a civil, nonprofit, educational corporation, chartered by and operating under the civil law of the

State of Indiana, totally directed by a largely lay board of trustees.

"To describe this as 'juridic control by the Church' would be simply untrue," he states.

The fact that the minority of priests on the campus wish to place their personal lives under the juridic control of the Church does not detract from professional academic freedom. Then Hesburgh, who has undoubtedly joined an intellectual renaissance to the resurgence of the football fortunes of the Fighting Irish, underscores this passage from Vatican II's Constitution on the Church in the Modern World as his guide:

"In order that they may fulfill their function, let it be recognized that all the faithful, whether clerical or lay, possess a lawful freedom of inquiry, freedom of thought and freedom of expressing their mind with humility and fortitude in those matters in which they enjoy competence."

Still, the theoretical issue of the relationship of theology as an autonomous academic discipline with the teaching authority of the Catholic Church is not totally resolved. There will be continuing friction until bishops and professors get to know each other better. Seminary-trained bishops have not experienced true academic life, and few professors understand how much importance the bishops assign to their role as guardians of the faith. If there is to be true intellectual dialogue on a Catholic campus, it cannot be achieved with one ideology inevitably destined for victory. This spells the end of protectionism.

The Hesburgh approach was significantly buttressed by twenty-six leaders in Catholic higher education who met at Land O'Lakes, Wisconsin, in 1967. The group's manifesto declared the Catholic university "must have true autonomy and academic freedom in the face of authority of whatever kind, lay or clerical, external to the academic community itself."

Accordingly, theological investigation must serve the ecumenical goals of collaboration and unity. There must be no outlawed books or subjects. The Catholic university must objectively criticize the Church.

To say all this, the educators summed up, "is simply to assert that institutional autonomy and academic freedom are essential conditions of life and growth and, indeed, of survival for Catholic universities as for all universities."

CHAPTER 11

A Pilgrim's Theology

A confrontation of theologians and hippies seems, on the surface, to offer little but a bizarre contrast in the divergencies of man. The one formally probes deeper into God's continuing revelation of himself; the other reveals a rejection of traditional forms in a new search for reality.

The two were thrust into coexistence briefly in August, 1967, when the Canadian bishops sponsored a theology congress that attracted the leading theologians in the Catholic Church. A constellation of forty-five experts and some 2,000 delegates assembled at the University of Toronto, whose campus engulfs Queen's Park, a hippie hangout. Each evening as the delegates flowed across the park, they could hear the hippies haltingly express their simple philosophy of love, non-violence, and scorning of middle-class values, including clean shirts, shoes, and haircuts.

"Christ is hip," a bearded young man proclaimed as a staid group of clerics in black suits stopped to listen. "Love, love, love" was his message.

During one of the lectures, an "elderly" hippie (he turned out to be 32) was observed sitting cross-legged on the floor. At the intermission, he was on his feet, asking for attention. Scattered applause and an occasional murmur of annoyance greeted his request.

The hippie explained why his friends were demonstrating in the park: they wanted an end to police brutality. He asked the theologians for their support. Most of them turned and left, but a group of priests stayed and took the hippie to dinner.

They were impressed: "He was great . . . he spoke seriously about the Bible and Jesus and love . . . the importance of loving people and treating them as individuals . . . you'd think he was a mystic."

Most of the hippies, with iconoclasm as their only weapon, simply ignored the passing strangers as if they were relics from another age. The theologians and delegates, for the most part, regarded the cult as an embarrassing intrusion on the world of erudition. The brief coexistence pointed up a valuable lesson. The professional theologians may be tuned in to the theory of the modern world, but the modern world is turning off a structured, incomprehensible religion.

Neither the hippies nor the theologians, by any means, speak for the full range of modern man. In fact, the hippies will doubtless evolve into some other form of social protest. But they do illustrate, even in their extremes, a growing rejection by modern man of religious forms that he believes are barriers to some far-off reality. Modern man still retains the respectability of a clean shirt and shoes, but he, too, increasingly questions the artificiality of so many of the forms in which religion has wrapped itself.

As one looks around the Christian churches on a Sunday morning, there is still strong evidence of a religious assent, at least in the cultural habit of physical presence. The crowded parking lots do not reveal, however, the interior questioning going on in many minds. Is God real for me? How do I talk to God? What does Christ really mean? What about my world, my job, my family, my worries—where does Christ fit into all these things?

These are the questions that the modern theologians are continually bringing to light as they try to strip away outdated cultural forms so that the timeless presence of a loving God becomes clear to men of all generations, colors, and mentalities. In their common search for the real thing (whether through diligent intellectual pursuit or the various forms of social protest), modern theology and modern man are more intimately linked than they have been in centuries.

Theology now takes into consideration all the learning in the avenues of modern life before making its judgments. But the verbalization of this theology is so formidable that it hovers as a cloud over the rushing, perplexed, pressured man of the 20th century instead of piercing through his confusion like a shaft of light. The impact of the communications media on the mysterious world of theology is only gradually forcing theologians to bridge the language gap between what they are saying and what everybody else understands.

There is more to this than just popularization. For the theology that now exists in the Catholic Church seems capable of ending forever the Counter-Reformation split of man into two parts—sacred and secular, holy and worldly, preserved and contaminated. The progressive theology that gave a foundation to the Second Vatican Council enables the Christian and the secular to become one. The modern Christian finds his holiness in the creativity of the world. The world is where he expresses his Christ-like humanity. The world is where he works out his redemption. The institutional Church teaches and guides and consoles him. But it does not smother or blind or constrict him. The Church is not in one corner, like a filling station, with the world a racetrack. The Church is not a supreme court, much less a detective agency. It is an animator, a leaven. World and Church are joined, with the Church developing new forms and styles just as the world progresses from age to age.

The Church of the new theology does not depend on power, pomp, or circumstance, but is a continuing witness and manifestation of God's presence in human affairs. The new Church, then, serves mankind out of genuine love, inspiring man to love his brother so that the completeness of human love will evoke a response to God's call to eternal love. The whole struggle of the Catholic revolution centers on this point: making this new concept of God's dynamic message to the world a living reality fast enough to show modern man that the Church can help him in his urgent search for inner peace, social justice, and love of something greater than himself.

The new theology burst into the open with the Council when churchmen, previously silenced by the Holy Office, suddenly swept into Rome and expounded their views to admiring and amazed bishops. These bishops in the remoteness of their far-flung dioceses had been vaguely aware that many things they were saying no longer made much sense. It was only at the Council that the many private opinions coalesced into a public opinion of such strength as to prevent further suppression.

The shocked defenders of unbending orthodoxy did not yield without a struggle. Various progressive theologians were forbidden by curial authorities to set foot in Rome during the Council sessions, only to be brought there by bishops as their advisers. Bookstores in Rome were forbidden to display their works. Superior generals of religious orders were warned to protect their subjects from the suspect teachings of such thinkers as Yves Congar, Karl Rahner, Hans Kung, and Joseph Ratzinger.

As was seen in Chapter 1, the heresy-hunting was resumed

after the bishops scattered at the end of the Council. However, the 1967 Synod of Bishops may have put a final end to the Curia's efforts to freeze theological thought in the static molds of the late Scholastics and Counter-Reformation.

Incredible as it seems today, the institutional Church was highly successful in maintaining thought-control until a few years ago. In the open society of the United States, anyone who suggested ten years back that the Friday abstinence was an idiosyncrasy of a subculture without religious significance, and should therefore be abolished, would have been stigmatized as having lost touch with the mind of the Church.

Liturgists like Father H. A. Reinhold and the Benedictines of Collegeville were dismissed as crackpots when they urged changes far more moderate than those to be shortly approved by the Council. In the early 1950s Catholics were expressly forbidden to have anything to do with the meeting of the World Council of Churches in Evanston, Illinois. And all his life Father John Courtney Murray, S.J., was regarded as suspect for propagating the views that the Council would write into its Declaration on Religious Freedom.

Also, in the early 1950s, there was living in obscurity in New York a man known to only a handful of Catholics. He had written many books. In obedience to his Jesuit superiors, however, the significant ones remained unpublished until after his death in 1955 at the age of 74. A member of the French Academy of Sciences, Teilhard de Chardin always insisted that he was no theologian and that his works concerned his abstruse specialization as a paleontologist.

But his life-long, worldwide study of fossils drove him to seek the human and religious meaning that lies behind the advance of the sciences and particularly of biology. This became apparent with the appearance a few months after his death of a book completed in 1947, *The Phenomenon of Man,* which provides a description of the evolution of the world, including man, and a tentative explanation of the significance of this evolutionary process.

This and a number of other books published in the following years offered the Catholic Church a way to reconcile itself with the surging life of humanity from which it had withdrawn into its post-Tridentine ghetto. Teilhard's method, however, required the Church to abandon the static view of the world that formed the cultural dress for its major teachings about God and religion. Thus it was that he laid the groundwork for the new theology which gives top emphasis to man in his existential search for a better material, moral, and spiritual life as his contribution to God's design for the individual and the race.

Such a concept was anathema to the Holy Office. It maintained the traditional view that God had made the world in a single act, giving to each thing its nature and functions, with man as the pinnacle of material creation, lord of everything else, but himself subject to a series of rules established by God.

This view reduced life to "a period of testing," an interval with no intrinsic values of its own. The man who observed the rules would be rewarded for his obedience, and the one who did not would be punished for his disobedience. It was an interpretation of the mystery of life acceptable in a primitive society in which man's control of his environment was marginal, serving to rationalize the apparent meaninglessness of the masses whose lives lacked material comfort and intellectual development. It became superfluous when man achieved control over the material world through science, and it became offensive when he acquired an understanding of himself as a rational being with inherent dignity and rights.

The dynamic interpretation of life on earth offered by Teilhard de Chardin has more appeal for modern man.

Teilhard saw creation as a continuing process, so that history represents God as engaged in producing a work of art that will be completed only at the end of time when all things are made perfect in Christ. The continuing creation does not come by the day-to-day intervention of God in the process, in the anthropomorphic way in which creation is described in Genesis, but by the action of forces inherent in things since the beginning of the creative process. Consequently, man is no longer to be thought of as playing in God's garden, still less as a plaything of God to be rewarded or punished according to the perfection with which he learns to jump through a moral hoop. He is God's associate in the creative process.

The Holy Office was quite right in its belief that acceptance of such an explanation of the place and function of man in the divine economy had serious theological implications and would end its monopolistic control of Catholic thought. Jesuit Robert North has reported that as recently as 1962, the year in which the Vatican Council began, American bishops received from the Apostolic Delegate, Egidio Vagnozzi, "a communication of the unofficial but firm will of the curial head of the Holy Office, Cardinal Ottaviani." They were told to refuse permission for any public lecturing on Teilhard, and to take other measures along the same lines "to discourage the current wave of interest, so that it would die a natural death."

The American bishops followed their orders, but the Holy Office could not control Pope John who, about the same time, was discussing the importance of Teilhard with Poet-President Leopold Sedar Senghor of Senegal. Indeed, it is not surprising, as Gary MacEoin observes in his book on the Council, *What Happened at Rome?*, "to find that Pope John shared Teilhard's positive attitude to the world, his awareness of the great reservoirs of goodness waiting to be tapped. He saw the world as already in Christ, so that the task of the Church was to make the world understand that fact. The Fathers echoed that belief in the message they addressed to the world early in the Council's first session."

The wave of interest in Teilhard's ideas, in consequence, did not die the natural death which the Holy Office had wished. The specific reason his ideas did not die was that they made sense to contemporary man in a way in which the traditional expression of the relationship between God and man had ceased to make sense.

Man today is conscious, above all, of the rapidity and ubiquity of change, of its dominant importance for him, and of his need to learn to live with it, because it promises to be the only constant in the world of the present and the future. The need for adaptation to constantly changing situations, which is basic to Teilhard's thought, is also a characteristic of the new theologians—men like Karl Rahner, Edward Schillebeeckx, and Bernard Haring—for whom he provided a scientific and philosophical framework.

This context of change is a basic clue to an understanding of the conflict raging in the Church today and threatening a revolutionary sundering of conservatives and progressives. Man's natural fear of the unknown is reinforced in the case of the Catholic by centuries of conditioning to urge him to retain the safe and established formulations of his beliefs. Yet his sense of self-preservation, even more basic, makes him realize that if everything is changing, he also must change simply in order to remain the same.

Karl Rahner's vision of the Christian of the future, for example, gives a good idea of what is involved. Projecting the trends he sees at work in the world today, he believes that the Christian Church will everywhere become a minority in an open and pluralist society, unfavored by the dominant ideology of that society, and unassisted by any social impetus toward Christian commitment. The Christian will be such by his own personal decision. His minister will have no publicly acknowledged status and will be recognized only by and for the ministry of service he offers.

This minority, however, will not be a ghetto, because it will not cut itself off defensively as an ark of salvation. Instead, it will offer itself to the entire community as "the sign of the salvation of those, who, as far as its historical structures are concerned, do not belong to it." Its missionary preaching will aim not at the salvation of those who would otherwise be lost, but at bringing those whom Rahner calls "anonymous Christians" to an explicit recognition of what they already are implicitly.

Such a conception of Christianity is essentially Teilhardian. It sees every act of development of the world, whether performed by a Christian or by a non-Christian, as a creative act. It sees the entire world as partaking of an implicit Christianity, i.e., a sanctified expression of man's communion with God.

In Chapter 7, I quoted Father Haring as telling a group of priests in Chicago that "the whole system of counting mortal sins has to die." Another of his favorite expressions is that we must get away from the magic of numbers and the mathematics of indulgences. His great contribution has been the substitution of human dignity and love in the place of legalism and fear as the bases for deciding the morality of human actions. He praises Pope John for stressing that the whole teaching office of the Church is pastoral, that is to say, directed to helping people live more Christian lives.

"All doctrine," he says, "has to be understood as a ministry for salvation. Moral teaching as a guideline for life must not only look to abstract principles but above all to persons and to the context, the world environment in which persons have to live."

Father Haring has had an enormous impact on attitudes toward marriage. He was particularly active as a theological expert at the Vatican Council, and his influence can be discerned in many parts of the Constitution on the Church in the Modern World. He points out, for example, that the Council never referred to marriage as a contract, not only because in the modern understanding of contracts the parties involved have full freedom in deciding their content, but also because today a contract means a mutual business arrangement to regulate impersonal rights and duties. What Father Haring stresses is that marriage is a covenant of love. Its sacramentality, he says, cannot be understood in a magic way.

"It is the constant action of Christ upon the mutual love. He purifies it. He appeals to the spouses to bestow upon themselves mutually a love which may help them to understand ever more the redeeming love of Christ."

In an important contribution to the birth-control discussion, Father Haring insists that the legalist moral theologians, who have argued that St. Thomas Aquinas settled the issue on the basis of the natural law by declaring that procreation is the primary end of marriage, are taking St. Thomas out of context and gravely misunderstanding him.

What St. Thomas meant by primary goal, he says, is what man "has in common with all the other animals," while secondary meant for him what is on the higher specific human level. "Primary, in consequence, by no means signifies the higher goal, and secondary does not mean a lower but rather a higher level."

Vatican II avoided all reference to primary and secondary goals when it developed a doctrine of responsible parenthood based on marriage as a covenant of love between two persons who have the right and duty to apply general moral principles to their own concrete situation.

This, says Father Haring, excludes "a concept of the confessor who has to take on his conscience all the decisions of the penitents and to impose his decision on them," as well as "the interference of the public authority in the most intimate decisions of persons."

He stresses that the Council admitted it had no concrete answer to the dilemma of a married couple who find themselves in a situation in which they judge that a new pregnancy is now undesirable, while requiring the intimacy of wedded life to retain the faithful exercise of love. Having analyzed various elements in the Council statement, he reaches two conclusions.

"First, it cannot be asserted that the method of birth regulation is blameworthy because it does regulate birth or hinder a new pregnancy efficaciously. But it can also not be asserted that all methods are good, if the necessity of birth regulation is evident to an upright conscience." The final decision as to which means are good can, he believes, be made only with the help of "the experts in modern sciences and the couples who are taught by their virtue and by their experience."

Such a teaching on birth control is obviously at variance with the only viewpoint permitted expression by the Holy Office before Vatican II—a viewpoint still maintained verbally in statements from Rome, including the famous assertion by Pope Paul that the magisterium is not in a state of doubt on the issue. It is, nevertheless, being expressed in ever more explicit language by the new theologians, men like Canadians Gregory Baum and Stanley Kutz, and Ireland's Enda McDonagh. It is also spelled out in the Dutch Catechism.

"Are all methods of regulation of births of equal value to the Christian conscience?" the Catechism asks. "The Council gave no answer to this question. It does, however, call on married people to ask themselves conscientiously whether the practices in question do, or fail to do, full justice to the great personal values which should be expressed in sexual intercourse and in the whole of married life. . . . The last word lies with the conscience, not with the doctor or the confessor. But reverence for life undoubtedly demands that no practices be chosen which could be harmful to health or the affective life."

The views on birth control expressed by the Congress of the Laity in Rome in October, 1967, as I noted earlier, reflect exactly this position. And, as I also noted, the use of contraceptive methods still disapproved by the traditional theologians on the basis of the teaching of Pope Pius XI and Pope Pius XII seems to be growing more universal among Catholic spouses.

The contemporary communications explosion enters here, as it does into the entire phenomenon of the new theology, in two ways. On the one hand, theological speculation can no longer be conducted behind closed doors or in a vacuum of public opinion, as was formerly the case. The moment some novel viewpoint or some proposed solution for a current problem is mentioned in a professional publication or at a congress of experts, it is broadcast in simplified form by the press, radio, and television to the educated and the uneducated of all the world.

On the other hand, any attempt by Rome to muzzle or censor the views of Haring, Schillebeeckx, Rahner, or any of the others whose names have become familiar to millions all over the world is itself subjected immediately to the spotlight of publicity. This ensures a quicker and wider diffusion of the offending views than under normal circumstances. It also subjects the would-be censor to a public odium which the Curia is increasingly anxious to avoid. The communications media have thus become an integral part of the Catholic revolution.

The Catholic press, meanwhile, is undergoing a basic transformation. The extraordinary interest generated among the masses for religious news has led to an intensive coverage in the general press. A study of *Paris-Match,* France's most important popular illustrated magazine, showed that during a period of more than one year 11 percent of all editorial space had been devoted to religious subjects. The proportion may not be as great in *Look, Life, Time, Newsweek,* or *The New York Times,* but in all of them the same growth of attention is visible. The Catholic press has followed suit, even when controlled by bishops who might prefer discreet silence.

It has also been compelled in self-defense to increase the professional level of its editorial help, and the new editors judge the news on the basis of public interest, not of chancery reaction. As more editors blossom forth in the spirit of the Vatican Council, with its stress on individual judgment under the inspiration of the charisms granted to all Christians, they are no longer afraid to present theological views contrary to those approved by the Church. They believe that the whole People of God constitute the Church, and that even in the past the people lived a fuller theological life than they were permitted to express.

These new editors use their publications not to make theological judgments, but to involve their readers in pertinent dialogue and discussion. This creates the conditions for a true public opinion in the Church and a revival of the concept of the active consensus of the faithful as the determinant of the belief of the Church.

The popular involvement in theology increases the urgency of an aspect to which Schillebeeckx has devoted much attention, namely, the reformulation of the truths of faith in contemporary language, as well as the determination of the importance or centrality of a particular belief.

The old theologians tended to place everything on the same level—the Resurrection of Christ, the virginity of Mary, the existence of angels, the existence of a personal devil, limbo, the real presence of Christ in the Eucharist, papal infallibility, the Incarnation, the pre-eminence of celibacy over marriage. They came as a package to be accepted in its entirety.

The new theologians have introduced two important modifications. They are less concerned about the intellectual formulation of belief, stressing instead that Christianity is a way of life rather than a complex of doctrines. And following Vatican II, they stress a hierarchy or order of truths, some central to Christianity—such as the Resurrection of Christ—others peripheral to or entirely unrelated to the deposit of faith, or at least of no importance to us here and now and consequently to be left open while we concentrate on more urgent issues.

Even the central truths must be theologically reinterpreted in order to make intelligible to those living in our cultural context the meaning of doctrines formulated to meet the situation of an entirely different cultural context. The Dutch Catechism, which is deeply impregnated with the thought and techniques of Schillebeeckx, provides many examples. As the bishops of The Netherlands say in the foreword, its purpose is to present anew the message that Jesus of Nazareth brought into the world, to make it sound as new as it is. "The whole message, the whole of the faith remains the same, but the approach, the light in which the faith is seen, is new."

Typical of the Schillebeeckx contribution to theological reformulation is his analysis of the meaning of the doctrine that Christ is truly present in the Eucharist. Until recently, in the traditional Catholic textbooks, the issues were discussed without any indication of awareness of what man has learned about the constitution of physical matter. A presentation assuming the objective validity of a culturally conditioned explanation of matter in terms of substance and accident is meaningless to people who know matter primarily as an accumulation of tremendous energy poised in vibrant tension.

To explain the technical term *transsubstantiation* for us, Schillebeeckx uses such equally technical terms as *trans-finalization* and *transsignification*. In the Dutch Catechism these concepts emerge in everyday language. "When we consider the matter in terms of present-day thought, one should therefore say that the reality, the nature of material things is what they are—each in its own way—for man. Hence it is the essence or nature of bread to be earthly food for man. In the bread at Mass, however, this nature becomes something quite different: Jesus' body, as food for eternal life. Body in Hebrew means the person as a whole. Bread has become Jesus' person. This is a mysterious presence. We must not imagine, for instance, that Christ's body enters our mouth in a very small edition, so to speak, just as in Nazareth he entered the house of Mary in actual life size. We must be equally on our guard against the opposite explanation, which would be purely 'symbolic,' as though Jesus were not really present. It is better to say that the bread is essentially withdrawn from its normal human meaning or definition, and has become the bread which the Father has given us, Jesus himself."

The issue that has most caught the popular imagination is the so-called "Death of God." This is an aspect of a problem mentioned above, namely, that the development of a culture controlling its environment to the extent we do today makes God superfluous for the tasks ascribed to him by less sophisticated men. We don't need God any more to explain the thunder or lightning, to stop an epidemic of smallpox, to steer a ship through uncharted seas. The "Death of God" theologians are convinced that the mythical, metaphysical, and religious god must die before we can once again be really open to the revelation of God.

The Dutch theologian Robert Adolfs adopts what is an increasingly popular view among theologians on the "Death of God" issue. He thinks that we do not have at our disposal the means to offer a satisfactory answer. "In our present situation, we must perhaps avoid using the word 'God,' " he says. "Perhaps we must learn to cultivate an attitude of listening and waiting receptivity towards the mastery that 'calls,' 'addresses' and 'invites' us."

Having said this, Adolfs goes on to make another important point. It is open to question, he says, whether the problem of God is in itself at the heart of our present critical situation or whether it is only a symptom of this situation. He quotes Schillebeeckx as having said that all the social surveys conducted by religious sociologists confirm the concrete experience of Schillebeeckx himself, namely, that the chief difficulty is not the problem of God, nor even Christ, but the Church.

"The main difficulty," Adolfs concludes, "is to be found in the form and mode of existence of the Church." He says that the Christian message is preached in such a way in our modern secular society that it has become unintelligible. "The jargon of the Church is possibly still understood in elevated ecclesiastical circles familiar with the traditional teaching of the Church, but in the world outside it is regarded at best as pious and irrelevant."

Why is the Church so persistent in clinging to its archaic and meaningless jargon? Because it is an integral part of its way of existence, Adolfs says. "The Church's teaching is out of tune with the modern age because the form itself of the Church is also a survival from a past age. This form has to be reinterpreted and refashioned in every new human and world situation. Everything points to the fact that it is almost certainly the form of the Church that is the real cause of the critical situation in which Christianity finds itself in the modern world."

Then, having traced the historical circumstances that caused the Church to become irrelevant to the great structures of modern society, while imprisoned within the system, he draws a grim conclusion. "It may be a rather exaggerated comparison to make, but the Church is in a similar position to the Indians in the United States. Their way of life could not be made to fit into modern American society and they have consequently been put into special reservations where 'they cannot do any harm.' So it is with the Church. She has become a 'religious reservation' with its own pattern of life. She can still exert some influence in the private sector of life, but outside this sector any effect that she may have is quickly neutralized."

For Adolfs—and he argues his thesis with much conviction in his famous book, *The Grave of God*—the solution is not to write the Church off, as English theologian Charles Davis did, but to purify it by returning it to its original spiritual purpose and humble condition. He uses the Greek word *kenosis* (emptying) to describe this condition, recalling Paul's description of Christ as having emptied himself by taking the existence of a servant upon himself.

"If the Church is to have a future, she must renounce all claims to power and all longing for power, all honor, worldly esteem and love of display. For Christ's sake, she will have to become 'poor' in the deepest, evangelical sense of the word. In order to win everything, she will have to be ready to lose everything. She will have to be a *Servant*—a Servant who will not use power to force men to action, but who will aim to rule only by love."

It is not difficult to see how the revolutionary ferment described in the previous chapters is a logical result of the new theology as lived by people who find themselves constrained by the kind of institution Adolfs describes.

The Vatican Council has frequently been criticized for avoiding a direct conflict between progressives and conservatives in the interest of consensus, coming up instead with a permissive formula enabling both sides to extract the interpretation each desired. No doubt, some ambiguities were the result of political compromise, but there was also the deeper problem that it would have been self-defeating for the progressive majority to impose its will on the conservative minority, since that would have been a denial of the basic principle of the new theology which motivated the majority.

We can consequently anticipate the continuation for a considerable time of the situation of conflict in this country, since it has become clear that the United States bishops are, with few exceptions, unable to respond to the revolution of rising expectations of Catholics, clerical and lay, at an acceptable rate of speed. Evidence of this was provided by the pastoral letter of the bishops issued in January, 1968. It was an attempt to move forward and discuss the Church in the light of the American experience, but it demonstrated principally the paternalistic and protective attitudes of the writers. It clearly demonstrated that they fear to lose control over much more than teaching.

Warning Catholics against becoming "prisoners of the present" and losing a sense of continuity amid Church reforms, the pastoral letter stated that to demean the Church of former ages is to diminish the Church of the present age and to impoverish the future. History has never recorded a "beneficent alternative" to the visible, institutional structure of the Church. Although the laity "must echo the authentic voice of Christ to the whole community," the laity are also responsible to the organized structure of the Church. Little has yet been said of how the laity can rebuild those structures that are outdated.

In an open letter in response to this pastoral in the *National Catholic Reporter,* Monsignor Joseph Gallagher told the bishops that nobody was listening to them while they polished brass on a sinking ship, least of all the best seminarians and the best young Catholics. "In a few harsh words: you seem to them almost hopelessly remote, institutional, establishment, bureaucratic, bourgeois, defensive, legalistic, real-estated, cigared, cadillaced, mansioned. You give few compelling signs of any consuming, Christ-like concern for non-institutional truth and justice, of open humility and penitence for past and present corporate sins, of trust in the Spirit. You do not candidly own up to the dilemma of the birth control issue, a dilemma which clashes with your comforting words about trust in the magisterium."

Monsignor Gallagher is a former editor of the *Catholic Review,* official newspaper of the Baltimore archdiocese. He was translation editor of the most widely used English translation of the documents of Vatican II, and he is professor of philosophy at the Baltimore seminary. The fact that people of his standing within the institutional Church are willing to express their views so frankly and do not lack the media in which to express them is one of the most significant signs of the restlessness now sweeping through the Church. Articulate criticism of the institution at the middle-management level is everywhere.

The new theology answers the questions of most of these critics, the Vatican Council in its broad formulations embraced it, but it is only grudgingly winning assent in practice. As the American bishops imply, there are fears that the new theology will lose contact with tradition in its eagerness to discern the signs of the times and find a language that has a cutting edge in the modern world. The "now" people want a "now" theology. There is an inevitable conflict between them and the bishops who see their role more as custodians of a Church nearly 2,000 years old than as pathfinders into the future.

The new theologians recognize that the world of the classicist no longer exists. In this new age, modern theology has become a collective, ecumenical effort to make the good news of God's call meaningful to all men. Theologians today have three tasks: to reflect on the word of God, to reflect on the nature and meaning of the Church, to reflect on the problems of contemporary humanity. The result must be a radical reorientation of the function of theology, for it cannot fulfill its office simply by being a defender of the denominational church looking in on itself.

Modern theology is concerned with a transformation of the human condition. This elevates the Church above the task of merely reforming its political involvements into a new level of participation with all men who sorrow and suffer. Thus, crucial questions are looming about the Church's correct attitude to armed revolutions to achieve social justice for the poor. Those who opposed the Vietnam war on grounds of conscience found strength for their position in the anti-war spirit of the Vatican Council. The Church has come to realize that the "just war" theory is untenable in the nuclear age. And yet there are some important theologians who are asking whether Christians should accept violence for the sake of gaining justice and liberty, or whether they should accept the status quo which is itself a form of violence against masses of poor who cannot achieve their human rights.

Father Johan-Baptist Metz, a German protégé of Karl Rahner, says that "if the status quo of a society contains as much injustice as would probably be caused by a revolutionary upheaval, a revolution in favor of justice and liberty for the sake of 'the least of our brothers' would be permissible even in the name of charity." But, he warns, the Church must forsake the use of power in order to be a critic of the society around it. Metz wants the Church to be a passionate critic of the powerful of this world wherever man has been treated contemptuously by man.

Father Francois Houtart, a Belgian theologian and demographer, deplores the fact that development in much of the world lags so far behind that of the rich, aggressive nations of the West. Latin America needs radical political changes of a kind that have been achieved only by armed revolt elsewhere.

"Are we as churchmen to accept violence, or are we to accept the status quo?" he asks.

In the underdeveloped countries, Houtart says, ostentatious expenditures by the Church are among the classic complaints. "The Catholic Church builds luxurious nunciatures in these countries, whose prestige function seems fundamental. Often, it is the government or certain families of the ruling oligarchy who volunteer to build and outfit these properties."

Then Houtart recounts a case history which dramatically captures the tension that exists on so many levels between theologians and the magisterium of the Church. "A Latin American government, whose people are struggling in dreadful misery, has offered a million dollars to build a new nunciature. Will the Nuncio have the courage to refuse, or will he come out of the affair with a red hat?"

Metz and Houtart are not advocating armed revolution, but recognizing its inevitability, and warning the Church that this is the last chance for it to identify itself with the poor instead of with the rich. Their theology is supported by at least sixteen bishops with dioceses in such Third World countries as Brazil, Algeria, Lebanon, and Laos who issued a joint letter backing radical reforms.

"Revolutions are and have been part of the evolution of the world," they said.

They scorned the fact that for a century the Church "has tolerated capitalism with its legalization of lending at interest and other practices that so little conform to the moral teaching of the prophets and the gospels."

They rejoiced at the development of new social systems.

301

"Christians have the duty to demonstrate that true social-ism is a full Christian life that involves a just sharing of goods and fundamental equality. . . . In this way we will stop people confusing God and religion with the oppressors of the poor and the workers which is what the feudal, cap-italist and imperialist systems are. These inhuman systems have engendered others which, intended to liberate the people, in fact oppress the individual if they fall into totali-tarian collectivism and religious persecution."

The Church should greet with joy and pride new social systems that respect not money concentrated in a few hands, but the workers, the laborers, and the peasants. It is simply not true that it is God's wish that rich men should enjoy the good things of this world by exploiting the poor; it is not true that God wishes a wretched destiny for the poor.

This Third World theology does not identify the Church with any given society or culture, let alone government. Rather, by standing back, it properly judges the ills and crimes of society in order to foster in love the struggle for justice. This theology gives man a sense of belonging to the human community and makes him conscious of the fact that God is concerned about land reform, an end to racial discrimination, equal opportunities in education, jobs, and housing. This is the theology that makes the Church rele-vant in modern society.

Certainly it will be attacked as "socialism" and "Marx-ism." The only reply to be made is that certain tenets of socialism and Marxism are identifiable with Christianity, and the Third World bishops are concentrating on the spread of justice to one billion persons who stand outside rich doors. The theology of justice stands apart from the political associations of both the Communist countries and the Western powers. It can fully succeed only when the in-stitutional Church shuns the favors and privileges of all societies.

The picture of the Christian who says his prayers in a quiet corner and quietly tries to refrain from sinning, while the world around him falls apart, is on the point of complete abandonment. The new theology emphasizes that the Church must be a sign for the poor, not only speaking in the idiom of our times, but manifesting itself as a servant.

Out of this pilgrimage with mankind, we can see that the Church has a future, says Hans Kung, one of the world's major theologians. Fulfilling its mission in the world is what gives the Church reality and purpose. It is God's grace that enables the Church "to overcome all the anxieties of the present, all the shortcomings, all the doubts, all the cares, all the hopelessness, all its illusions that it can redeem itself, all the wretchedness of the Church and the world."

The Church does have a future, Kung maintains. "It has *the* future. This is the eighth day which passes description and cannot be foreseen, the day on which God will complete his work of creation, the Church will reach the goal of its pilgrimage, and the world will recognize its Lord."

CHAPTER 12

Conclusion: The Christian Prophecy

The Catholic revolution has now pushed ahead too far to be stopped. But the Church is still far from the promised land of conciliar reform. Will the revolution abort?

The Church is changing at a faster rate of speed than ever before. But the world and the attitudes of all the people in it are changing even faster. Can the Church ever catch up, or is it destined to lag farther and farther behind?

The Church passed through the most important Council in its history, which underscored the freedom and responsibility of all its members. But the bishops are still stressing their authority over institutional machinery. Is reform incompatible with the structure of the institution?

The 1960s brought us the Council, the open window, a universal consensus to push the Church forward, agonizing doubts about how to do it and how rapidly, emotional reactions from both reactionaries and progressives, and finally a great question mark over the credibility of the Church. Does it have the courage to march relentlessly down the path of reform to an unknown future? That is the most important question as the most tumultuous decade since the Reformation draws to a close.

The answers must take the form of bold, positive steps forward if the Church is to retain the interest, dedication, commitment, and hope of its members. Already, disillusionment and skepticism have set in, producing unprecedented public defections and a wave of silent schisms. Despite advances during the 1960s that were undreamed of before the decade began, there is a great depression in the Church.

A public view of the Synod is banned. Experimental liturgies are banned. Nuns' new apostolates are banned. The Dutch Catechism is banned. None of these actions is in the open spirit of Vatican II. Rather, it is in the defensive spirit of Trent. It represents a heavy-handed ecclesiastical mentality that does not trust Catholic people to be mature and responsible.

This mentality will gradually fade ("a lot of problems are solved by funerals," Pope John used to say), but the damage that it is doing to the credibility of the Church in the meantime is enormous. It is directly responsible for the widening of the gap between the forces of renewal and the institutional Church. This cleavage is already producing a new kind of de-institutionalized Catholic, one who is still a believer but is not affected by what the institution says or does.

We can say that the Catholic revolution has been a success in the sense that it would be inconceivable for the Church to return to the old regime; a pre-conciliar institution could not be maintained. At the same time, the revolution is not achieving real, lasting success because a completely reformed institution is unattainable in the foreseeable future. The weight of scholasticism, legalism, and clericalism has been simply too great for the Church to make a rapid recovery. There are too many issues to be handled, too many substructures to be altered, too many vested interests to be placated, for the Church to be smoothly transformed from a dominating institution to an animating influence.

Yet, there is good reason for saying that if the Church were updated with greater speed, chaos would result. The confusion and the crises are bad enough, but the Church has been saved from being torn asunder by the acrobatic skill of Pope Paul. Of what use would a full-speed-ahead, damn-the-torpedoes reform be if shipwreck were sure to follow?

However enticing the prospect, the Church could not tolerate two Pope Johns in a row. John, the innovator, had to be followed by Paul, the consolidator, in order for the Council to take root in the life of the Church. Caution, however, is not an attractive quality to those who fret because their own spiritual lives are in a state of crisis.

"Those are my twenty years you're playing around with" is the common reply to bishops who insist that reforms take a generation to come to fruition.

The Church before Vatican II depended largely on form and externals. Regular Sunday Mass. No meat on Friday. No birth control. The law thus superseded internal convictions. When the Council began stripping away the externals to get at the bare Christ of the faith, it was a nerve-shattering experience for many people who had depended on props far more than they realized. The probing of doctrine and questioning of discipline upset them, and the bishops accordingly recoiled from too much openness.

Yet it was precisely this forthrightness that aided other Catholics in their search for a post-conciliar spirituality that could be integrated into their human existence. These Catholics no longer look to spiritual "exercises" to keep fit. What they desire is a faith that helps them to see that life itself is a religious practice, to achieve a way of existence that ends the dichotomy between religion and life. Faith then ceases to be a comfort. It is a constant challenge, raising haunting questions about the human condition around us, the poverty, the racial discrimination, the underdeveloped countries. Catholics at this level are less concerned with the "churchy" qualities of renewal and are eager for the Church to shed all the institutional trivia that prevents it from being a powerful conscience and critic of the social ills in the world.

Despite the advances made by the Synod (and they are not inconsiderable, despite the poor public opinion of the Synod because of its closed nature), the institution is starting to mean less and less to more and more people. As soon as the mortal-sin penalty for missing Sunday Mass is removed—it will never be able to stand up against the inroads of the new theology—the exodus from Sunday liturgy will become pronounced. Great numbers of people are bored in church, and there is no denying it. Declining numbers will injure the financial structure of the parishes and dioceses, and the schools, already reeling under the vocation shortage, will be dealt another blow.

All this is part of the Church's suffering which must be endured if reform is to become reality. The price of the Catholic revolution is fewer numbers in the Church, shortages of priests and sisters, harder times, confusion, and even despair. But there is no way around these minefields. Balanced progress is the only solution. That is clearly not fast enough for the many who want to be done immediately with the constraints of the institution, while it will be too fast for the multitudes who have not yet absorbed the changes already here. A mammoth crisis of conscience is on the horizon.

Accordingly, the next ten years are sure to be even more dizzying than were the 1960s. The pressure for change will win over the pressure of tradition, but no matter what is changed, it will not be enough for the growing numbers who have already decided that the institution has lost its meaning for them. When the present college generation, already disenchanted with institutional religion, is added to this group, the adherents of the institution will find themselves a minority within the Church. This very development will goad the institution to a new round of innovation.

Obviously, bishops will have to be elected by the clergy and people if co-responsibility in Church government is to have any meaning. But who will do the electing? Is it a responsible act to let anyone vote? Is it realistic to expect the Church to function as a pure democracy? Structures are needed to bring representatives of the People of God into one setting and decide such important matters as elections. Parish councils will lead to diocesan and national councils. The days of the laity meeting on one side of the street and the hierarchy on the other will be ended, as the fusion of the baptized, each with an infused priesthood, becomes a reality. The consensus of the faithful will be sought before the bishops issue declarations. Bishops' Synods, for their part, will become permanent, and will take over the election of popes.

In the Church of the future, inter-communion with other faiths may be commonplace; married clergy will most likely be permitted; the barrier against women in the ministry will be lowered; there will be a variety of liturgies; and big churches will no longer be constructed.

Will all this be sufficient to fully modernize the Church? It will not. For the laborious process involved in these achievements will use up the little time the Church has left for the real modernizing required. The Church must turn its attention and energies outward if it has any hope of influencing the Third World that will soon be a majority of mankind.

Achieving an interior harmony will amount to little if the Church fails to be a vibrant witness of love and service among the millions of oppressed who daily become poorer while the rich get richer. The Church must find new ways of saying to the black and brown and yellow millions that Christ loves them. The old ways, in which a Latin culture was superimposed on a supposedly pagan people, were a travesty of the true meaning of the incarnate Christ.

That is why the decision of Cardinal Leger of Montreal to throw off the burden of administration and devote the rest of his life to being a simple priest among African lepers is so significant. Leger, the innovator, is a living prophecy of the Christian message. It is in this simple act that we see the power of the Christian light shining on a frightened world.

Selected Bibliography

ABBOTT, Walter M., S.J. (General Editor), *The Documents of Vatican II* (New York: Guild Press, 1966).

ADOLFS, Robert, *The Grave of God* (New York: Harper & Row, 1966).

ARMSTRONG, April Oursler, *What's Happening to the Catholic Church* (New York: Doubleday, 1967).

BAUM, Gregory, O.S.A., *The Future of Belief Debate* (New York: Herder and Herder, 1967).

BEA, Augustin Cardinal, and VISSER'T HOOFT, Willem A., *Peace Among Christians* (New York: Herder and Herder, 1967).

BEA, Augustin Cardinal, *The Way to Unity After the Council* (New York: Herder and Herder, 1967).

BEKKERS, W. M., *God's People on the March* (New York: Holt, Rinehart and Winston, 1966).

BONHOEFFER, Dietrich, *Letters & Papers from Prison* (London, England: S.C.M. Press, 1953).

BORDELON, Marvin, Msgr. (Editor), *The Parish in a Time of Change* (Notre Dame: Fides, 1967).

BORROMEO, Sister M. Charles, C.S.C. (Editor), *The New Nuns* (New York: New American Library, 1967).

BOYD, Malcolm (Editor), *The Underground Church* (New York: Sheed & Ward, 1968).

Brown, Robert McAfee, *The Ecumenical Revolution* (New York: Doubleday, 1967).

Callahan, Daniel J., Oberman, Heiko A., O'Hanlon, Daniel J., S.J. (Editors), *Christianity Divided* (New York: Sheed & Ward, 1961).

Callahan, Daniel, *The Mind of the Catholic Layman* (New York: Charles Scribner's Sons, 1963).

Callahan, Daniel, *The New Church* (New York: Charles Scribner's Sons, 1966).

Callahan, Daniel (Editor), *The Secular City Debate* (New York: The Macmillan Company, 1966).

Cavallari, Alberto, *The Changing Vatican* (New York: Doubleday, 1967).

Cox, Harvey (Editor), *The Church Amid Revolution* (New York: Association Press, 1967).

Cox, Harvey, *The Secular City* (New York: The Macmillan Company, 1965).

Davis, Charles, *A Question of Conscience* (London: Hodder and Stoughton, 1967).

DuBay, William H., *The Human Church* (New York: Doubleday, 1966).

Dunphy, William (Editor), *The New Morality* (New York: Herder and Herder, 1967).

Ellis, John Tracy, *Perspectives in American Catholicism* (Baltimore: Helicon, 1963).

Evoy, John J., S.S., and Christoph, Van F., S.J., *The Real Woman in the Religious Life* (New York: Sheed & Ward, 1967).

Fesquet, Henri, *Catholicism: Religion of Tomorrow?* (New York: Holt, Rinehart and Winston, 1964).

Fesquet, Henri, *The Drama of Vatican II* (New York: Random House, 1967).

FICHTER, Joseph H., *America's Forgotten Priests—What They Are Saying* (New York: Harper & Row, 1968).

FISHER, Desmond, *The Church in Transition* (London: Geoffrey Chapman, 1967).

FUCHS, Lawrence H., *John F. Kennedy and American Catholicism* (New York: Meredith Press, 1967).

GREELEY, Andrew M., *The Catholic Experience* (New York: Doubleday, 1967).

GREELEY, Andrew M., *The Hesitant Pilgrim* (New York: Sheed & Ward, 1966).

GREENSPUN, William B., C.S.P., and NORGREN, William A. (Editors), *Living Room Dialogues* (New Jersey: National Council of the Churches of Christ in the U.S.A. and Paulist Press, 1965).

GREENSPUN, William B., C.S.P., and WEDEL, Cynthia C. (Editors), *Second Living Room Dialogues* (New Jersey: Friendship Press, National Council of the Churches of Christ in the U.S.A. and Paulist Press, 1967).

GUITTON, Jean, *The Pope Speaks* (New York: Meredith Press, 1967).

HARDON, John A., S.J., *The Hungry Generation* (Maryland: The Newman Press, 1967).

HASSENGER, Robert, *The Shape of Catholic Higher Education* (Chicago: The University of Chicago Press, 1967).

HAUGHTON, Rosemary, and HEENAN, Cardinal, *Dialogue* (New York: Sheed & Ward, 1967).

HEBBLETHWAITE, Peter, *"Inside" the Synod Rome, 1967* (New York: Paulist Press Deus Books, 1968).

HORTON, Douglas, *Toward an Undivided Church* (New York: Association Press, 1967).

HOUTART, Francois, *The Eleventh Hour* (New York: Sheed & Ward, 1968).

HOYT, Robert G. (Editor), *Issues That Divide the Church* (New York: The Macmillan Company, 1967).

KAVANAUGH, Father James, *A Modern Priest Looks at His Outdated Church* (New York: Trident, 1967).

KELLY, George A., *The Christian Role in Today's Society* (New York: Random House, 1967).

KENNEDY, Eugene C., M.M., *Fashion Me a People* (New York: Sheed & Ward, 1967).

KERNER, Otto (Chairman), *Report of the National Advisory Commission on Civil Disorders* (New York: Bantam Books, Inc., 1968).

KIRVAN, John J., C.S.P., *The Restless Believers* (New Jersey: Deus Books Paulist Press, 1966).

KUHNS, William, *In Pursuit of Dietrich Bonhoeffer* (Dayton, Ohio: Pflaum Press, 1967).

KUNG, Hans, *The Church* (New York: Sheed & Ward, 1967).

LALLY, Francis F., Msgr., *The Catholic Church in a Changing America* (Boston: Little, Brown, 1962).

LYONS, Bernard, *Parish Councils* (Techny, Illinois: Divine Word Publications, 1967).

MACEOIN, Gary, *New Challenges to American Catholics* (New York: P. J. Kenedy & Sons, 1965).

MACEOIN, Gary, *What Happened at Rome?* (New York: Holt, Rinehart and Winston, 1966).

McAVOY, Thomas T., C.S.C. (Editor), *Roman Catholicism and the American Way of Life* (Notre Dame: University of Notre Dame Press, 1960).

McGOEY, John H., S.F.M., *The Uncertain Sound* (Toronto: Longmans Canada Limited, 1967).

McGURN, Barrett, *A Reporter Looks at American Catholicism* (New York: Hawthorn Books, 1967).

McKENZIE, John L., S.J., *Authority in the Church* (New York: Sheed & Ward, 1966).

MIDDLETON, Neil (Introduction), *Catholics and the Left* (Springfield, Ill.: Templegate, 1966).

MILLEAU, Thomas V., *Ghetto Fever* (Milwaukee: Bruce Publishing Company, 1968).

MILLER, John H. (Editor), *Vatican II: An Interfaith Appraisal* (Notre Dame: University of Notre Dame Press, 1966).

MURPHY, Francis X., C.S.S.R., and MacEOIN, Gary, *Synod '67, A New Sound in Rome* (Montreal: Palm Publishers, 1968).

NORTH, Robert S.J., *Teilhard and the Creation of the Soul* (Milwaukee: Bruce Publishing Company, 1967).

NOVAK, Michael, *The Open Church* (New York: The Macmillan Company, 1962).

O'GARA, James (Editor), *The Postconciliar Parish* (New York: P. J. Kenedy & Sons, 1967).

OSBORNE, William, *The Segregated Covenant* (New York: Herder and Herder, 1967).

OUTLER, Albert C., *Methodist Observer at Vatican II* (New York: Newman Press, 1967).

RAHNER, Karl, *The Church after the Council* (New York: Herder and Herder, 1966).

REEDY, John L., C.S.C., and ANDREWS, James F., *The Perplexed Catholic* (Notre Dame: Ave Maria Press, 1966).

RICHARD, Robert L., S.J., *Secularization Theology* (New York: Herder and Herder, 1967).

RYAN, Mary Perkins, *Are Parochial Schools the Answer?* (New York: Holt, Rinehart and Winston, 1963).

RYNNE, Xavier, *Letters From Vatican City* (New York: Farrar, Straus, 1963).

RYNNE, Xavier, *The Second Session* (New York: Farrar, Straus, 1964).

RYNNE, Xavier, *The Third Session* (New York: Farrar, Straus, & Giroux, 1965).

RYNNE, Xavier, *The Fourth Session* (New York: Farrar, Straus, & Giroux, 1966).

SHANNON, William V., *The American Irish* (New York: The Macmillan Company, 1966).

THORMAN, Donald J., *The Christian Vision* (New York: Doubleday, 1967).

THORMAN, Donald J., *The Emerging Layman* (New York: Doubleday, 1962).

WAKIN, Edward, and SCHEUER, Father Joseph F., *The De-Romanization of the American Catholic Church* (New York: The Macmillan Company, 1966).

YZERMANS, Vincent A., Msgr., *American Participation in the Second Vatican Council* (New York: Sheed & Ward, 1967).

A New Catechism—Catholic Faith for Adults (New York: Herder and Herder, 1967).

Afterword

As this book was about to go to press, Pope Paul brought down his long-awaited birth control encyclical, *Humanae Vitae* (Of Human Life). "Every marital act," he declared in the document's key sentence, "must remain open to the transmission of life."

Thus, after five years of theological debate, the Pope reaffirmed the traditional Church teaching and once more shut the door on all artificial means of contraception. The Pope rested his argument on the belief that birth control is contrary to the natural law, which he feels the Church cannot renounce, but only guard and interpret. He supported responsible parenthood, but insisted that the rhythm method was the only device permissible in the eyes of the Church.

The significance of the Pope's decision is that he overruled the recommendation for liberalization made by a majority of his own study commission (composed of theologians, scientific experts, and married couples), the specific request for change made by many important cardinals and bishops and the Third World Congress for the Lay Apostolate, and the published opinions of scores of theologians around the world who hold that the Catholic Church's teaching has been wrong.

The encyclical is not, of course, infallible, as theologians everywhere pointed out immediately in the most concentrated attack on papal teaching in modern times. In fact, within twenty-four hours, 87 theologians in the United States signed a statement declaring that the encyclical "betrays a narrow and positivistic notion of Papal authority," because it does not take into consideration the thinking of large segments of not only the Catholic Church, but other religious communities within Christianity.

Instead of resolving the birth control issue, the encyclical brought to a head, as nothing else has done, the whole question of the limits of papal authority. The Vatican was stunned when theologians in Europe and North America took to the communications media to insist that Catholics may dissent from authoritative, non-infallible teachings of the Magisterium when sufficient reasons for doing so exist. In other words, Catholics who believe in contraception are confronted with the unhappy choice of following their consciences or doing what the Pope tells them to do.

In going against the body of thought within the Catholic Church, Pope Paul has seriously damaged his prestige and position. The crisis of authority within the Church has now reached an intensity that no one thought possible when Vatican II ended. The repercussions of *Humanae Vitae* will be enormous; millions of parents will disregard the Pope's teaching and lose interest in the changing Church; the defection of priests who find it impossible to pass on this key moral teaching will increase; ecumenical progress will be seriously retarded; collegiality will be scoffed at, since the bishops obviously were excluded from the decision-making; and worst of all, youth around the world will feel confirmed in their quick judgments that the Church is not relevant to the problems of modern man.

The Catholic Revolution has taken a critical turn.

Index

Christian Family Movement, 99, 109

Christian Institute for People, 229

Ciappi, Louis, Father, 17–18

Clark, Tom C., 80

Cody, John, Cardinal, 199–200, 201

Cogley, John, 12, 248–249, 269–270

Colgate Rochester Divinity School, 79, 83–84

College of St. Thomas, 272–273

Colombo, Carlo, Bishop, 19

Commission on Ecumenical and Interreligious Affairs of the National Conference of Catholic Bishops, 135

Commonweal, xxi–xxii, 117, 152, 249

Community of John XXIII, 109–112, 118, 169

Concern Committee, 161–162

Confraternity of Christian Doctrine, 267, 270

Congar, Yves, 284

Congregation for Christian Education (formerly Congregation of Seminaries and Universities), 26

Congregation for Religious, 218, 228, 231

Congregation for the Doctrine of the Faith (formerly Holy Office), 6, 13, 14, 16–18, 19, 23, 127, 291

Congregation of Rites, 114–115

Congregation of Seminaries and Universities (see Congregation for Christian Education)

Connolly, Thomas, Bishop, 276

Constitution on the Church in the Modern World, 58, 103–104, 125–126, 129, 148, 242–243

Constitution on the Liturgy, 128–129

Conway, William, Cardinal, 1, 5, 50

Cooke, Terence J., Archbishop, 204

Cordeiro, Joseph, Archbishop, 19

Corita, Sister, 235

Cornell, Tom, 34

Cort, John, 35, 40

Council of the Laity, 39, 51–52, 292

Cox, Harvey, 235, 278

Critic, 151, 208

Curran, Charles E., Father, 237, 274–276

Cushing, Richard, Cardinal, 59, 276

Dallas, 112–113

Daly, Mary, 157–158, 249

Daughters of the Cross, 229

Davis, Charles, xvii, xviii, 297

Dearden, John, Archbishop, 3, 28, 40, 59, 61, 118

Declaration on Christian Education, 261

Declaration on Non-Christian Religions, 144–145

Declaration on Religious Freedom, 285

Decree on Ecumenism, 129–130, 144

Decree on the Laity, 104

Decree on the Pastoral Office of Bishops, 104

De Roo, Remi, Bishop, 231

Des Marais, Philip, 266

Detroit, 61–62, 118–122, 124–125, 264–265

Doepfner, Julius, Cardinal, 4, 18–19, 26

Donnelly, John F., 165–166

Donohue, James C., Monsignor, 263, 265

Drane, James, Father, 195

DuBay, William, Father, 68, 106, 195, 198

Eastman Kodak, 76

Eaton, Evelyn, 226, 228

Ecumenical Directory, 123–124, 133

Edelby, Archbishop, 19

The Education of Sister Lucy, 220

Ellis, John Tracy, Monsignor, x

Felici, Cardinal, 5, 25

Fichter, Joseph, Father, 190, 191, 207

FIGHT (Freedom, Integration, God, Honor, Today), 76–77, 78

Finks, David, Father, 76–77, 78, 89

Flahiff, George, Archbishop, 4

Fontinell, Eugene, 150

Ford, Henry, II, 68–69

Fordham University, 136, 271, 277

Fournier, Dick, Father, 120–122

Kirvan, John J., Father, 238, 243–247

Knight, David M., 276

Koenig, Franziskus, Cardinal, 4

Koob, C. A., Father, 266–267

Koop, Pedro, Bishop, 187, 188

Krol, John, Cardinal, 3–4, 40, 153, 275

Kuess, Barbara (formerly Sister Marie Bernadette), 226–227

Kung, Hans, 206, 284, 303

Kutz, Stanley, 291

Land O'Lakes, Wisconsin, 279

Landis, Dennis, 159–162

Leger, Paul-Emile, Cardinal, 4, 17, 309

Leger Community, 118

Leo XIII, Pope, 134

Leo, John, 185

Levesque, Louis, Archbishop, 4

Life, 223

Life Is Worth Living, 68

Lindbeck, George, 134–135, 140–141

Liturgical Conference, 114, 116

Liturgical Consilium, 114–115

Living Room Dialogues, 135

London Tablet, 15, 22

Loretto Sisters, 210–214, 220–221, 224, 271

Luce, Clare Boothe, 68–69

Lyons, Bernard, 169

McBride, Alfred, Father, 191

McCann, Cardinal, 17

McCarthy, Eugene, 98

McCarthy, James, 168–169

McCaw, John E., 138

McCluskey, Neil G., Father, 273

McCormack, Arthur, Father, 52–53, 55–56

McDivitt, James, 37

McDonagh, Enda, 291

McDonald, William J., Bishop, 274–275, 276

MacEoin, Gary, 232, 287–288

McGrath, John J., Father, 277

McGrath, Mark, Bishop, 4, 19

McGucken, Joseph T., Archbishop, 162

McHale, Kathleen A., 250, 251

McIntyre, James, Cardinal, 106, 195, 231–232

McKenzie, John L., Father, 184

McManus, Ora, Father, 204–205

Madeleva (Wolff), Sister, 220

Maione, Romeo, 41–44, 50, 56–57

Manhattan College, 247–248, 272–273

Marais, Philip des, 266

Marie Bernadette, Sister (Barbara Kuess), 226–227

Markham, John, Father, 264–265

Mater et Magistra, 58, 155

Maximos IV Saigh, Patriarch, 11

Mealey, Margaret, 155–157

Meaney, Daniel, 34, 66–67

Medical Missions Sisters, 222

Mejia, Jorge, Father, 22

Metz, Johan-Baptist, Father, 300–302

Meyer, Albert, Cardinal, 199

Meyer, Bertrande, Sister, 219–220

Michel, Virgil, Father, 204

Milwaukee, 62, 229

The Mind of the Catholic Layman, 117

A Modern Priest Looks at His Outdated Church, xvii, 171

Moran, Gabriel, Brother, 253

Muckenheim, Maryellen, Sister, 221, 234–235

Mundelein, George, Cardinal, 199

Muñoz Vega, Cardinal, 17, 19, 24

Murphy, F. X., Father, 21–22

Murray, John Courtney, Father, 204, 285

National Association for Pastoral Renewal, 185, 190–193

National Association of Laymen, 147–148, 159–165, 169

National Association of the Laity (see National Association of Laymen)

National Catholic Conference for Interracial Justice, 63–64

National Catholic Educational Association, 220, 266–267

Rossi, Peter H., 262–263, 268–269
Roy, Maurice, Cardinal, 51–52, 53, 54
Rubin, Ladislaus, Bishop, 5–6
Rumschlag, Mary Catherine, 226
Ryan, John, Father, 204
Ryan, Mary Perkins, 257
Rynne, Xavier, 21–22

Saigh, Maximos IV, Patriarch, 11
St. Agnes' Parish, Detroit, 264
St. Albert the Great (Dominican community), 186
St. Bridget's Church, Rochester, 76–77
St. Francis College, 272–273
St. Joan's International Alliance, 157
St. John Fisher College, 92–93
St. John's Abbey and University, Collegeville, Minn., 136
St. Louis, 94–98, 167–169
St. Louis Review, 153, 165
St. Louis University, 271, 272–273, 277–278
St. Mark's Church, Kansas City, 135
St. Roch's Parish, St. Louis, 167–169
St. Thomas College, 272–273
Scharper, Philip, 257, 258
Schillebeeckx, Edward, 186, 246, 288, 292, 293–295, 296
Secretariat for Non-Believers, 141
Secretariat for Promoting Christian Unity, 123–125, 130–131, 133, 137
Senghor, Leopold Sedar, 287
Seper, Franjo, Cardinal, 18, 19–20, 23–24
Servants of God, 90–92, 98
Shannon, James P., Bishop, 102–106, 108, 189–190
Shaughnessy, Jim, 118–119
Shaw, George Bernard, 278
Shaw, Russell, 266–267
Sheehan, James, Father, 61
Shehan, Lawrence, Cardinal, 4, 40, 153, 276
Sheen, Fulton J., Bishop, 4, 68–93, 145
Shields, Mrs, John D., 50
Siri, Giuseppe, Cardinal, 9

Sister Formation Conference, 220
Sisters for Christian Service, 229–230
Sisters of Loretto, 210–214, 220–221, 224, 271
Sisters of the Holy Child of Jesus, 222
Sisters of the Humility of Mary (formerly Sisters of the Holy Humility of Mary), 222
Sisters of the Immaculate Heart of Mary, 231–233
Society for the Propagation of the Faith, 75–76
Spellman, Francis, Cardinal, 65, 69, 88
Sponsa Christi, 218
Sprehe, Paul, 109
Stransky, Thomas, Father, 133
Stritch, Samuel, Cardinal, 199–204
Suenens, Leo, Cardinal, 3, 17, 19, 154
Swiss Guard, 37
Syllabus of Eighty Erroneous Propositions, 16
Syllabus of Errors, 13

Taguchi, Paul Yoshigoro, Bishop, 19
Tannenbaum, Marc H., Rabbi, 79
Teilhard de Chardin, Pierre, 82, 249, 286–289
Temple B'rith Kodesh, Rochester, 79
Thant, U, 49
Thomas Aquinas, Saint, 290
Thorman, Donald J., 102
The Times (London), 22
To Tell the Truth, 226
Toms River, New Jersey, 112
Topel, Bernard, Bishop, 153
Toronto, 169
Toronto, University of, 281–282
Trenton, 112
Tucson, Arizona, 165
Tulsa, Oklahoma, 112
Twin Circle, 152

Union Theological Seminary, 136, 206
United Nations, 43, 49–50

324

United States Bishops' Conference, 40, 162, 166, 231–232
United States Council of Catholic Women, 50
United States Riot Commission, 63, 77, 161, 263
University of Toronto, 281–282
Urbani, Giovanni, Cardinal, 4

Vagnozzi, Egidio, Father, 287
Van den Huevel, Albert, 140
Vatican Congregation for Religious, 218, 228, 231
Vatican Congregation of Rites, 114–115
Vega, Muñoz, Cardinal, 17, 19, 24
Veronese, Vittorino, 50
Veuillot, Cardinal, 19
Villanova University, 272–273
Villot, Jean, Cardinal, 3, 5
Visser't Hooft, Willem A., 143–144

Walsh, Jean, 94–95
Walsh, Joe, 94–95
Walsh, Joseph L., Father, 254–255
Ward, Barbara, 53, 55, 155
Washington, D.C., 113
Wayne State University, 237–240

Weaver, Robert C., 77
Webster College, 210–211, 213, 223, 270–271
Wedel, Cynthia, 135
Westhampton Beach, Long Island, 270
What Happened at Rome? 287–288
White, Sister Ann Richard, 210–215, 220–221, 224
Wilson, William T., 249–250, 251, 252
Wolff, Madeleva, Sister, 220
Woodstock College, 206
Work, Martin, 164–167, 169–170
World Council of Churches, 127, 132, 135, 140, 141, 142, 143, 144, 285
World Congress for the Lay Apostolate, 31, 33, 35, 36, 37, 39, 40, 41, 42, 44, 48, 49, 50, 51, 52, 55, 56, 57, 58, 63, 66, 133, 153, 154, 161, 292
Wree, Doug, 119
Wright, John J., Bishop, 4, 14, 19, 40, 169

Zoungrana, Paul, Cardinal, 19